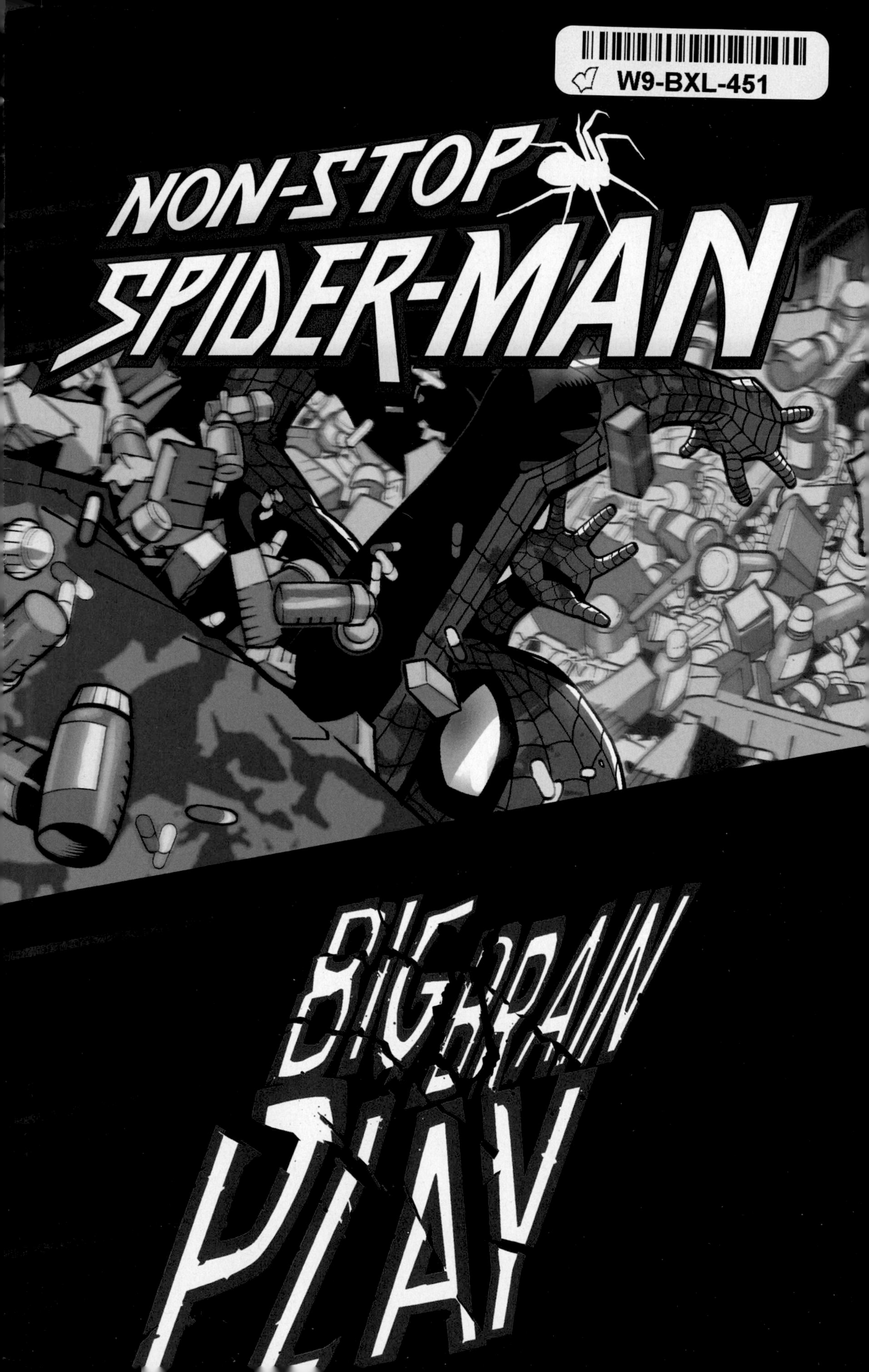
NON-STOP
SPIDER-MAN
BIG BRAIN
PLAY

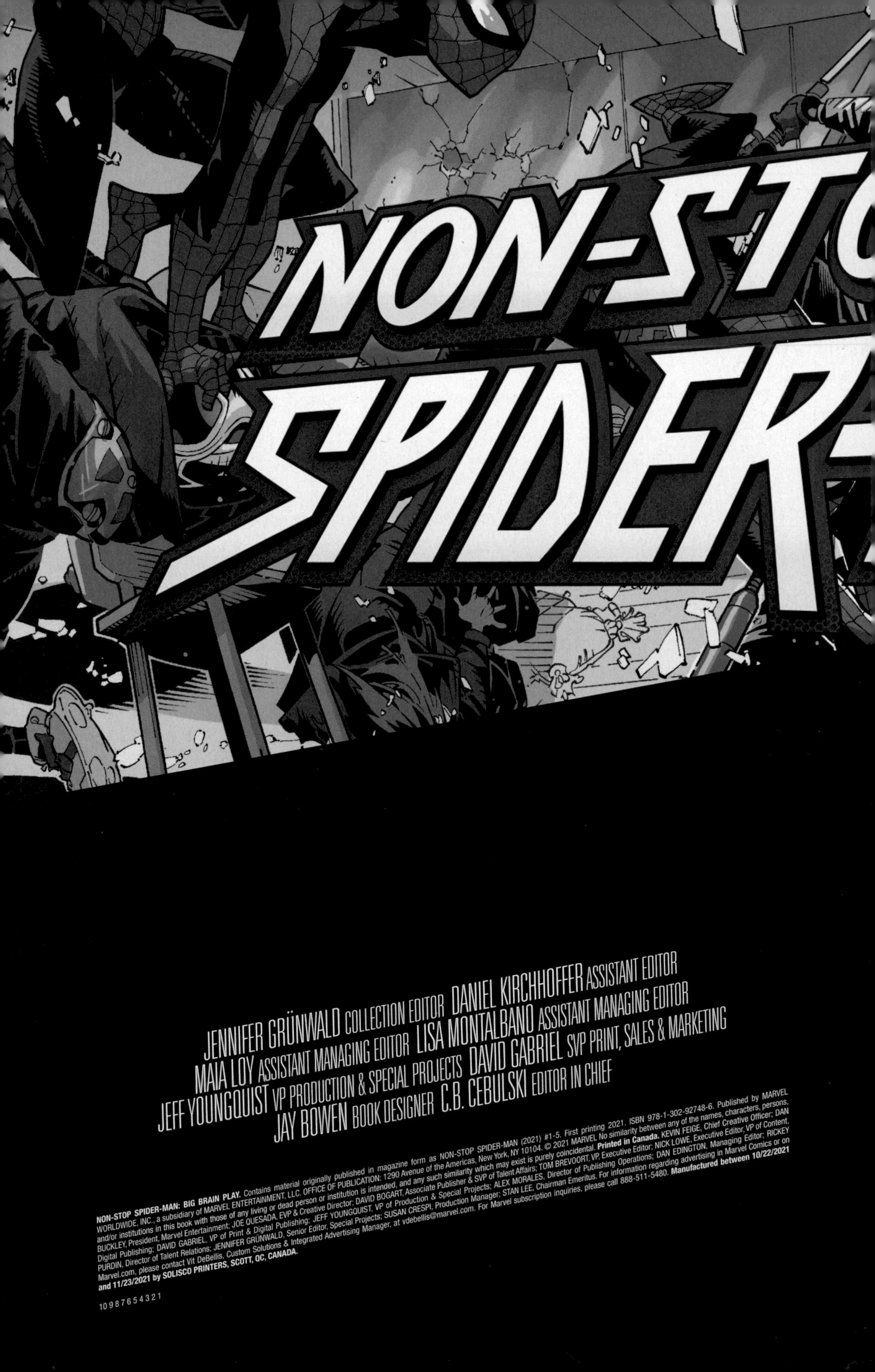

JENNIFER GRÜNWALD COLLECTION EDITOR DANIEL KIRCHHOFFER ASSISTANT EDITOR
MAIA LOY ASSISTANT MANAGING EDITOR LISA MONTALBANO ASSISTANT MANAGING EDITOR
JEFF YOUNGQUIST VP PRODUCTION & SPECIAL PROJECTS DAVID GABRIEL SVP PRINT, SALES & MARKETING
JAY BOWEN BOOK DESIGNER C.B. CEBULSKI EDITOR IN CHIEF

NON-STOP SPIDER-MAN: BIG BRAIN PLAY. Contains material originally published in magazine form as NON-STOP SPIDER-MAN (2021) #1-5. First printing 2021. ISBN 978-1-302-92748-6. Published by MARVEL WORLDWIDE, INC., a subsidiary of MARVEL ENTERTAINMENT, LLC. OFFICE OF PUBLICATION: 1290 Avenue of the Americas, New York, NY 10104. © 2021 MARVEL No similarity between any of the names, characters, persons, and/or institutions in this book with those of any living or dead person or institution is intended, and any such similarity which may exist is purely coincidental. **Printed in Canada.** KEVIN FEIGE, Chief Creative Officer; DAN BUCKLEY, President, Marvel Entertainment; JOE QUESADA, EVP & Creative Director; DAVID BOGART, Associate Publisher & SVP of Talent Affairs; TOM BREVOORT, VP, Executive Editor; NICK LOWE, Executive Editor, VP of Content, Digital Publishing; DAVID GABRIEL, VP of Print & Digital Publishing; JEFF YOUNGQUIST, VP of Production & Special Projects; ALEX MORALES, Director of Publishing Operations; DAN EDINGTON, Managing Editor; RICKEY PURDIN, Director of Talent Relations; JENNIFER GRÜNWALD, Senior Editor, Special Projects; SUSAN CRESPI, Production Manager; STAN LEE, Chairman Emeritus. For information regarding advertising in Marvel Comics or on Marvel.com, please contact Vit DeBellis, Custom Solutions & Integrated Advertising Manager, at vdebellis@marvel.com. For Marvel subscription inquiries, please call 888-511-5480. **Manufactured between 10/22/2021 and 11/23/2021 by SOLISCO PRINTERS, SCOTT, QC, CANADA.**

10 9 8 7 6 5 4 3 2 1

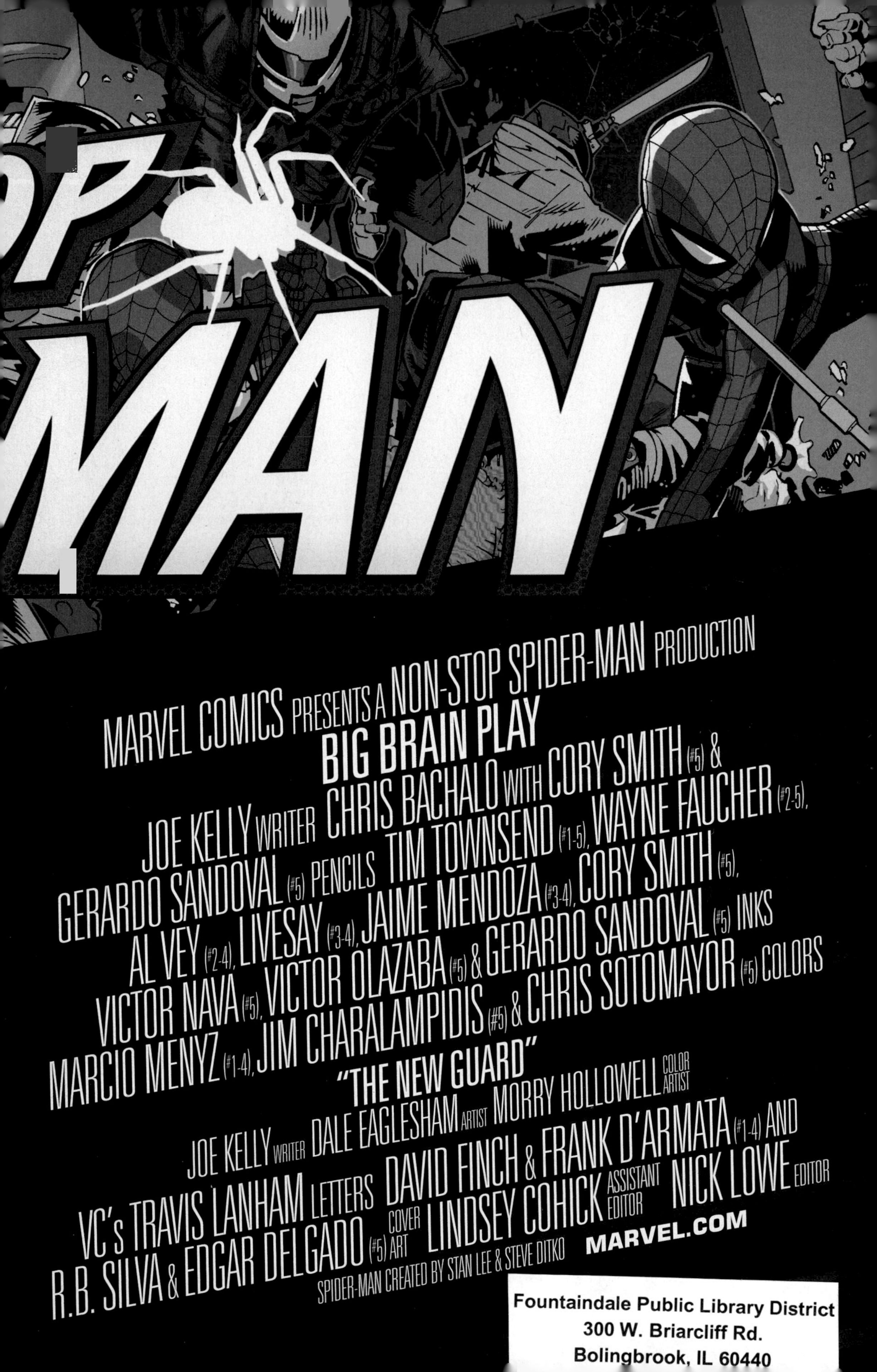
MAN

MARVEL COMICS PRESENTS A NON-STOP SPIDER-MAN PRODUCTION

BIG BRAIN PLAY

JOE KELLY WRITER CHRIS BACHALO WITH CORY SMITH (#5) & GERARDO SANDOVAL (#5) PENCILS TIM TOWNSEND (#1-5), WAYNE FAUCHER (#2-5), AL VEY (#2-4), LIVESAY (#3-4), JAIME MENDOZA (#3-4), CORY SMITH (#5), VICTOR NAVA (#5), VICTOR OLAZABA (#5) & GERARDO SANDOVAL (#5) INKS MARCIO MENYZ (#1-4), JIM CHARALAMPIDIS (#5) & CHRIS SOTOMAYOR (#5) COLORS

"THE NEW GUARD"

JOE KELLY WRITER DALE EAGLESHAM ARTIST MORRY HOLLOWELL COLOR ARTIST

VC's TRAVIS LANHAM LETTERS DAVID FINCH & FRANK D'ARMATA (#1-4) AND R.B. SILVA & EDGAR DELGADO (#5) COVER ART LINDSEY COHICK ASSISTANT EDITOR NICK LOWE EDITOR

SPIDER-MAN CREATED BY STAN LEE & STEVE DITKO

MARVEL.COM

1. BIG BRAIN PLAY
CHAPTER ONE

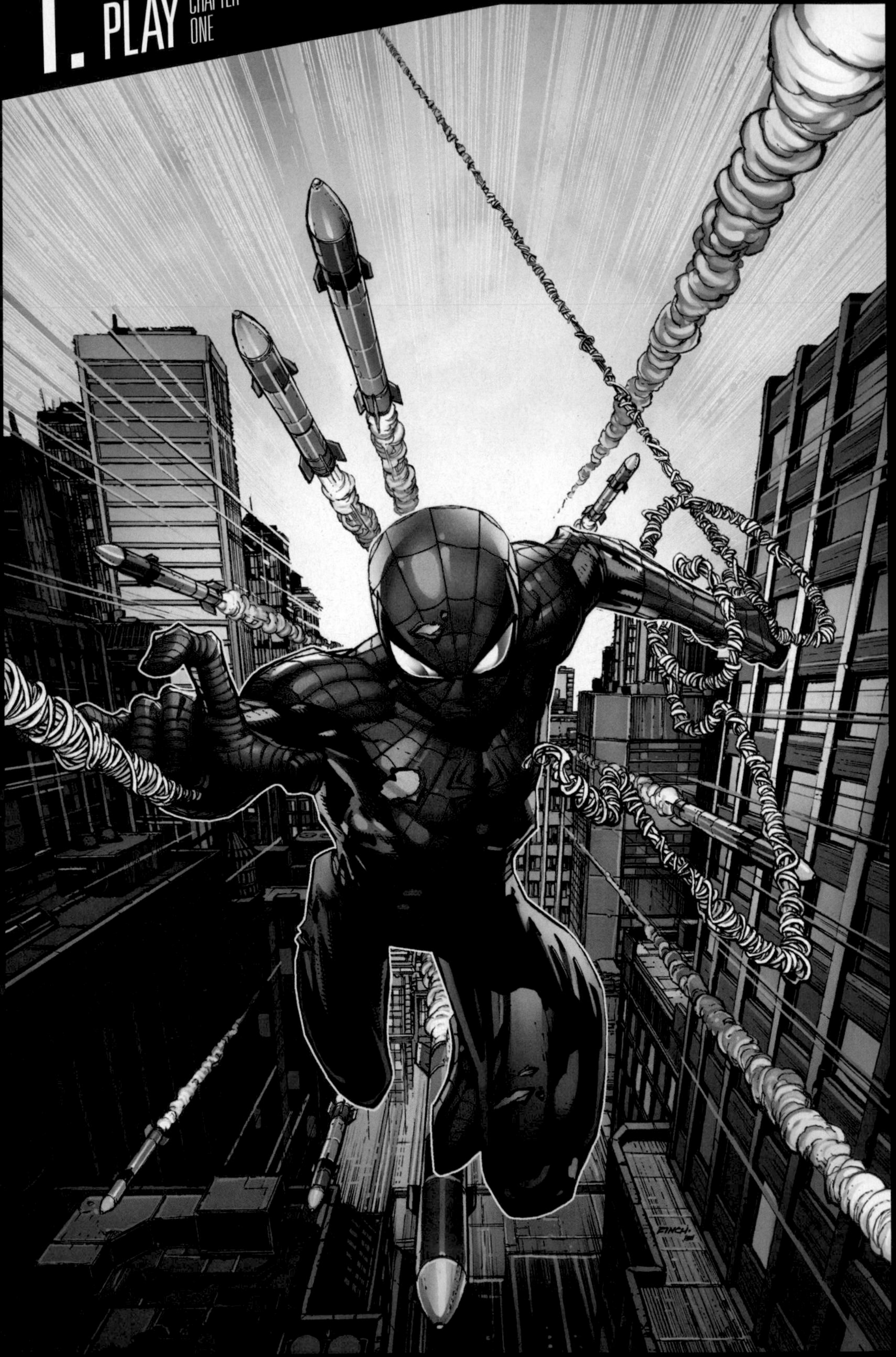

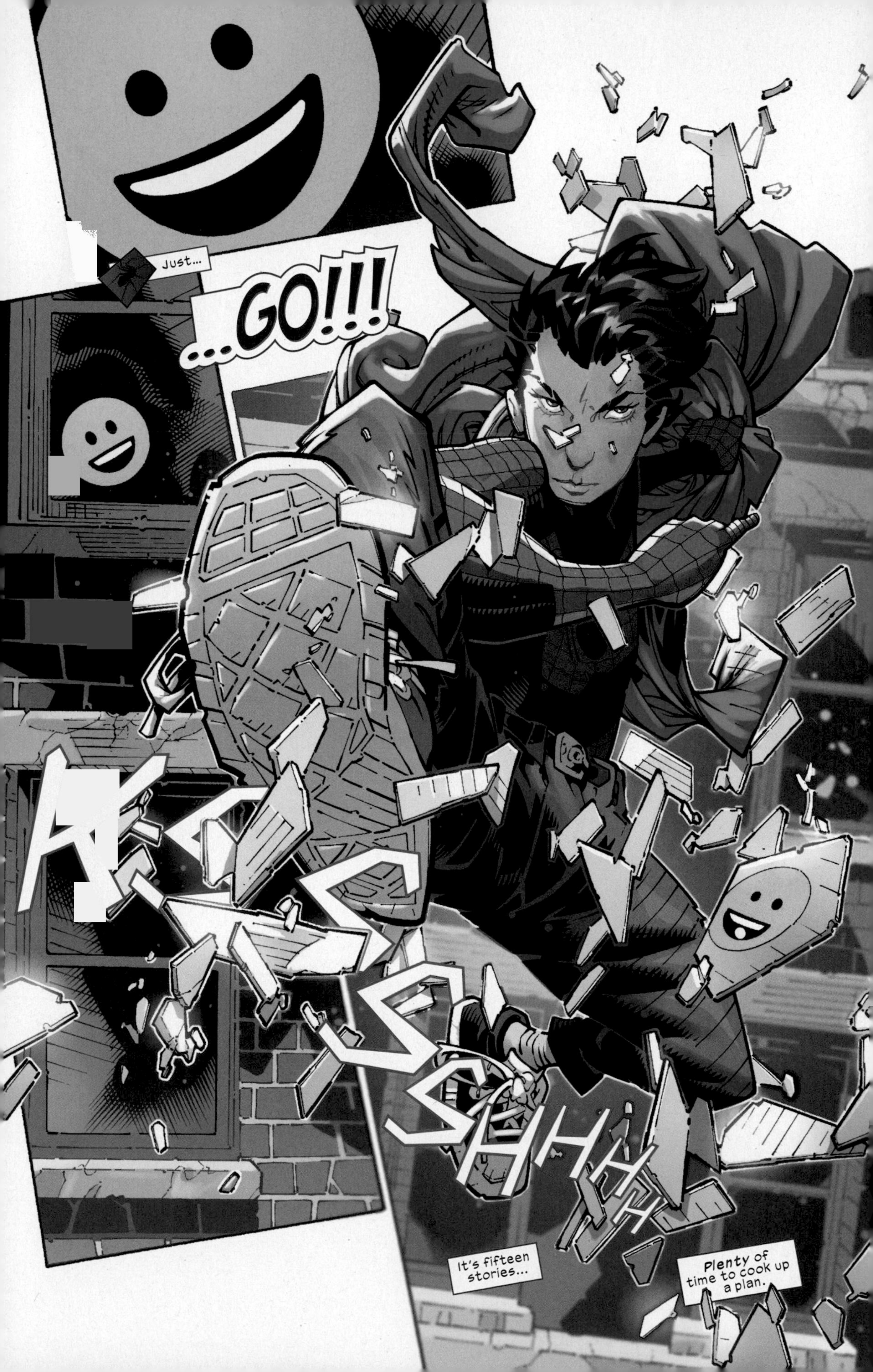

Just...
...GO!!!
It's fifteen stories...
Plenty of time to cook up a plan.

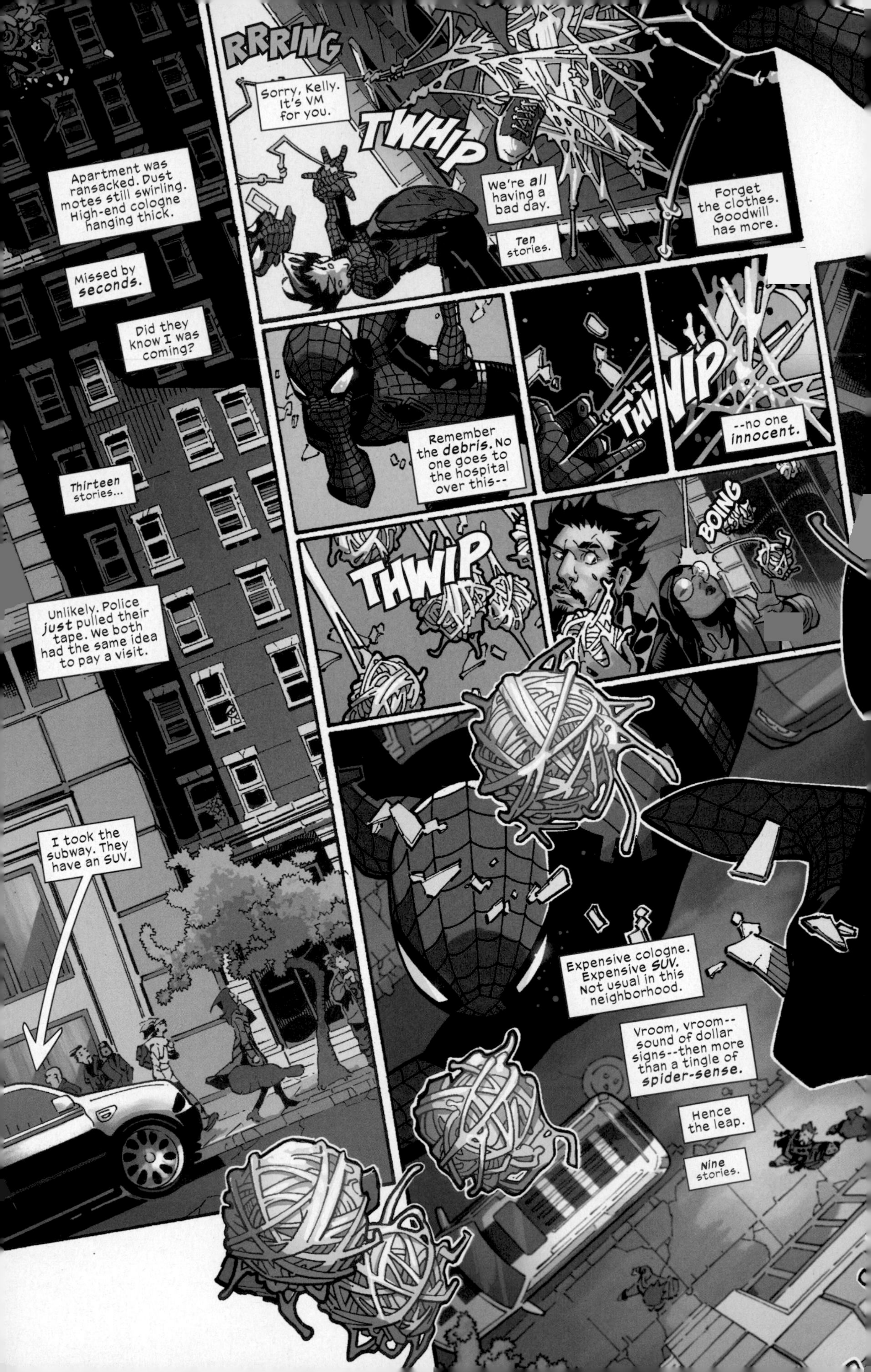

RRRING
Sorry, Kelly. It's VM for you.
TWHIP
We're all having a bad day.
Ten stories.
Forget the clothes. Goodwill has more.
Apartment was ransacked. Dust motes still swirling. High-end cologne hanging thick.
Missed by seconds.
Did they know I was coming?
Thirteen stories...
Unlikely. Police just pulled their tape. We both had the same idea to pay a visit.
I took the subway. They have an SUV.
Remember the debris. No one goes to the hospital over this--
THWIP
--no one innocent.
THWIP
BOING
Expensive cologne. Expensive SUV. Not usual in this neighborhood.
Vroom, vroom--sound of dollar signs--then more than a tingle of spider-sense.
Hence the leap.
Nine stories.

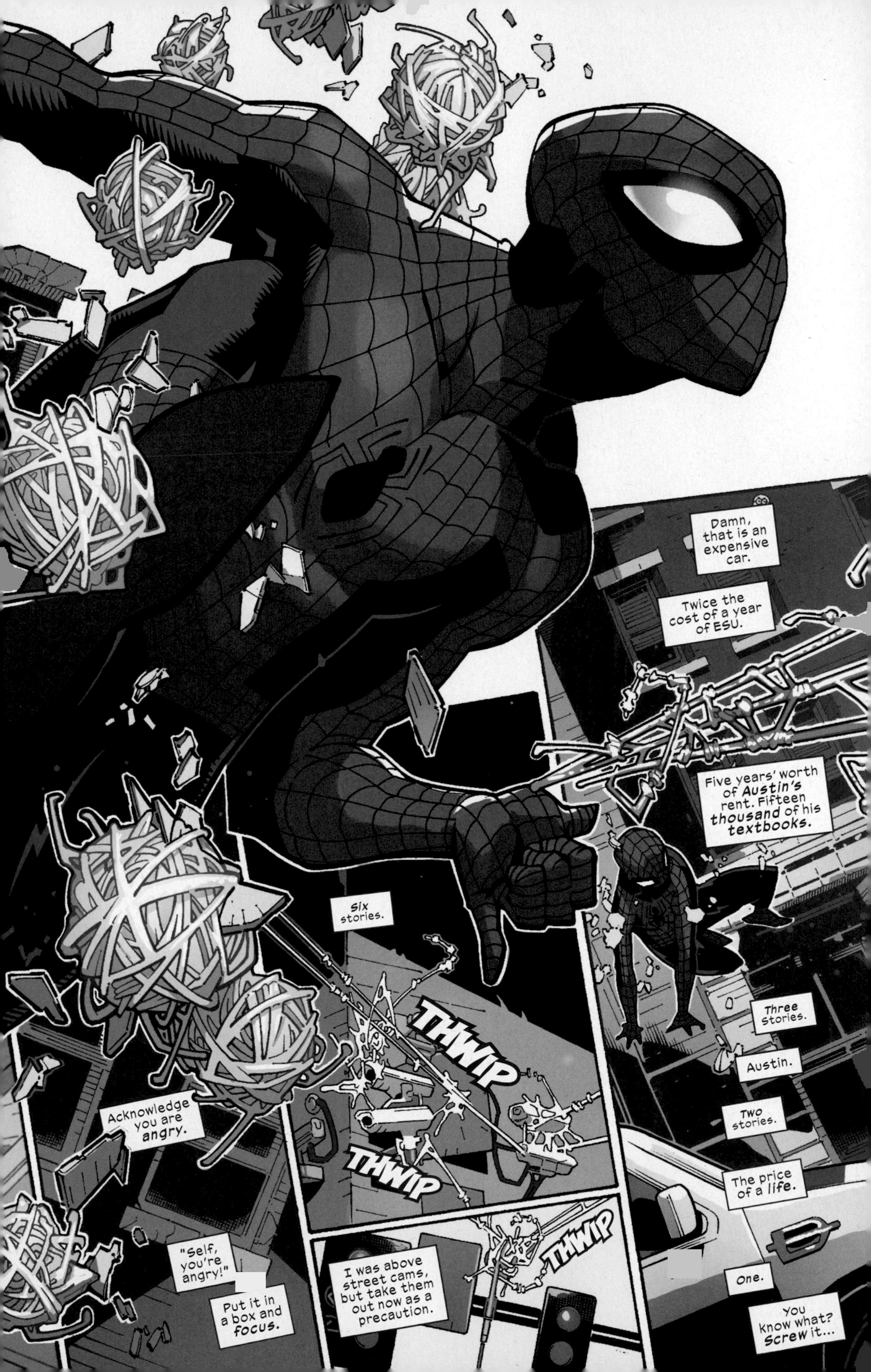

Damn, that is an expensive car.
Twice the cost of a year of ESU.
Five years' worth of Austin's rent. Fifteen thousand of his textbooks.
Six stories.
THWIP
THWIP
Three stories.
Austin.
Two stories.
The price of a life.
Acknowledge you are angry.
"Self, you're angry!"
Put it in a box and focus.
I was above street cams, but take them out now as a precaution.
THWIP
One.
You know what? Screw it...

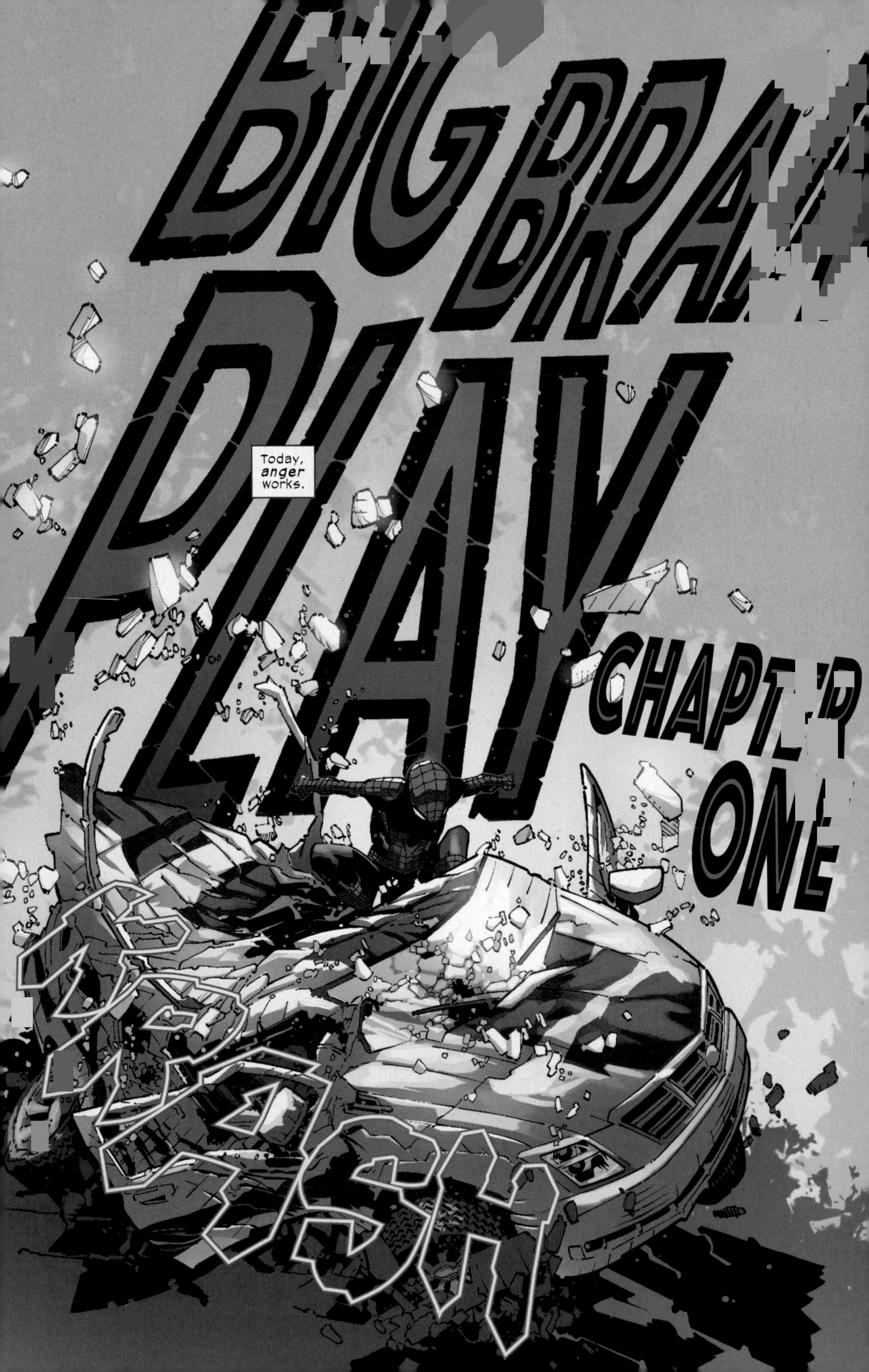
BIG
PLAY
Today, anger works.
ONE

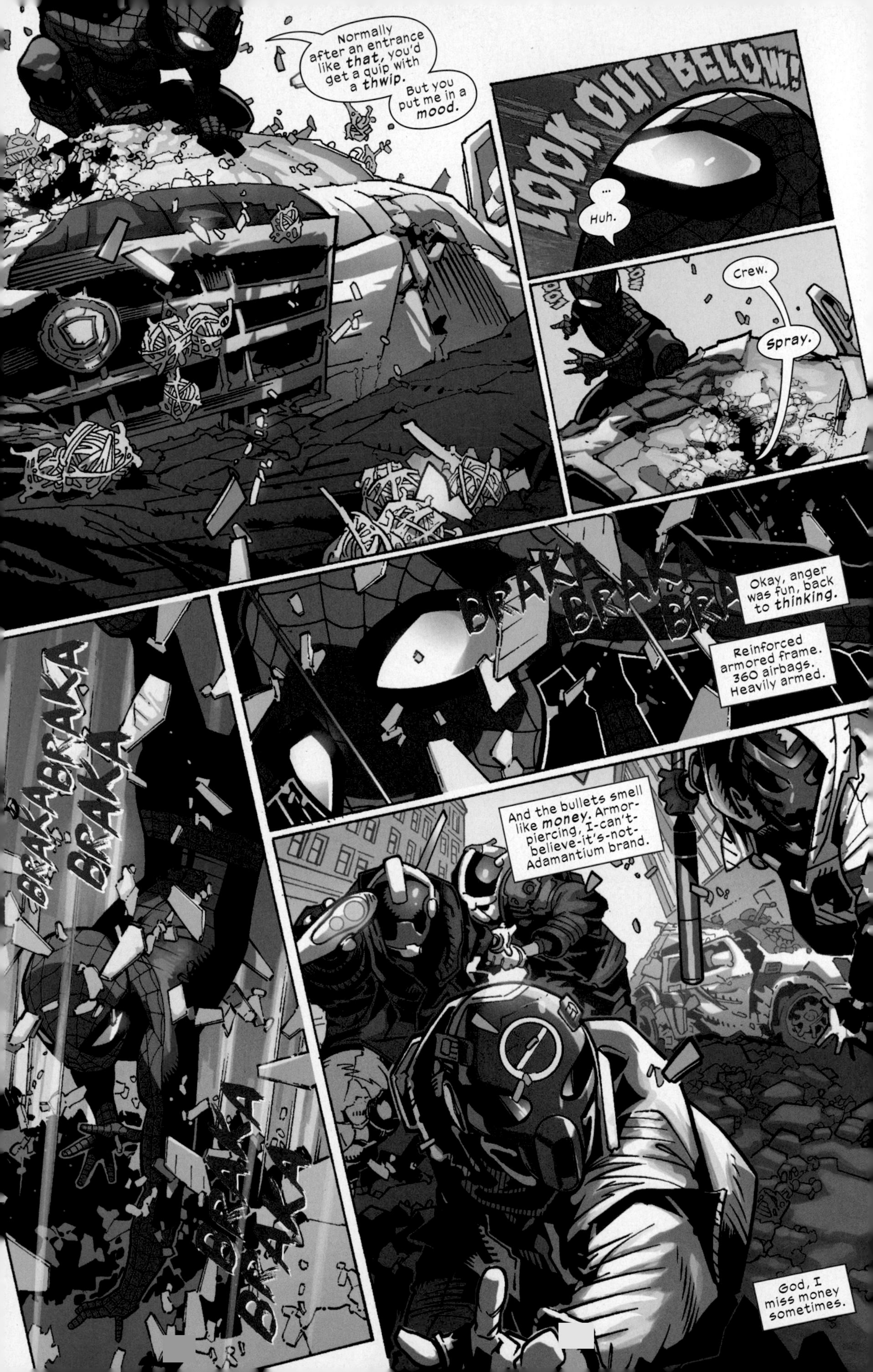

Normally after an entrance like *that*, you'd get a quip with a *thwip*.
But you put me in a *mood*.
LOOK OUT BELOW!
...
Huh.
Crew.
Spray.
BRAKA BRAKA BRA
Okay, anger was fun, back to *thinking*.
Reinforced armored frame. 360 airbags. Heavily armed.
BRAKABRAKA BRAKA
BRAKA BRAKA
And the bullets smell like *money*. Armor-piercing, I-can't-believe-it's-not-Adamantium brand.
God, I miss money sometimes.

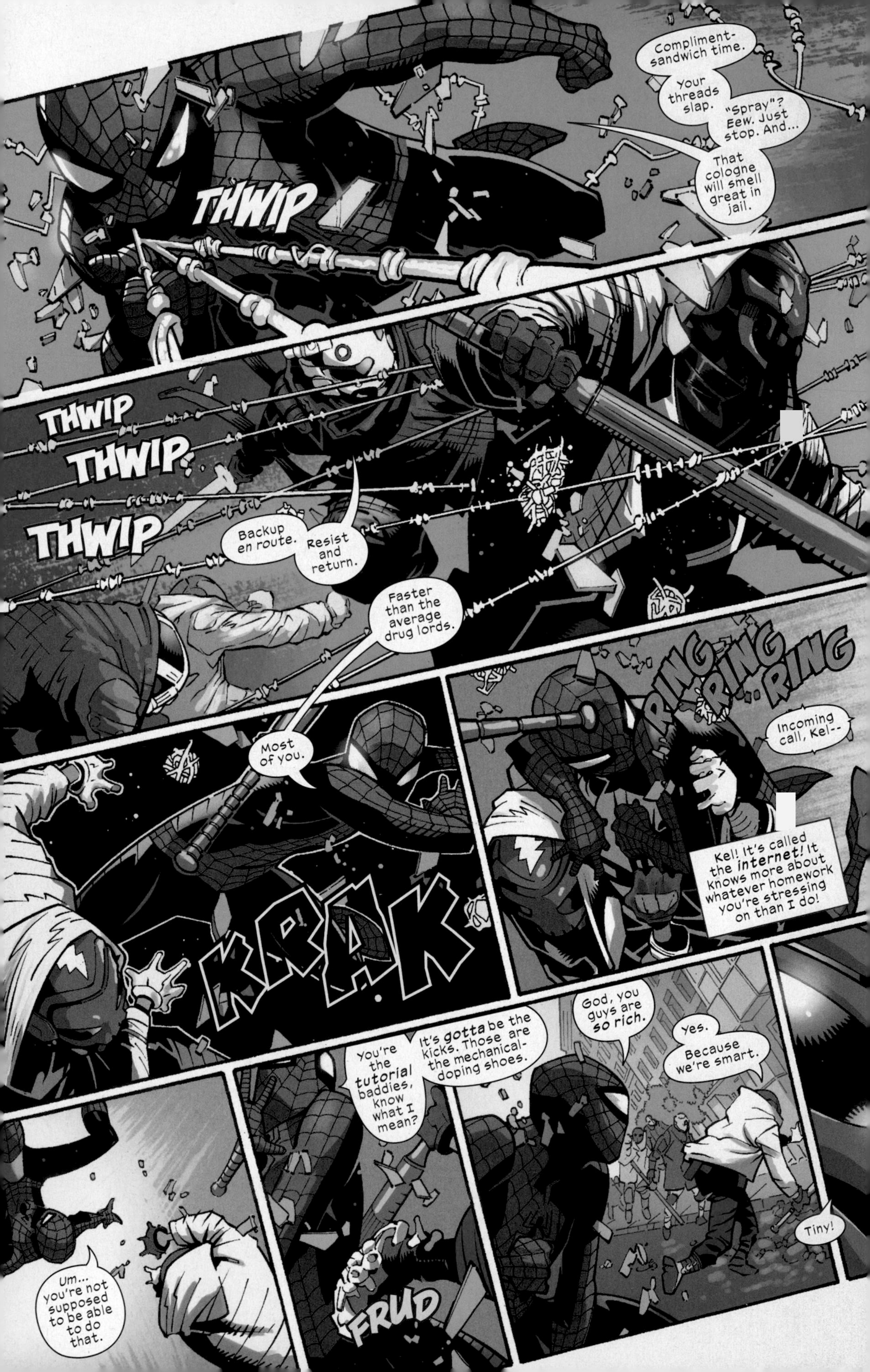

Compliment-sandwich time.
Your threads slap.
"Spray"? Eew. Just stop. And...
That cologne will smell great in jail.
THWIP
THWIP
THWIP
THWIP
Backup en route.
Resist and return.
Faster than the average drug lords.
Most of you.
KRAK
RING RING RING
Incoming call, Kel--
Kel! It's called the internet! It knows more about whatever homework you're stressing on than I do!
Um... you're not supposed to be able to do that.
You're the tutorial baddies, know what I mean?
It's gotta be the kicks. Those are the mechanical-doping shoes.
FRUD
God, you guys are so rich.
Yes.
Because we're smart.
Tiny!

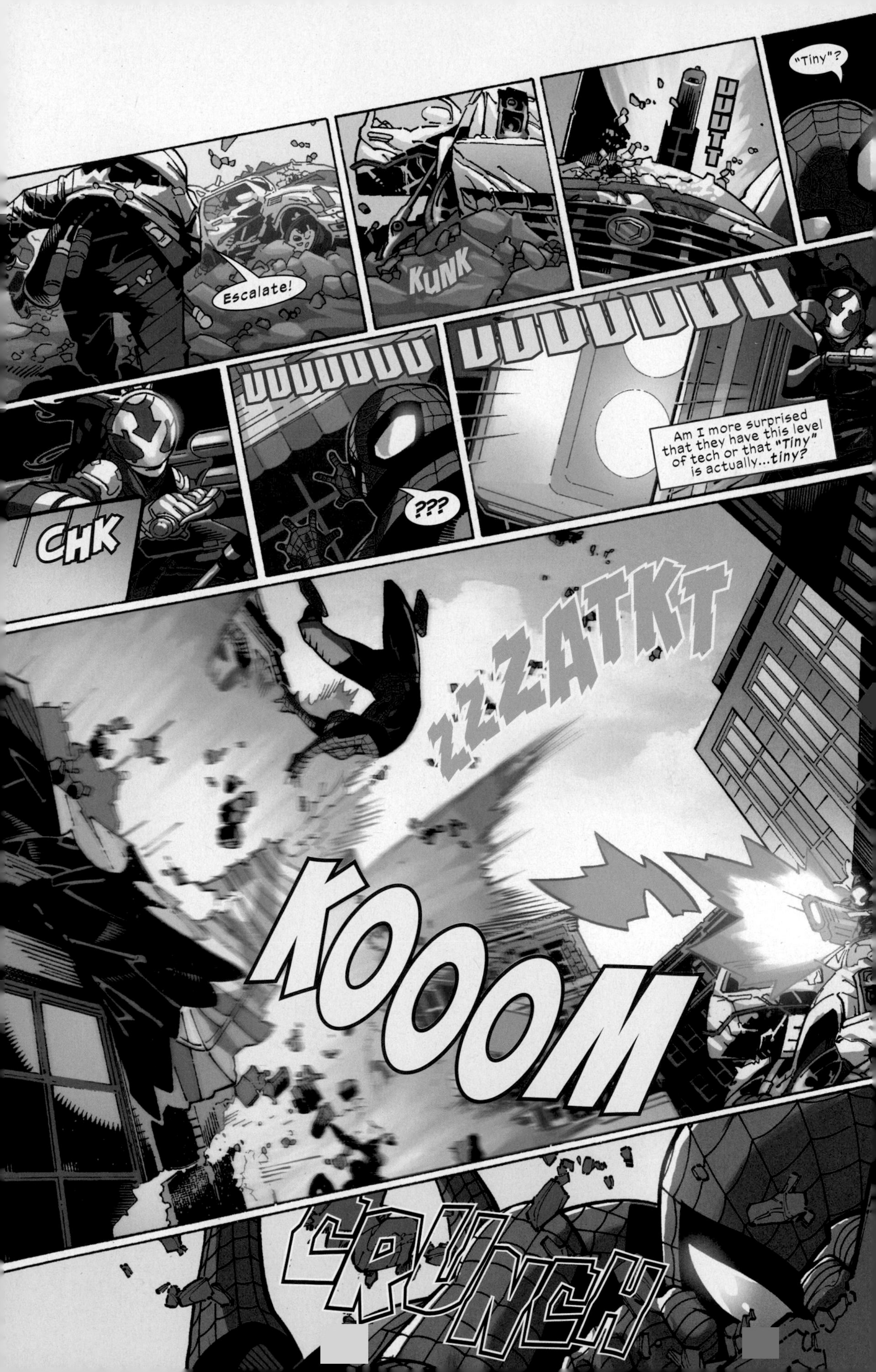

Escalate!
KUNK
UUUTT
"Tiny"?
UUUUUUU
UUUUUUUU
???
Am I more surprised that they have this level of tech or that "Tiny" is actually...tiny?
CHK
ZZZATKT
KOOOM
CRUNCH

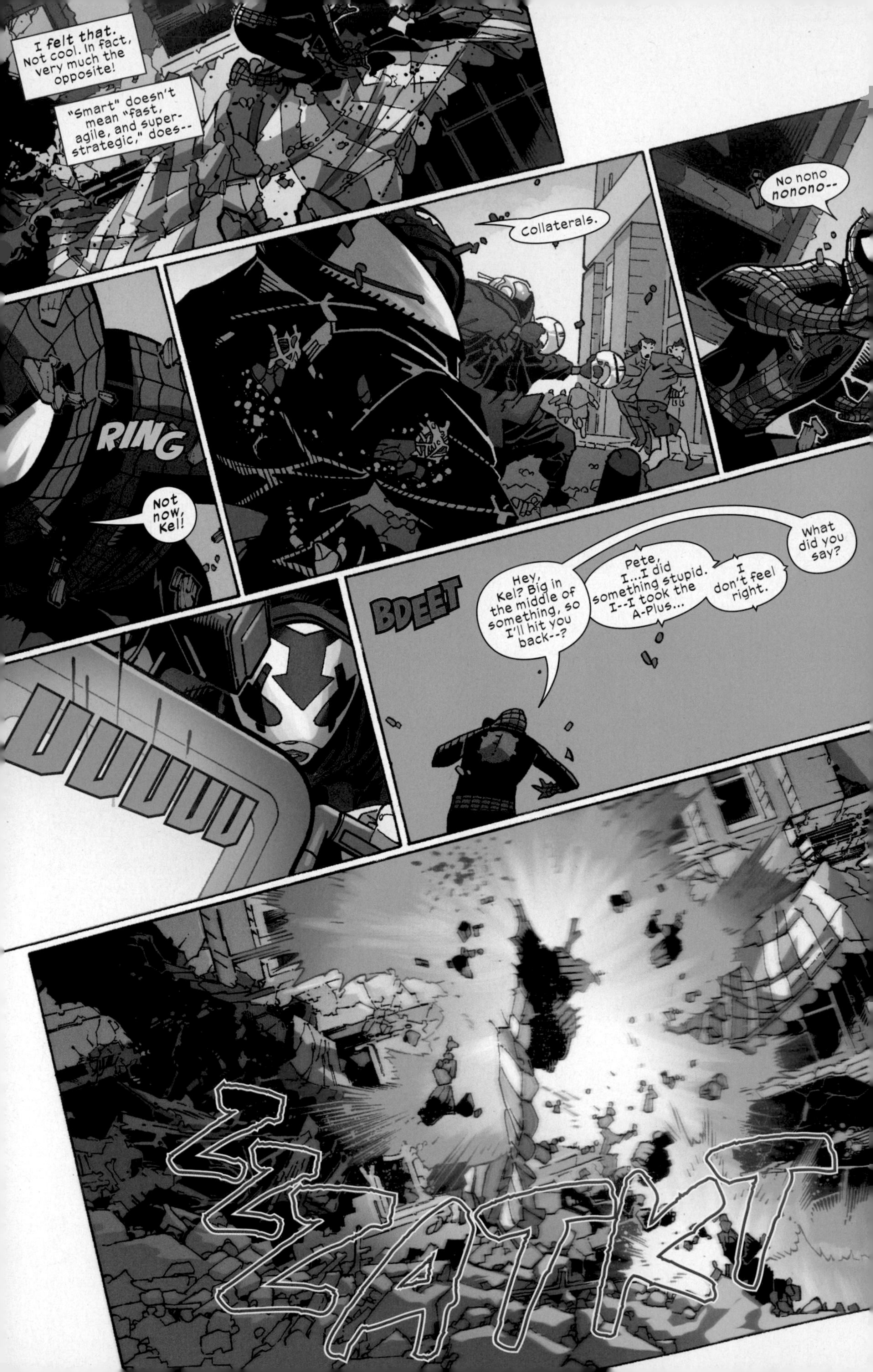
I felt that. Not cool. In fact, very much the opposite!
"Smart" doesn't mean "fast, agile, and super-strategic," does--
Collaterals.
No nono nonono--
RING
Not now, Kel!
BDEET
Hey, Kel? Big in the middle of something, so I'll hit you back--?
Pete, I...I did something stupid. I--I took the A-Plus...
I don't feel right.
What did you say?
UUUUU
ZZATKT

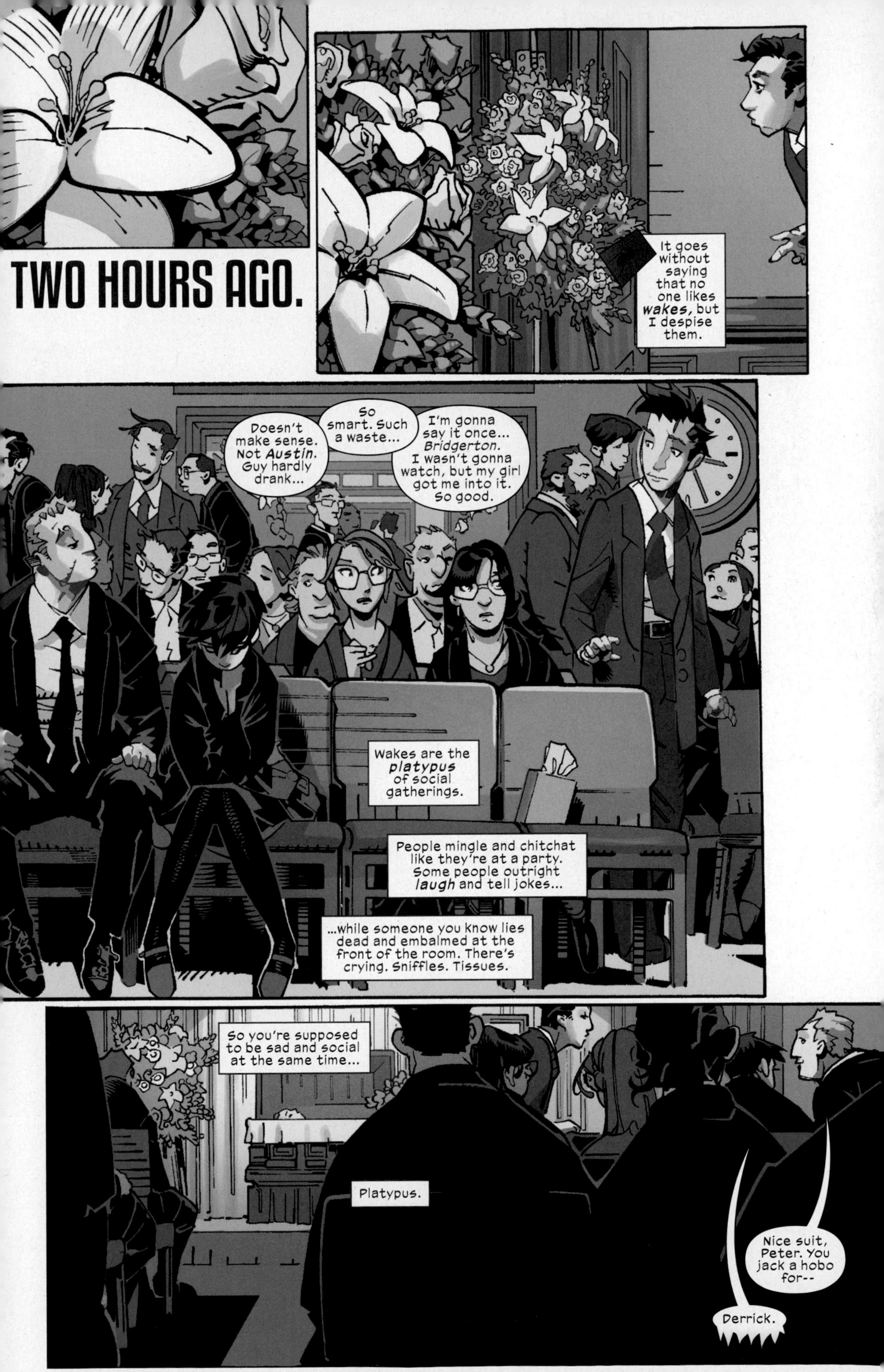
TWO HOURS AGO.
It goes without saying that no one likes *wakes,* but I despise them.
Doesn't make sense. Not *Austin*. Guy hardly drank...
So smart. Such a waste...
I'm gonna say it once... *Bridgerton.* I wasn't gonna watch, but my girl got me into it. So good.
Wakes are the *platypus* of social gatherings.
People mingle and chitchat like they're at a party. Some people outright *laugh* and tell jokes...
...while someone you know lies dead and embalmed at the front of the room. There's crying. Sniffles. Tissues.
So you're supposed to be sad and social at the same time...
Platypus.
Nice suit, Peter. You jack a hobo for--
Derrick.

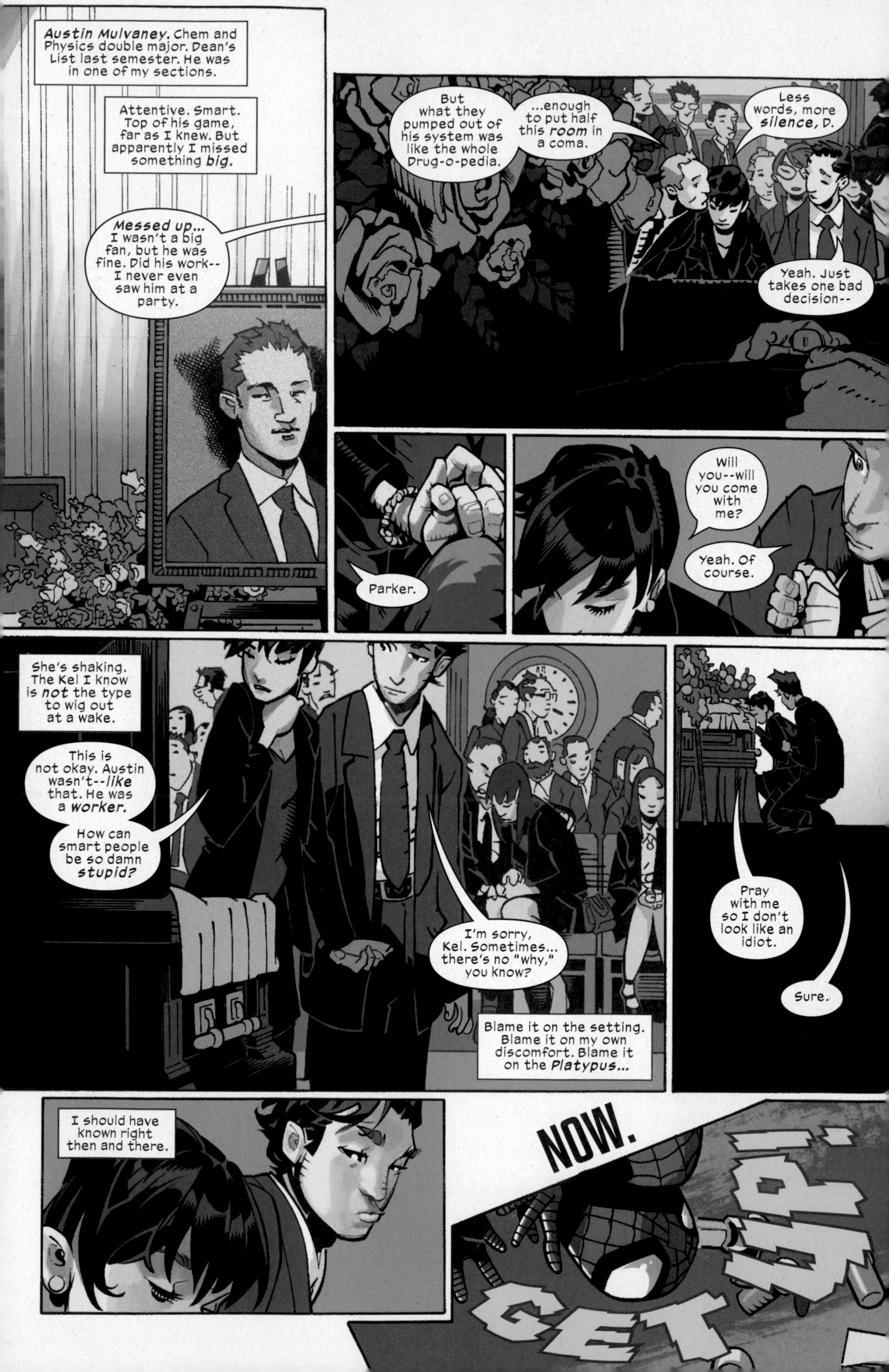

Austin Mulvaney. Chem and Physics double major. Dean's List last semester. He was in one of my sections.
Attentive. Smart. Top of his game, far as I knew. But apparently I missed something big.
Messed up... I wasn't a big fan, but he was fine. Did his work-- I never even saw him at a party.
But what they pumped out of his system was like the whole Drug-o-pedia.
...enough to put half this room in a coma.
Less words, more silence, D.
Yeah. Just takes one bad decision--
Parker.
Will you--will you come with me?
Yeah. Of course.
She's shaking. The Kel I know is not the type to wig out at a wake.
This is not okay. Austin wasn't--like that. He was a worker.
How can smart people be so damn stupid?
I'm sorry, Kel. Sometimes... there's no "why," you know?
Blame it on the setting. Blame it on my own discomfort. Blame it on the Platypus...
Pray with me so I don't look like an idiot.
Sure.
I should have known right then and there.
NOW.
GET IT!

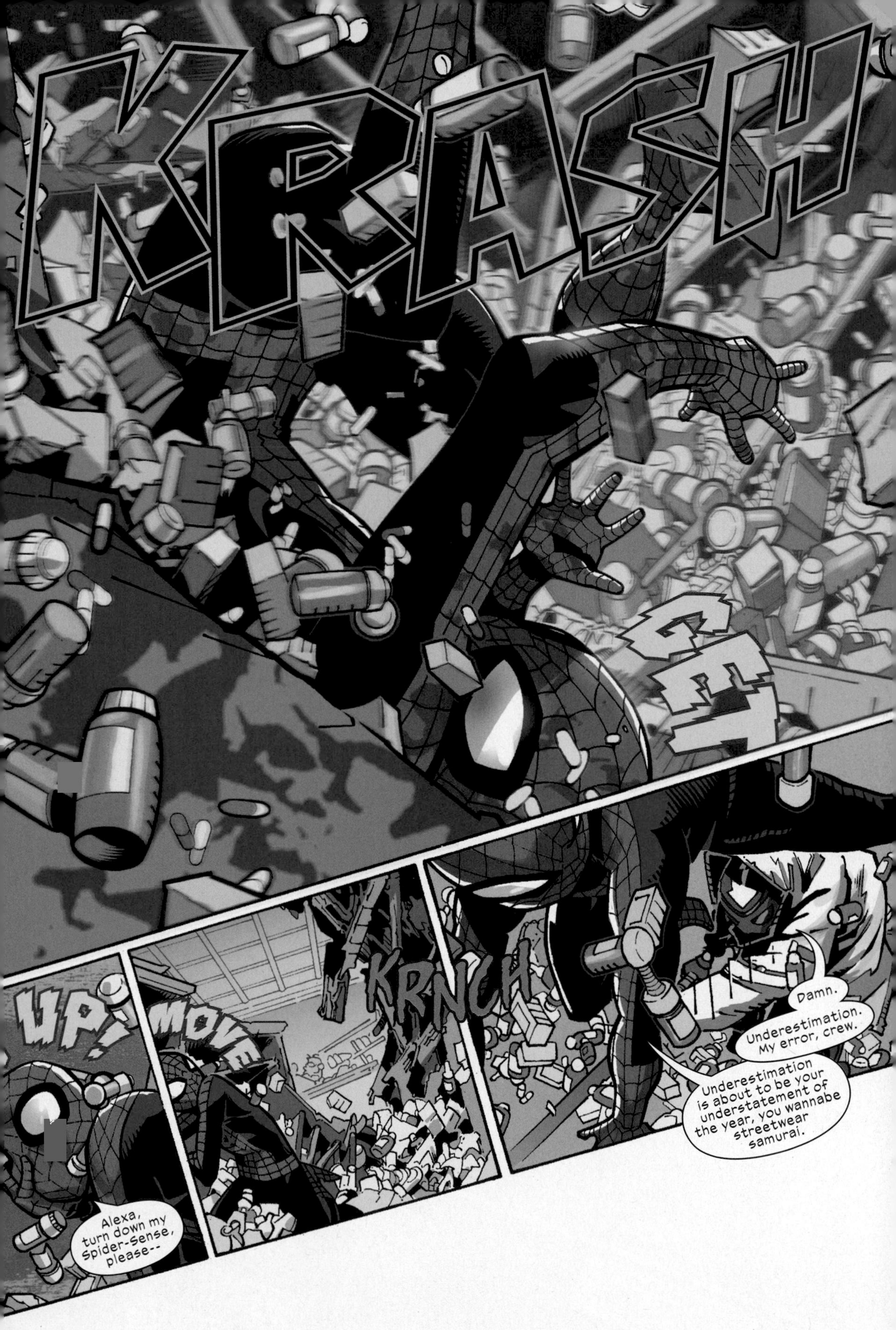
KRASH
UP!
MOVE
KRNCH
Alexa, turn down my Spider-Sense, please--
Damn.
Underestimation. My error, crew.
Underestimation is about to be your understatement of the year, you wannabe streetwear samurai.

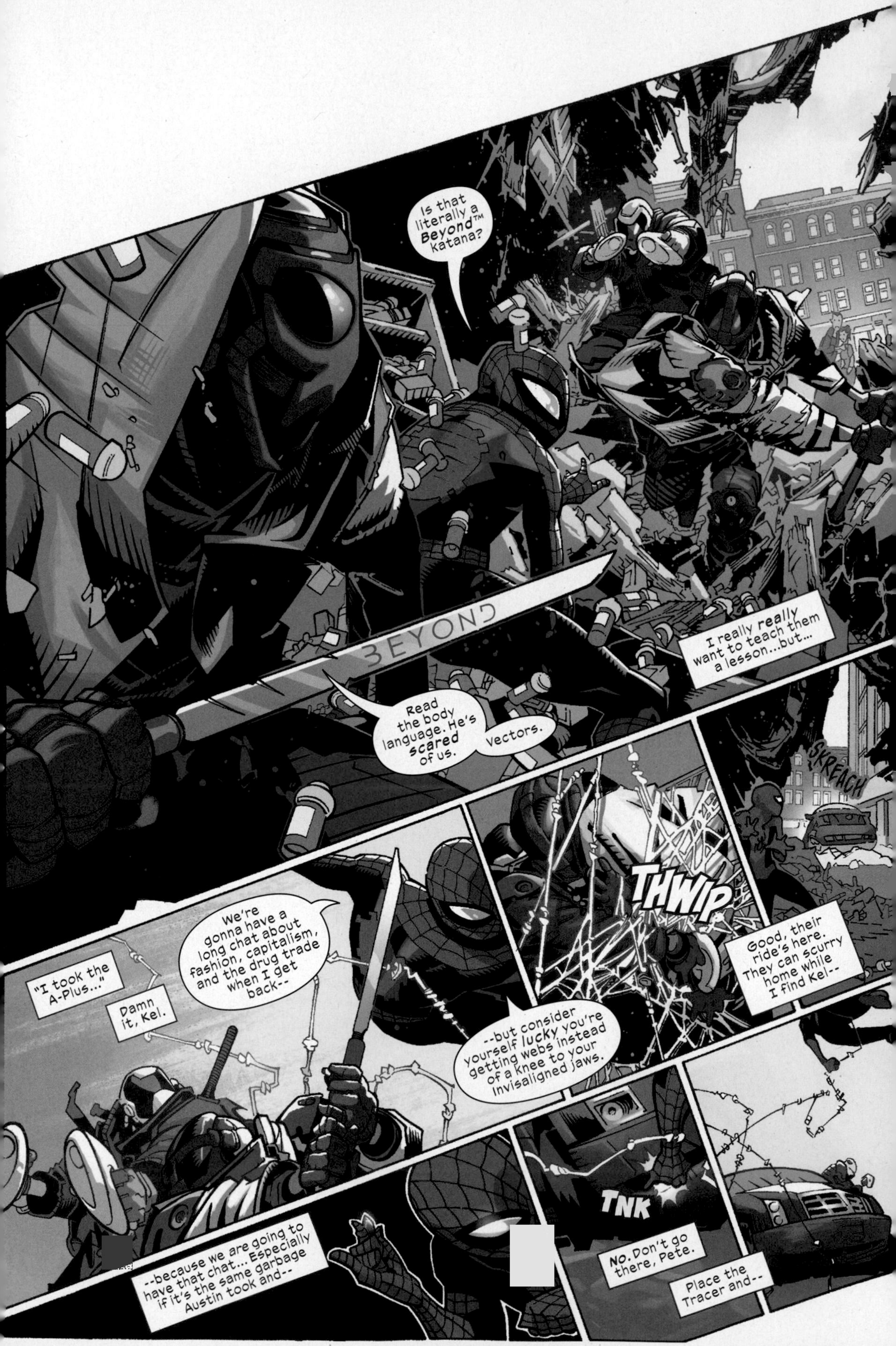

Is that literally a Beyond™ Katana?
BEYOND
I really really want to teach them a lesson...but...
Read the body language. He's scared of us.
Vectors.
SKREACH
THWIP
Good, their ride's here. They can scurry home while I find Kel--
"I took the A-Plus..."
Damn it, Kel.
We're gonna have a long chat about fashion, capitalism, and the drug trade when I get back--
--but consider yourself lucky you're getting webs instead of a knee to your Invisaligned jaws.
TNK
--because we are going to have that chat... Especially if it's the same garbage Austin took and--
No. Don't go there, Pete.
Place the Tracer and--

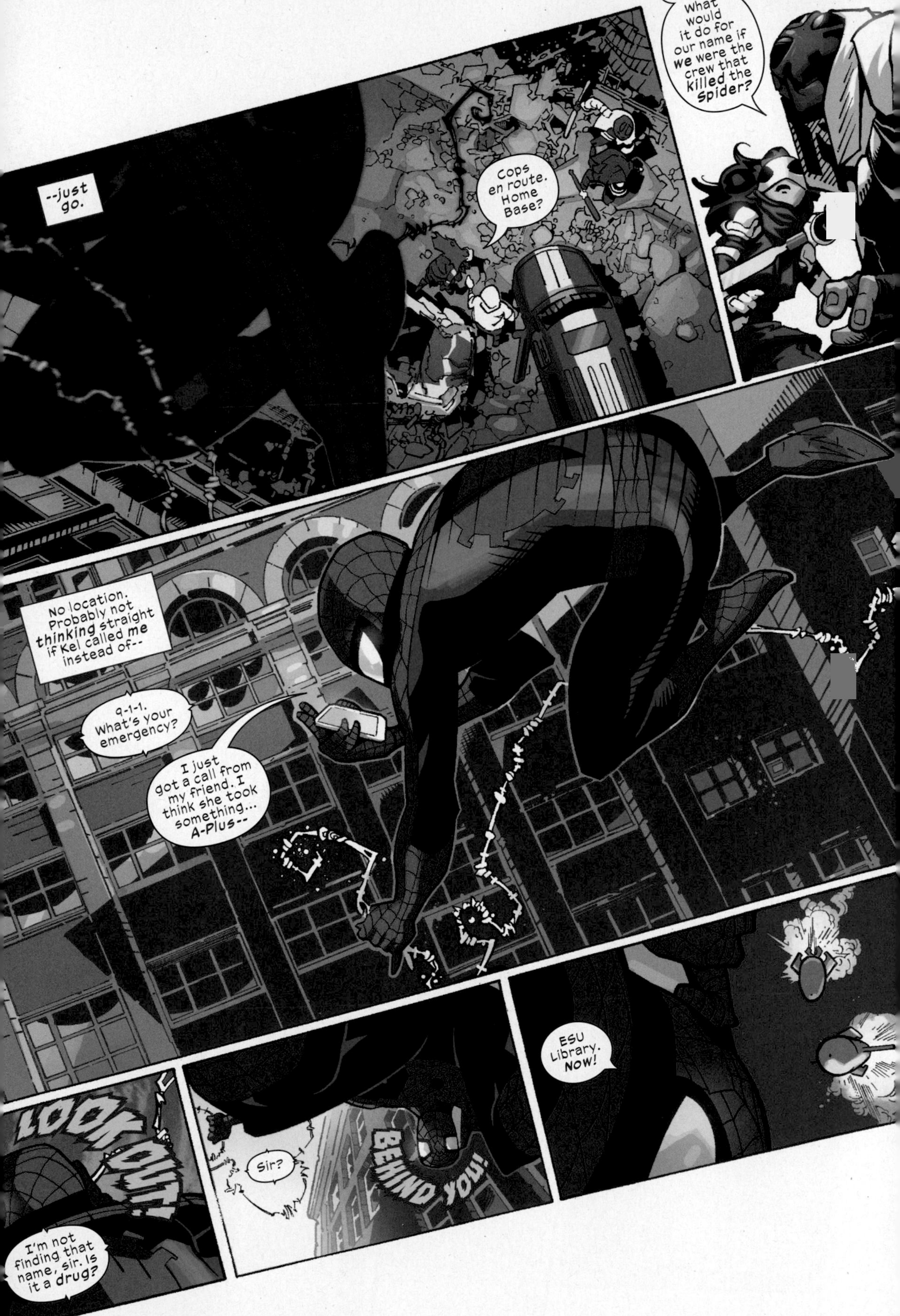
--just go.
Cops en route. Home Base?
...
What would it do for our name if we were the crew that killed the Spider?
No location. Probably not thinking straight if Kel called me instead of--
9-1-1. What's your emergency?
I just got a call from my friend. I think she took something... A-Plus--
ESU Library. NOW!
LOOK OUT!
I'm not finding that name, sir. Is it a drug?
Sir?
BEHIND YOU!

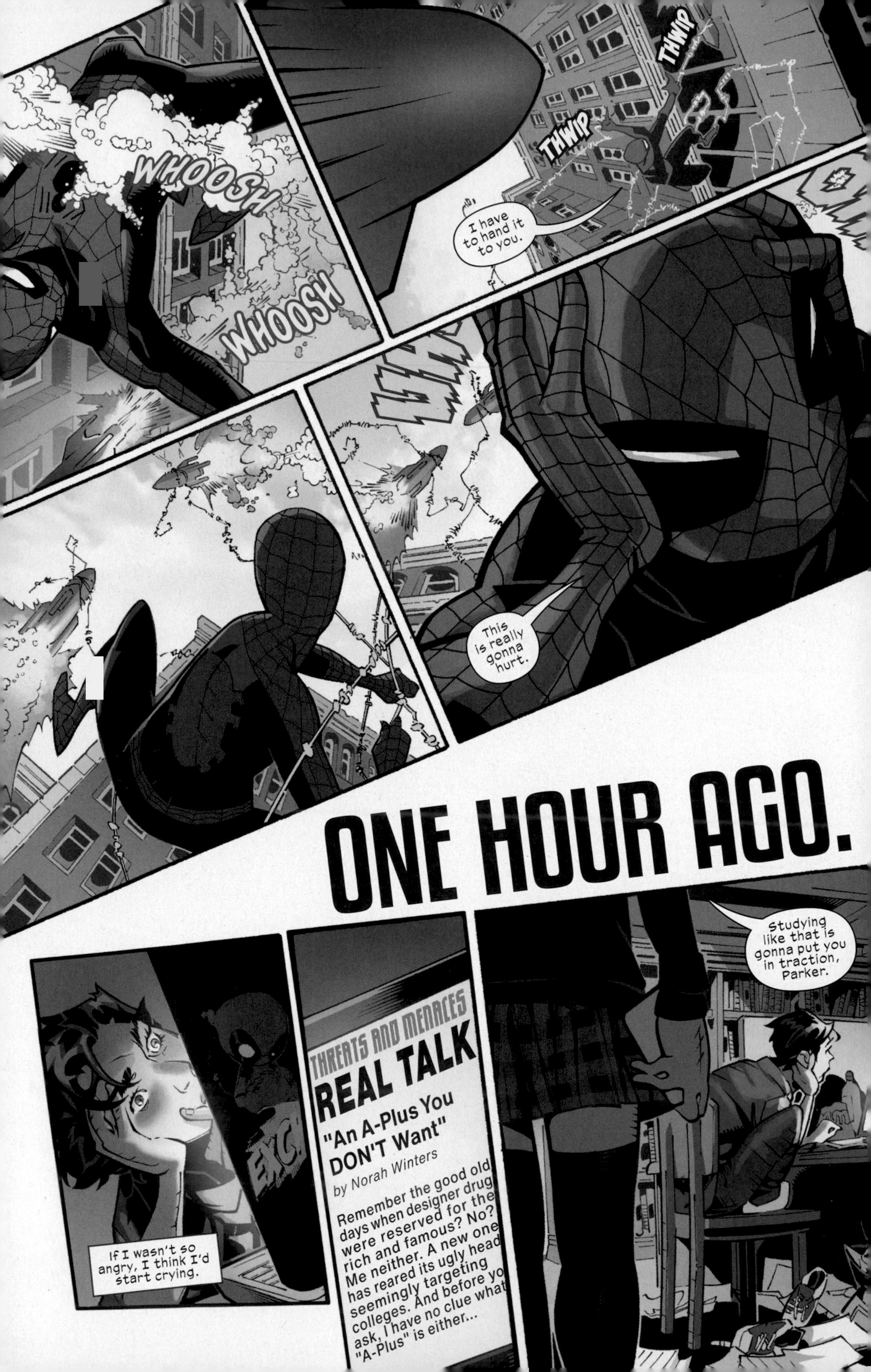
WHOOSH
WHOOSH
THWIP
THWIP
I have to hand it to you.
This is really gonna hurt.
ONE HOUR AGO.
If I wasn't so angry, I think I'd start crying.
THREATS AND MENACES
REAL TALK
"An A-Plus You DON'T Want"
by Norah Winters
Remember the good old days when designer drugs were reserved for the rich and famous? No? Me neither. A new one has reared its ugly head seemingly targeting colleges. And before you ask, I have no clue what "A-Plus" is either...
Studying like that is gonna put you in traction, Parker.

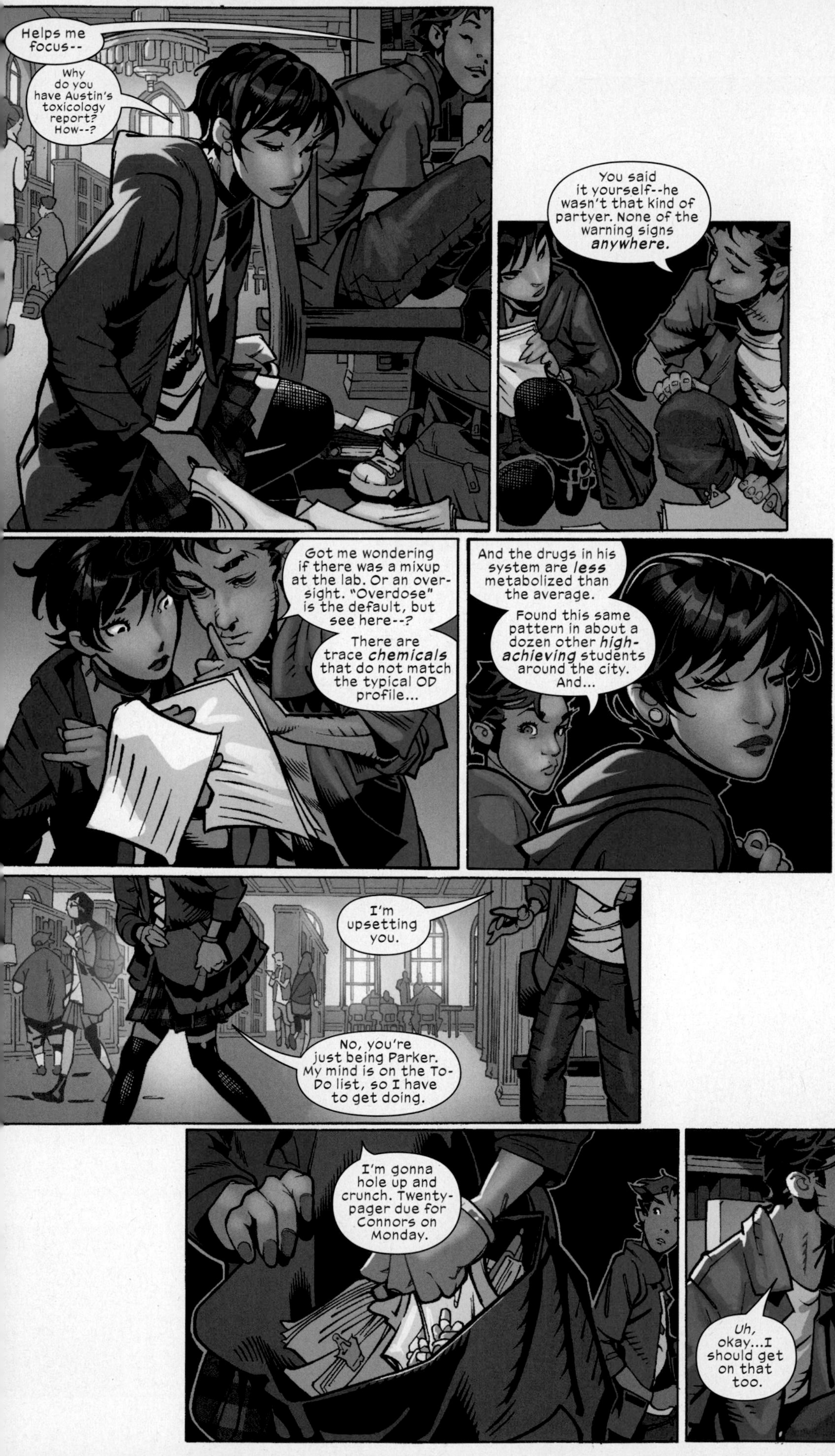

Helps me focus--
Why do you have Austin's toxicology report? How--?
You said it yourself--he wasn't that kind of partyer. None of the warning signs *anywhere.*
Got me wondering if there was a mixup at the lab. Or an oversight. "Overdose" is the default, but see here--?
There are trace *chemicals* that do not match the typical OD profile...
And the drugs in his system are *less* metabolized than the average.
Found this same pattern in about a dozen other *high-achieving* students around the city. And...
I'm upsetting you.
No, you're just being Parker. My mind is on the To-Do list, so I have to get doing.
I'm gonna hole up and crunch. Twenty-pager due for Connors on Monday.
Uh, okay...I should get on that too.

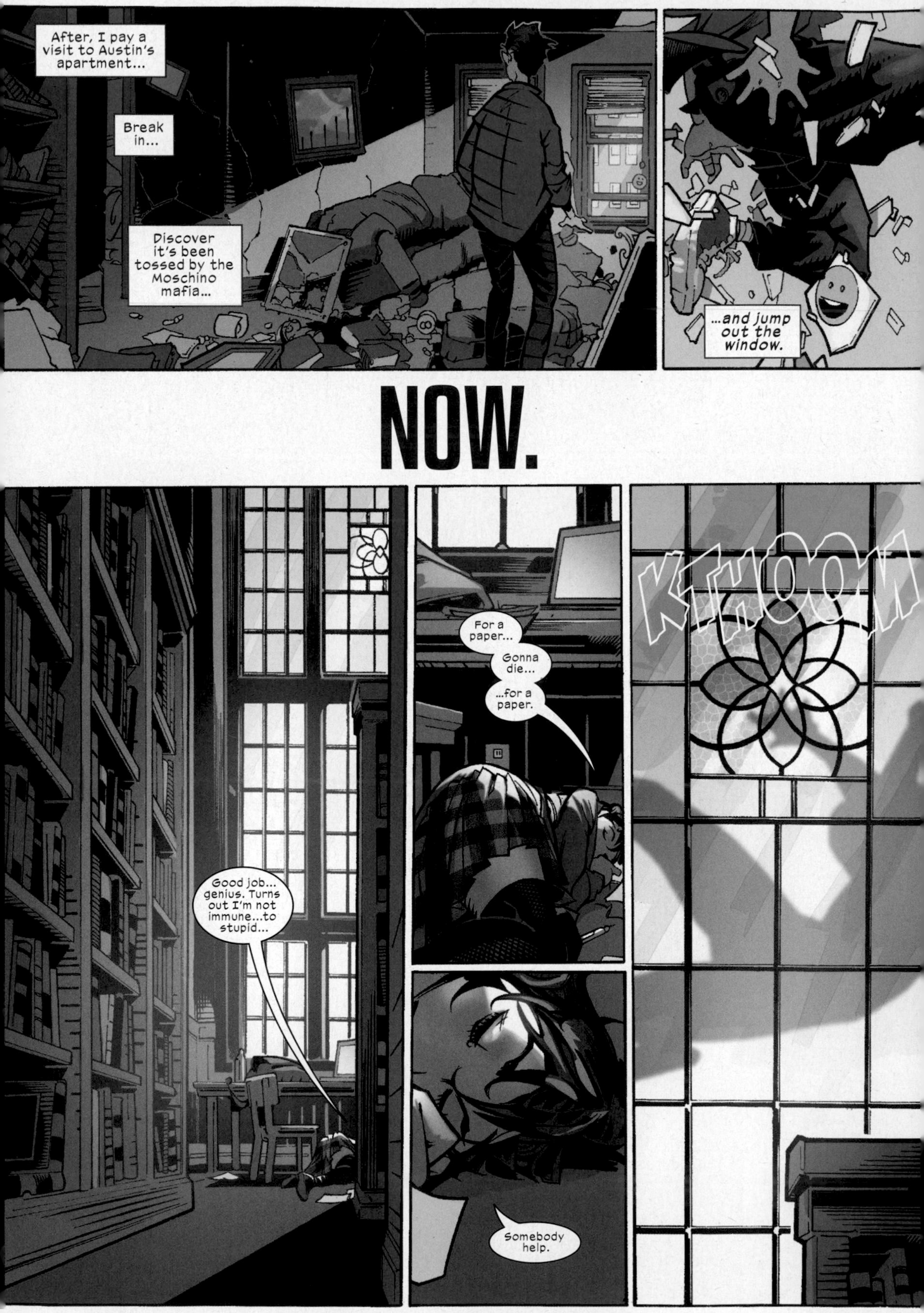
After, I pay a visit to Austin's apartment...
Break in...
Discover it's been tossed by the Moschino mafia...
...and jump out the window.
NOW.
Good job... genius. Turns out I'm not immune...to stupid...
For a paper...
Gonna die...
...for a paper.
Somebody help.
KTHOOM

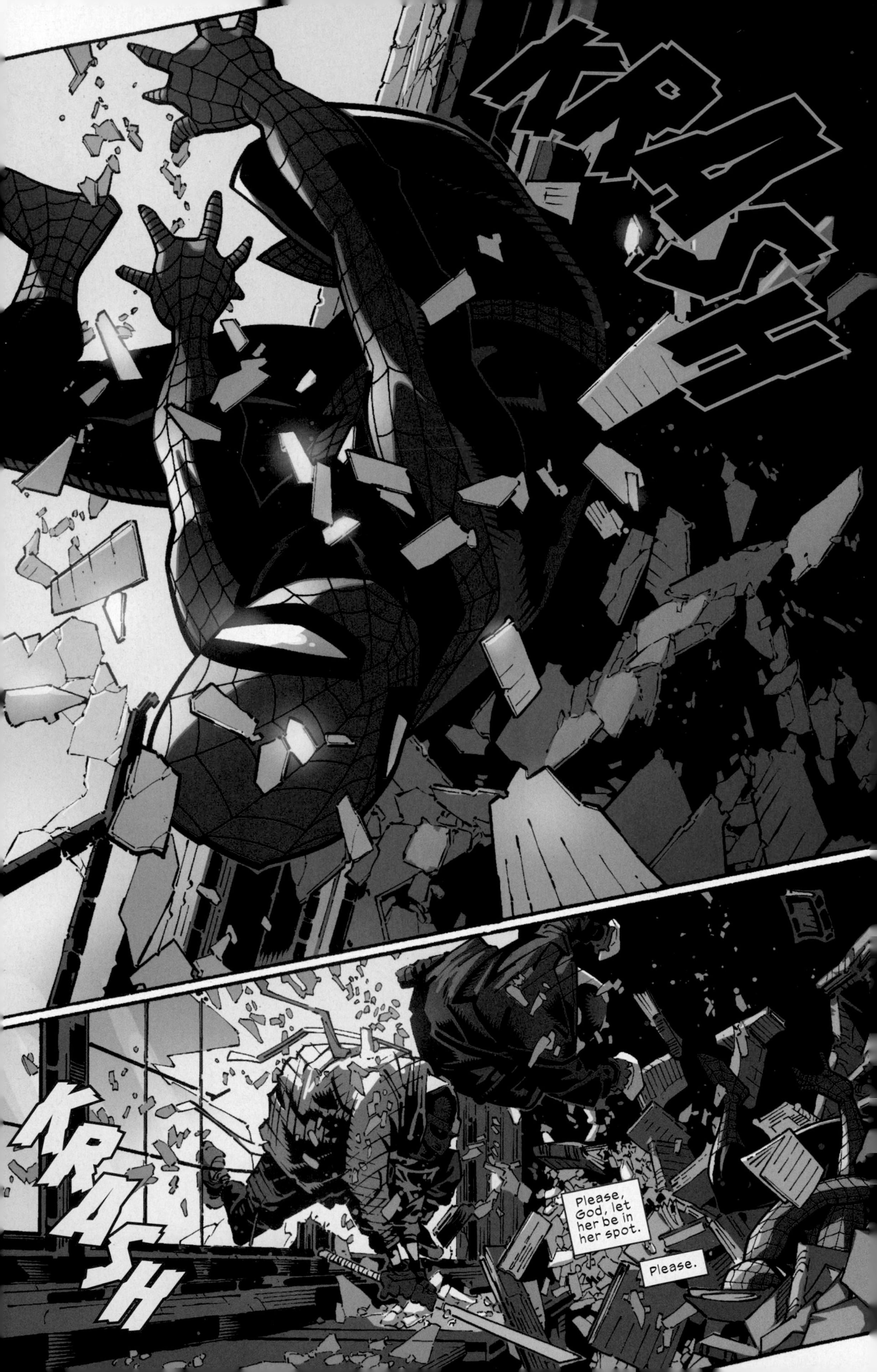
KRASH
KRASH
Please, God, let her be in her spot.
Please.

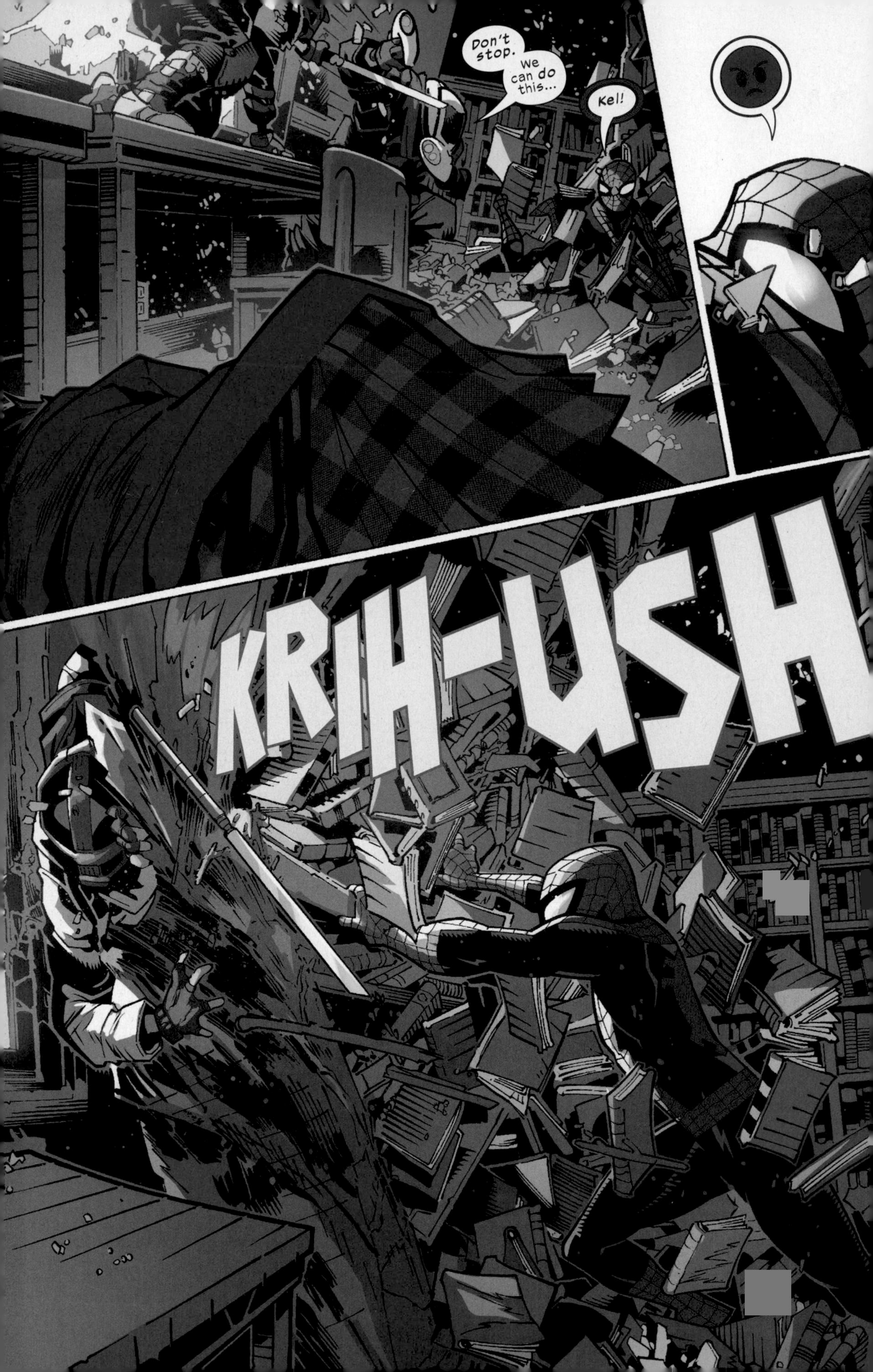

Don't stop. We can do this...
Kel!
KRIH-USH

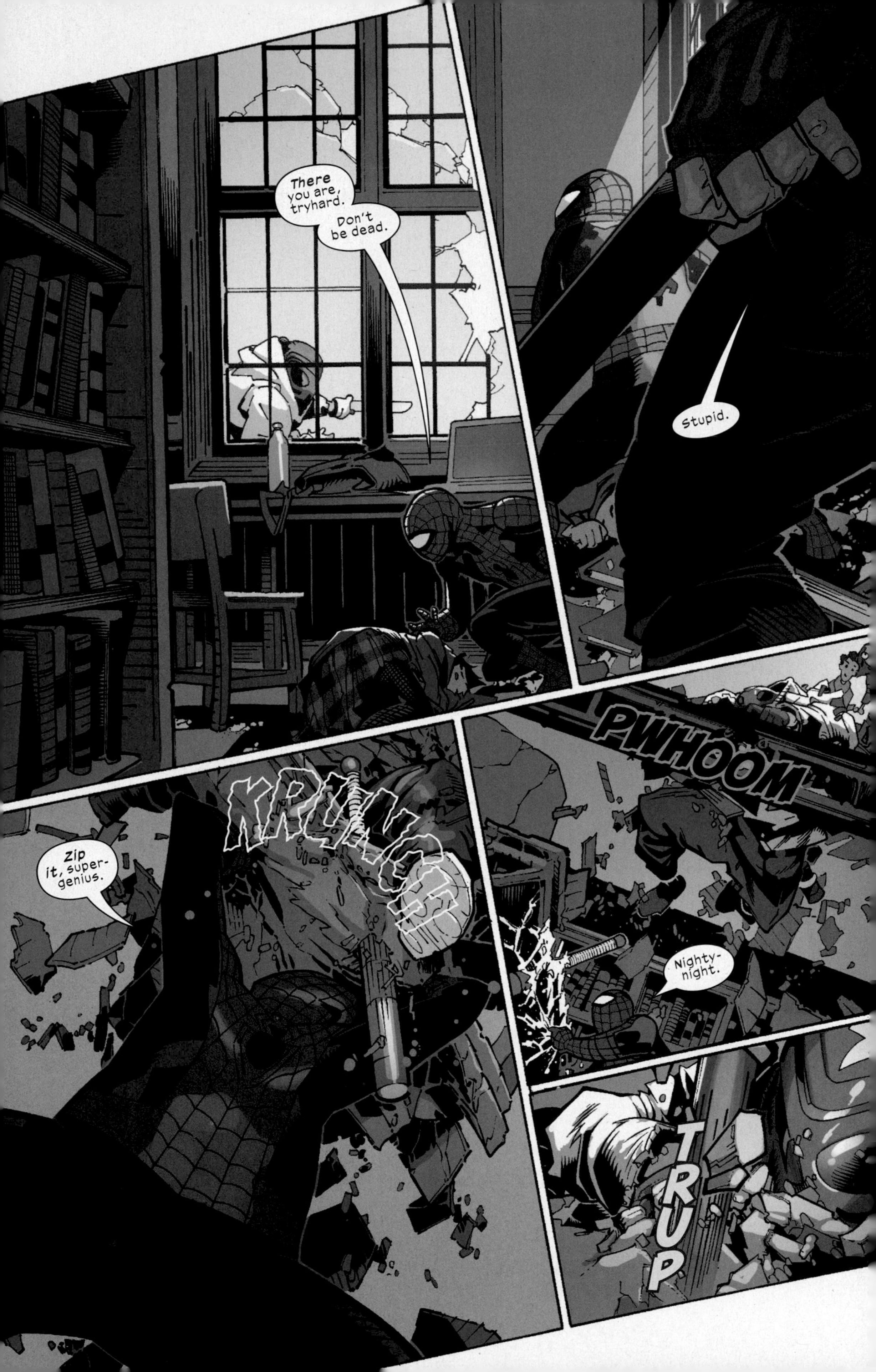
There you are, tryhard.
Don't be dead.
Stupid.
PWHOOM
KRUNCH
Zip it, super-genius.
Nighty-night.
TRUP

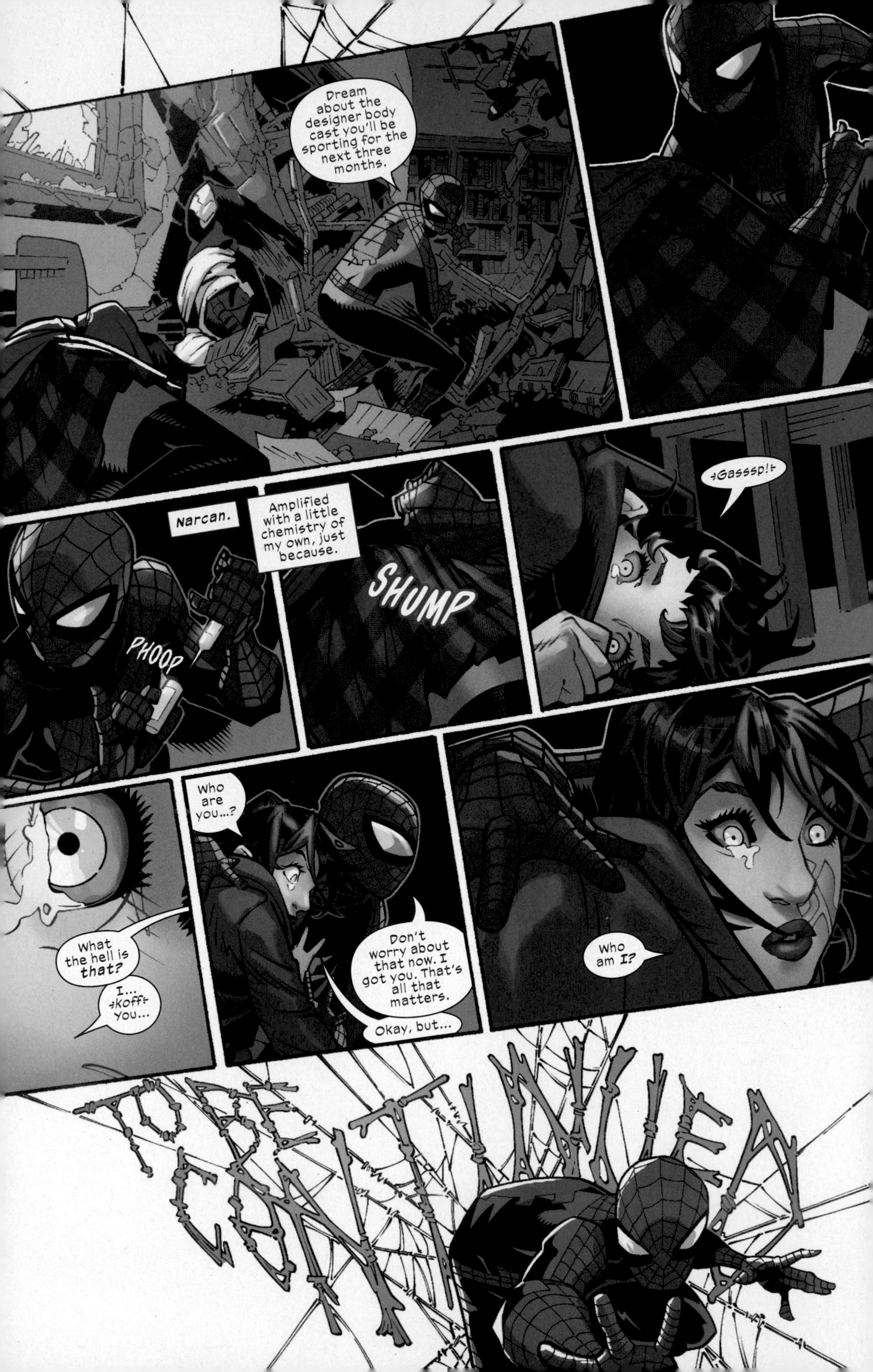
Dream about the designer body cast you'll be sporting for the next three months.
Narcan.
Amplified with a little chemistry of my own, just because.
PHOOP
SHUMP
-Gasssp!-
What the hell is that?
I... -koff- you...
Who are you...?
Don't worry about that now. I got you. That's all that matters.
Okay, but...
Who am I?
TO BE CONTINUED

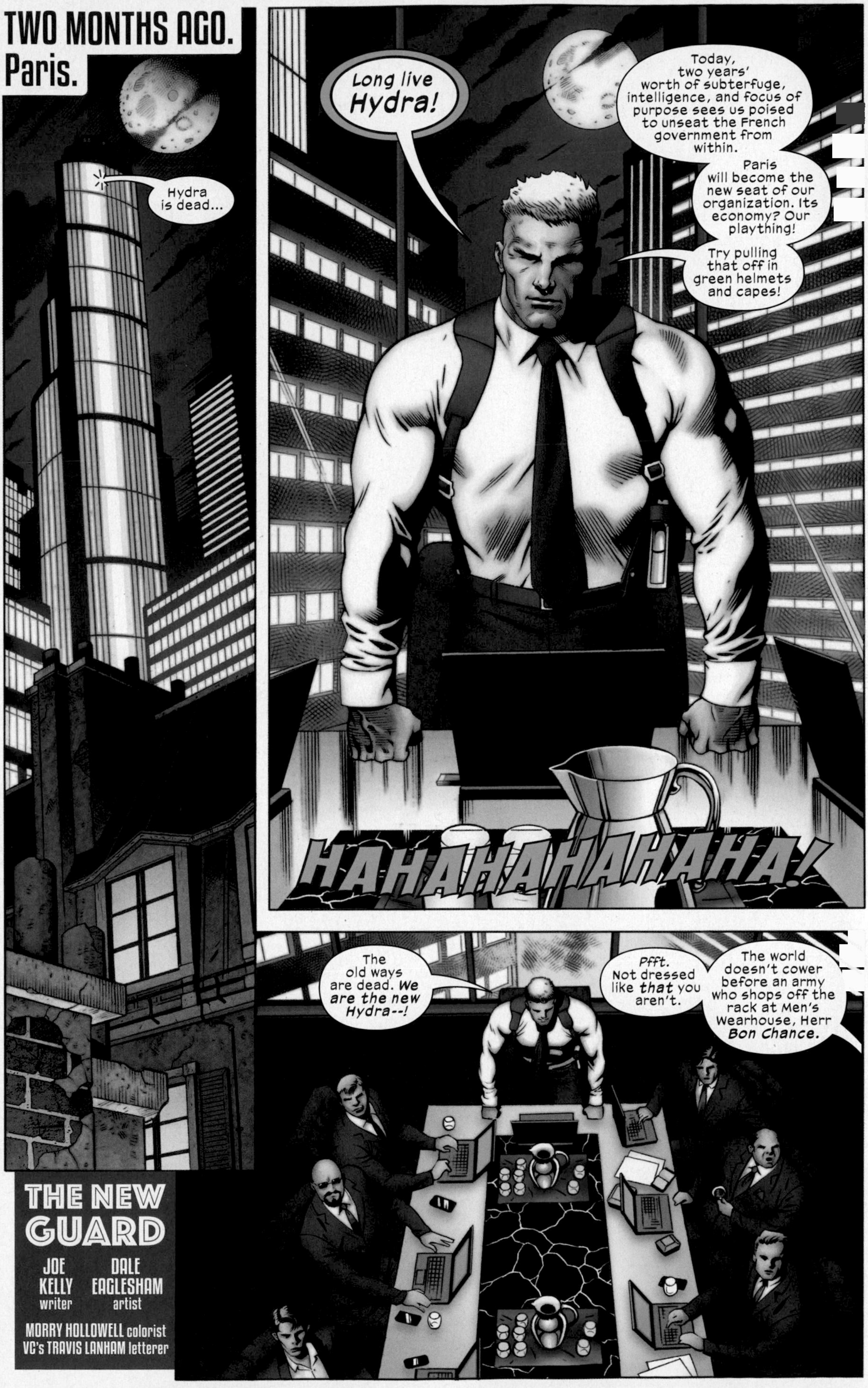
TWO MONTHS AGO.
Paris.
Hydra is dead...
Long live Hydra!
Today, two years' worth of subterfuge, intelligence, and focus of purpose sees us poised to unseat the French government from within.
Paris will become the new seat of our organization. Its economy? Our plaything!
Try pulling that off in green helmets and capes!
HAHAHAHAHAHAHA!
The old ways are dead. We are the new Hydra--!
Pfft. Not dressed like that you aren't.
The world doesn't cower before an army who shops off the rack at Men's Wearhouse, Herr Bon Chance.
THE NEW GUARD
JOE KELLY writer
DALE EAGLESHAM artist
MORRY HOLLOWELL colorist
VC's TRAVIS LANHAM letterer

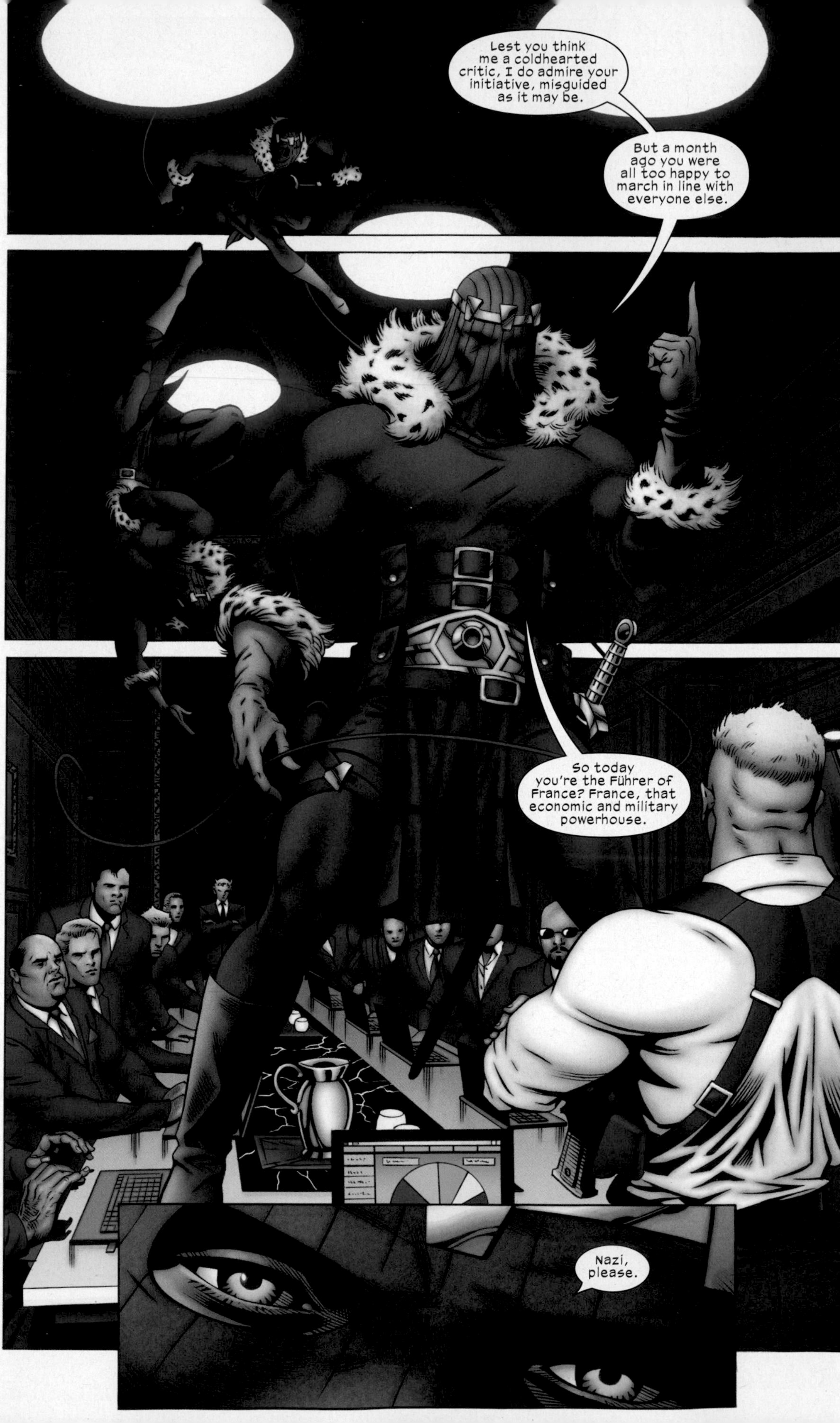
Lest you think me a coldhearted critic, I do admire your initiative, misguided as it may be.
But a month ago you were all too happy to march in line with everyone else.
So today you're the Führer of France? France, that economic and military powerhouse.
Nazi, please.

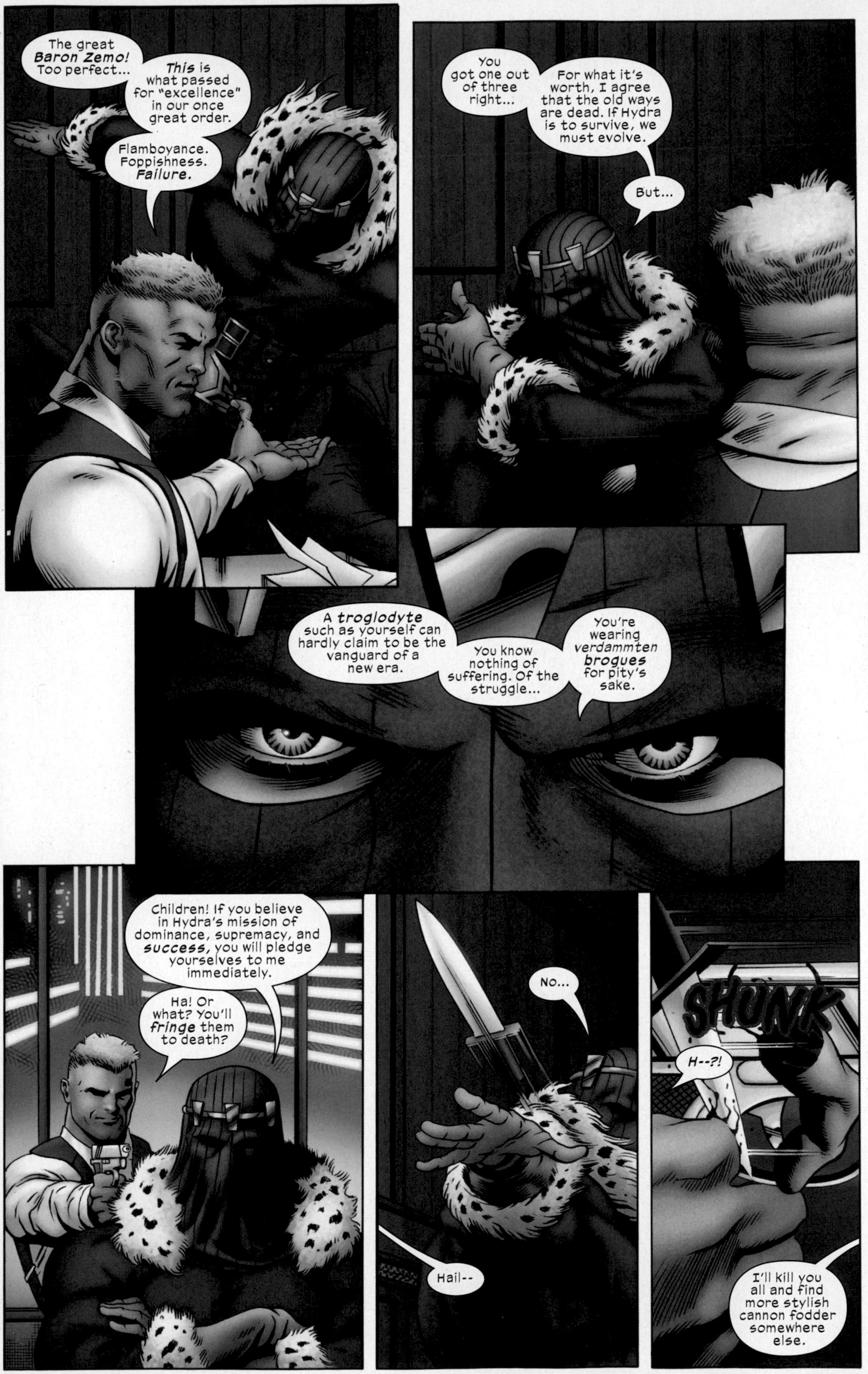

The great Baron Zemo! Too perfect...
This is what passed for "excellence" in our once great order.
Flamboyance. Foppishness. Failure.
You got one out of three right...
For what it's worth, I agree that the old ways are dead. If Hydra is to survive, we must evolve.
But...
A troglodyte such as yourself can hardly claim to be the vanguard of a new era.
You know nothing of suffering. Of the struggle...
You're wearing verdammten brogues for pity's sake.
Children! If you believe in Hydra's mission of dominance, supremacy, and success, you will pledge yourselves to me immediately.
Ha! Or what? You'll fringe them to death?
No...
Hail--
SHUNK
H--?!
I'll kill you all and find more stylish cannon fodder somewhere else.

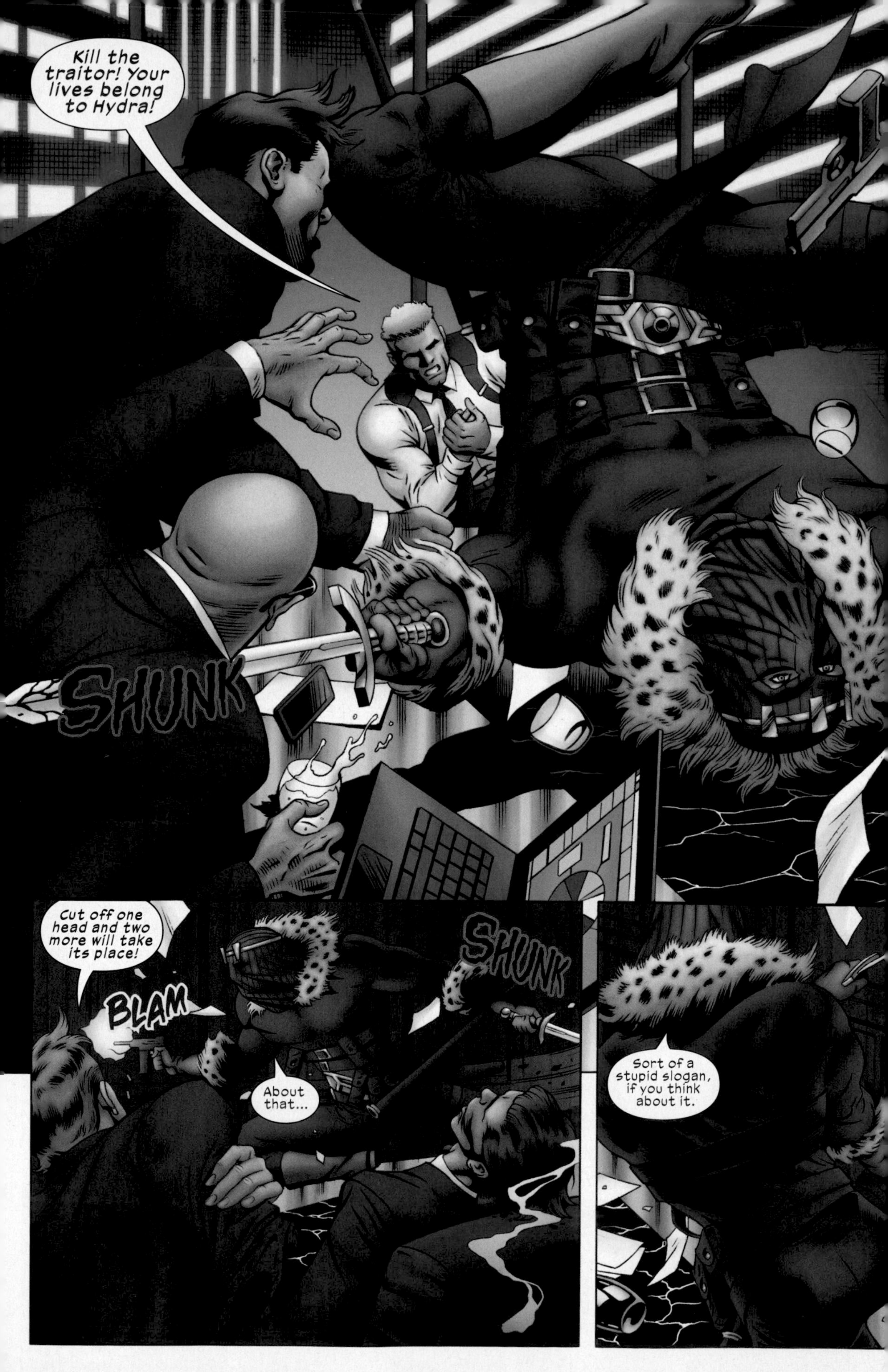
Kill the traitor! Your lives belong to Hydra!
SHUNK
Cut off one head and two more will take its place!
BLAM
SHUNK
About that...
Sort of a stupid slogan, if you think about it.

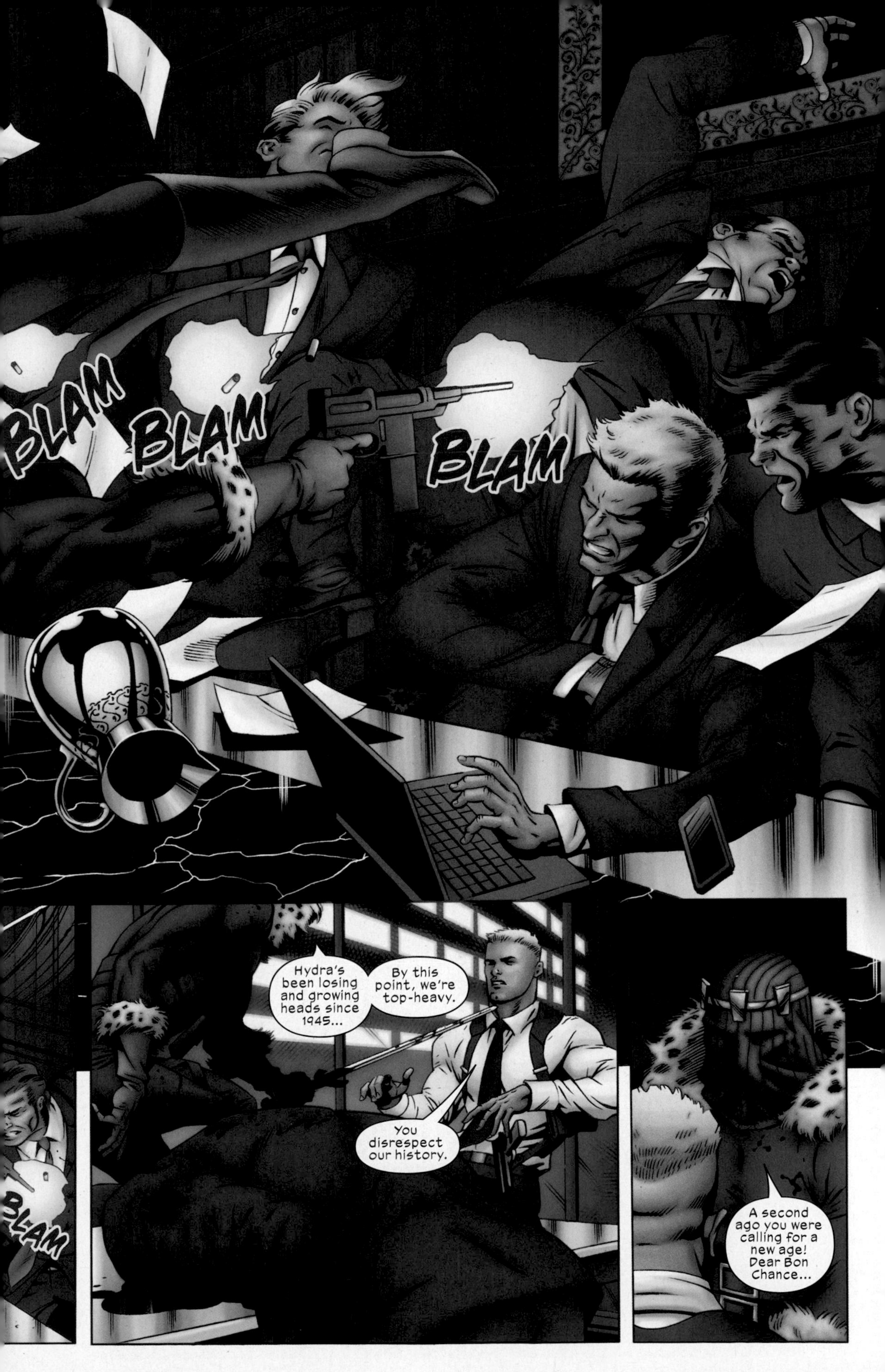
BLAM
BLAM
BLAM
Hydra's been losing and growing heads since 1945...
By this point, we're top-heavy.
You disrespect our history.
BLAM
A second ago you were calling for a new age! Dear Bon Chance...

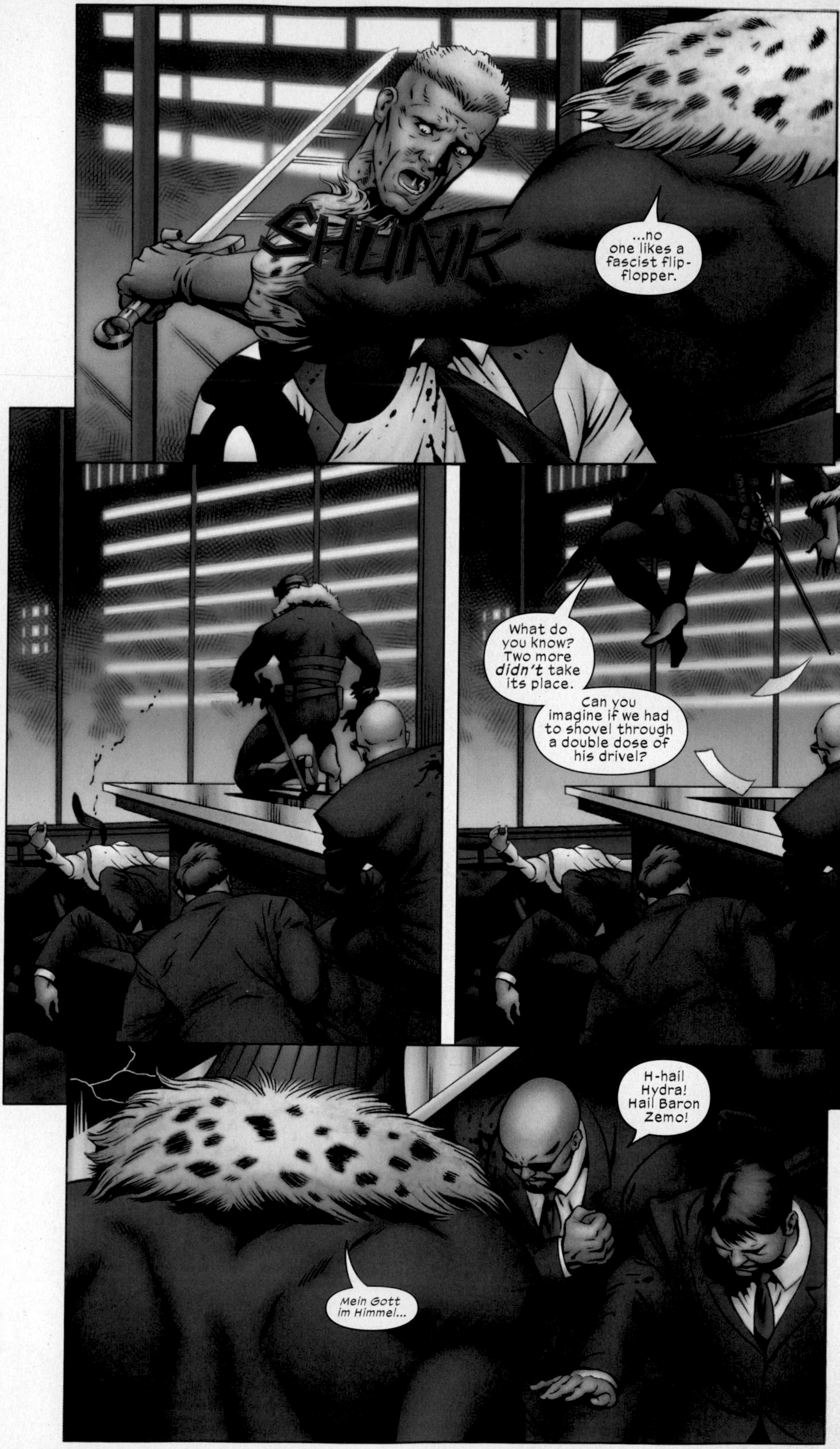
SHUNK
...no one likes a fascist flip-flopper.
What do you know? Two more *didn't* take its place.
Can you imagine if we had to shovel through a double dose of his drivel?
H-hail Hydra! Hail Baron Zemo!
Mein Gott im Himmel...

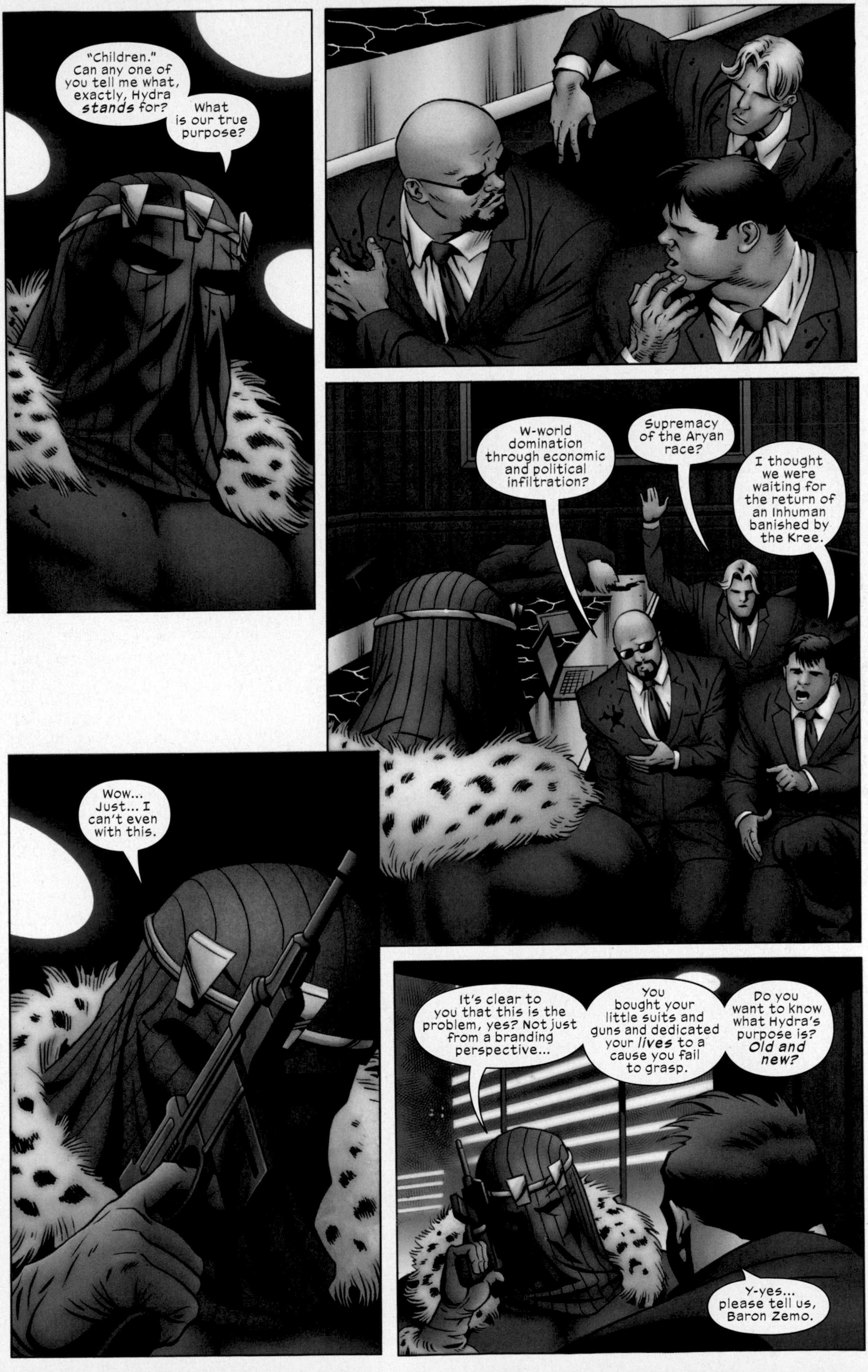
"Children." Can any one of you tell me what, exactly, Hydra *stands* for?
What is our true purpose?
W-world domination through economic and political infiltration?
Supremacy of the Aryan race?
I thought we were waiting for the return of an Inhuman banished by the Kree.
Wow... Just... I can't even with this.
It's clear to you that this is the problem, yes? Not just from a branding perspective...
You bought your little suits and guns and dedicated your *lives* to a cause you fail to grasp.
Do you want to know what Hydra's purpose is? *Old and new?*
Y-yes... please tell us, Baron Zemo.

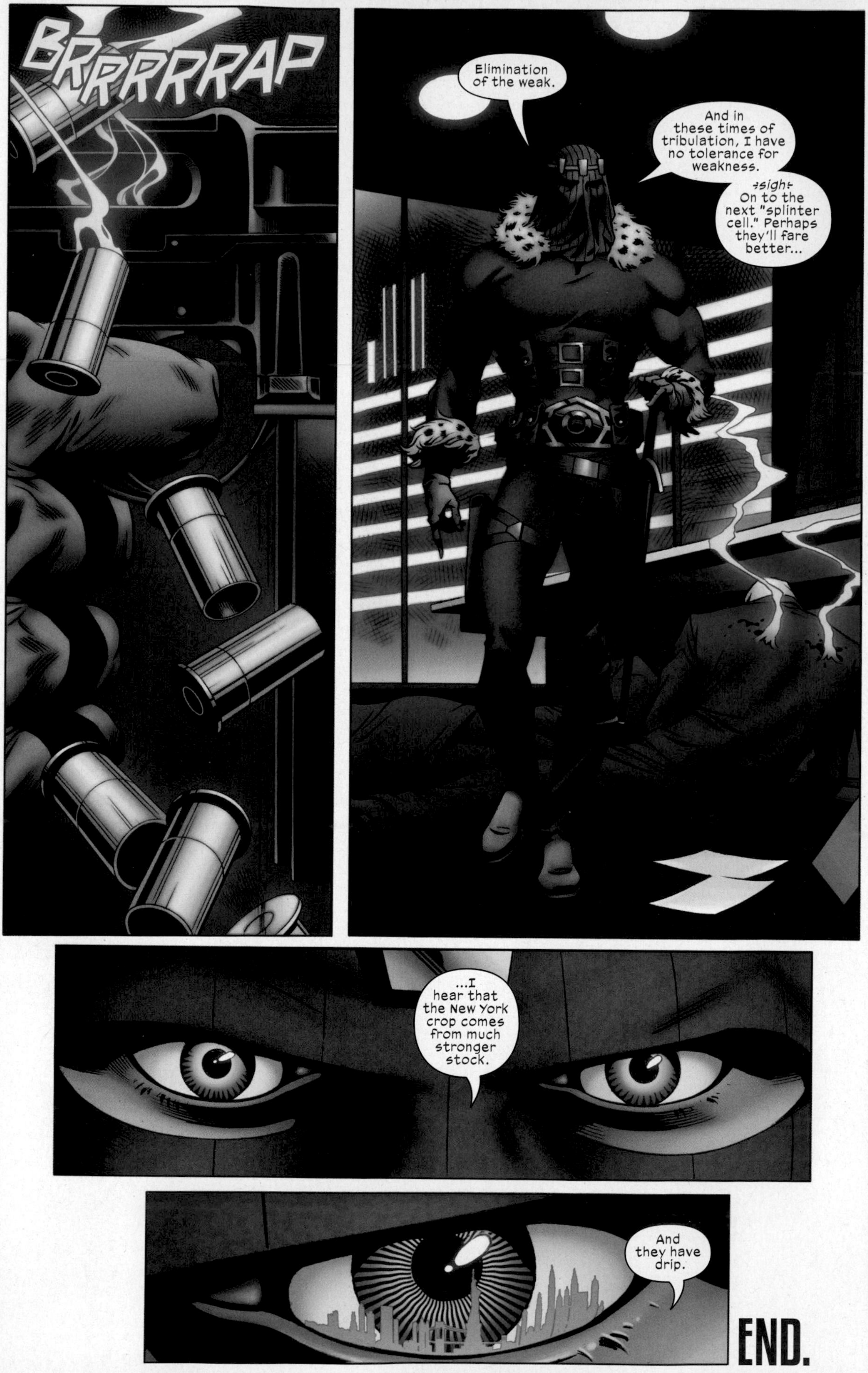
BRRRRRAP
Elimination of the weak.
And in these times of tribulation, I have no tolerance for weakness.
sigh On to the next "splinter cell." Perhaps they'll fare better...
...I hear that the New York crop comes from much stronger stock.
And they have drip.
END.

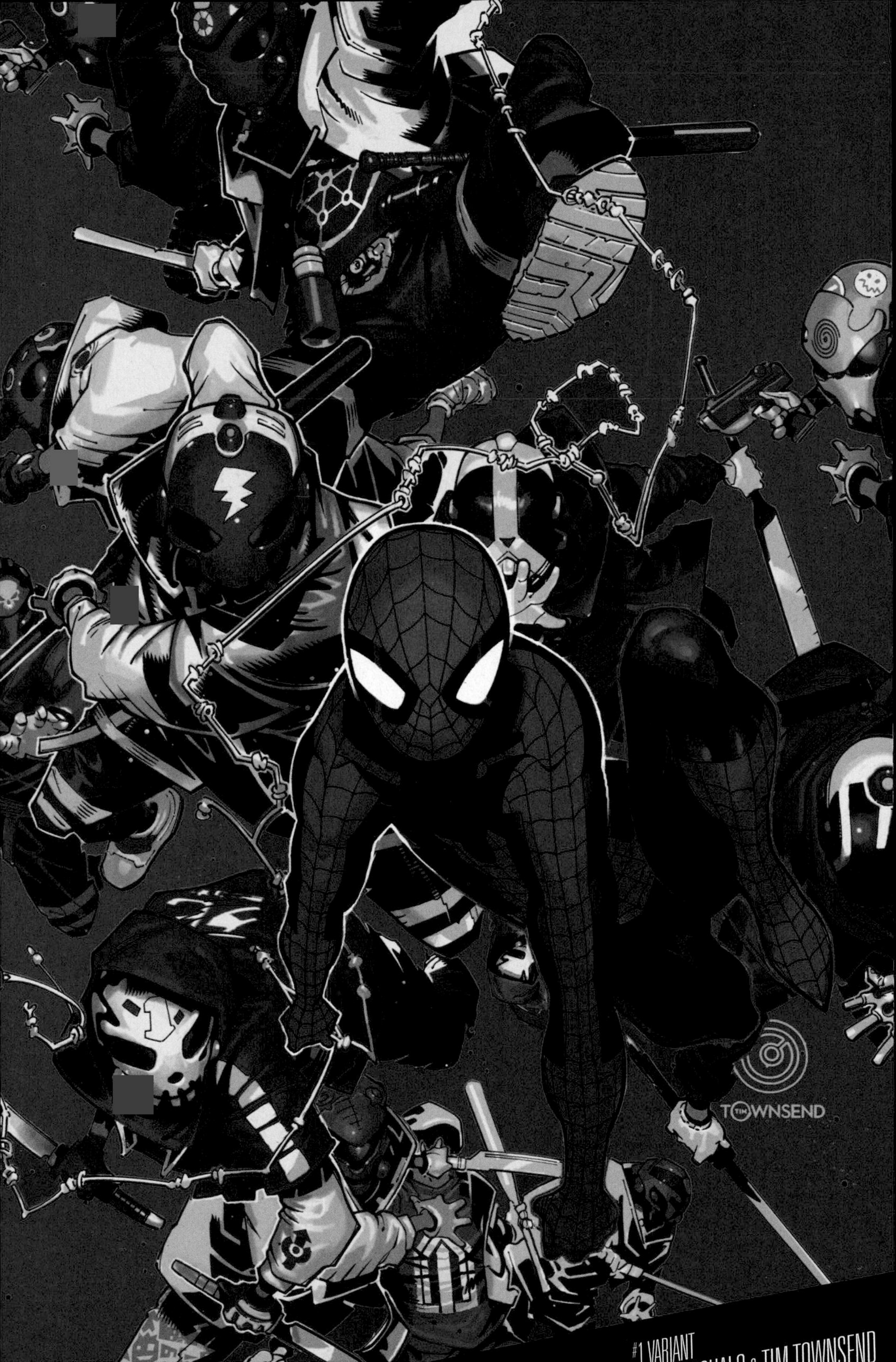
TOWNSEND

#1 VARIANT
CHRIS BACHALO & TIM TOWNSEND

2. BIG BRAIN PLAY
CHAPTER TWO

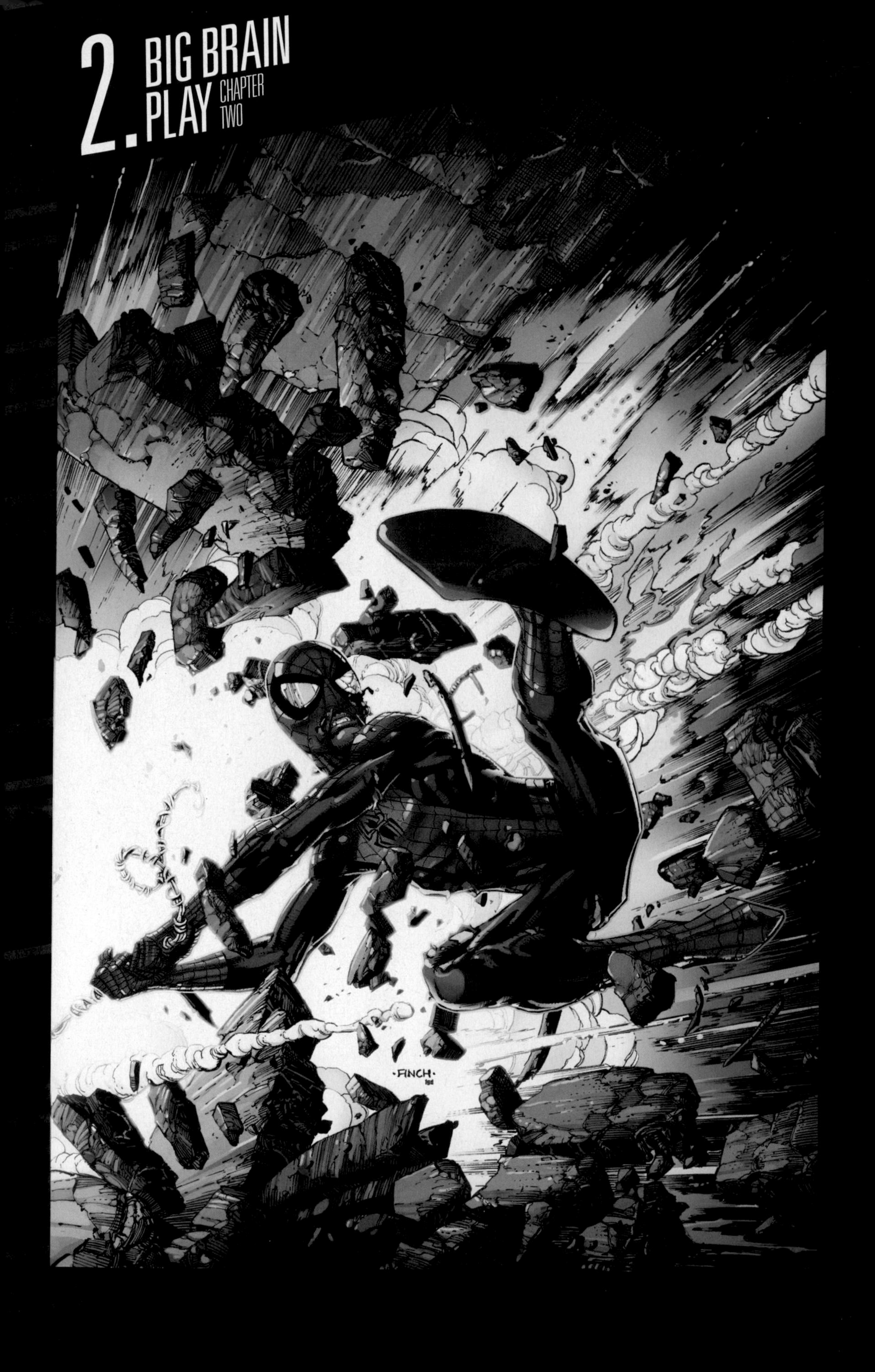
FINCH

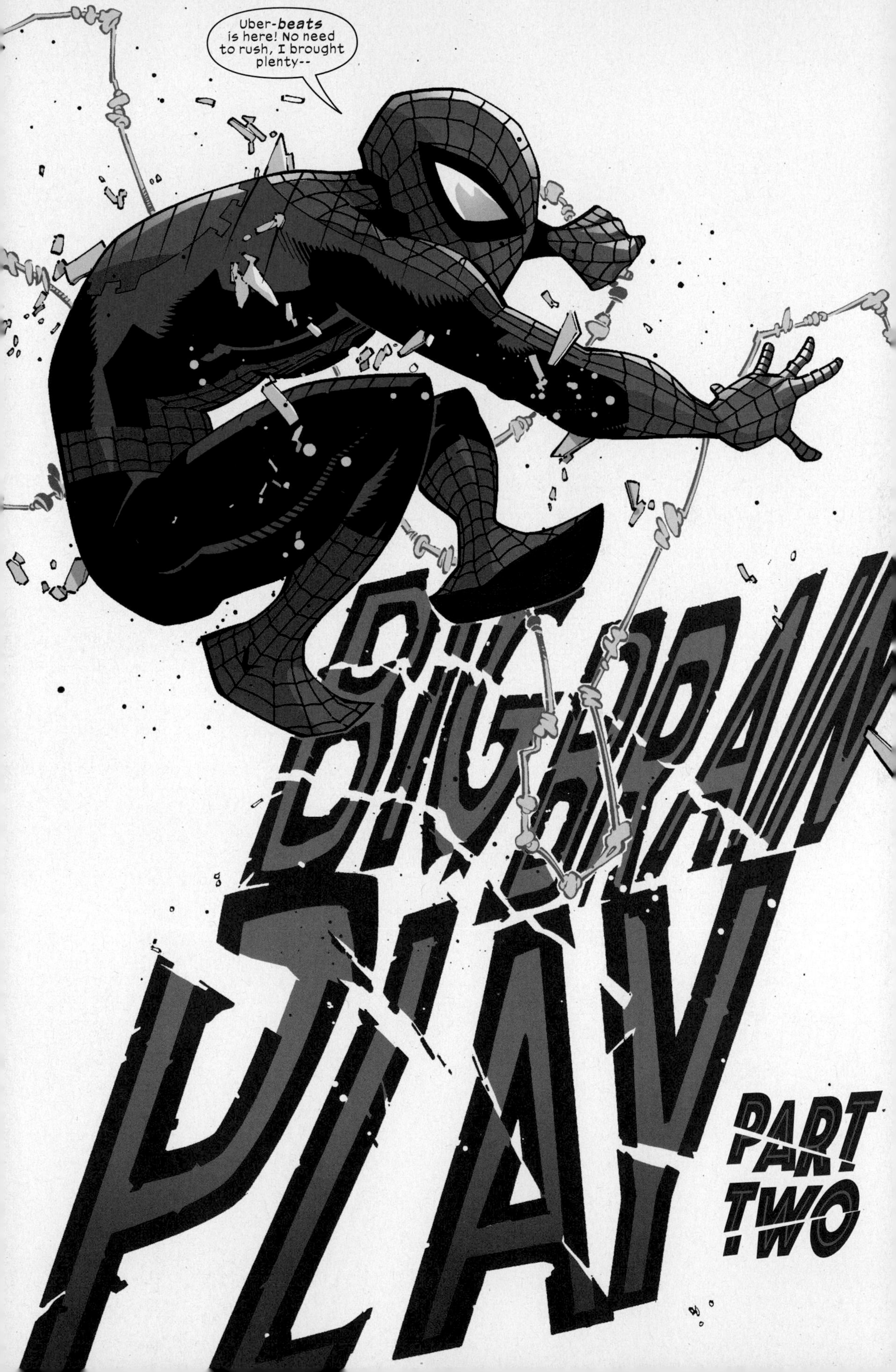
Uber-*beats* is here! No need to rush, I brought plenty--
BIG BRAIN PLAY
PART TWO

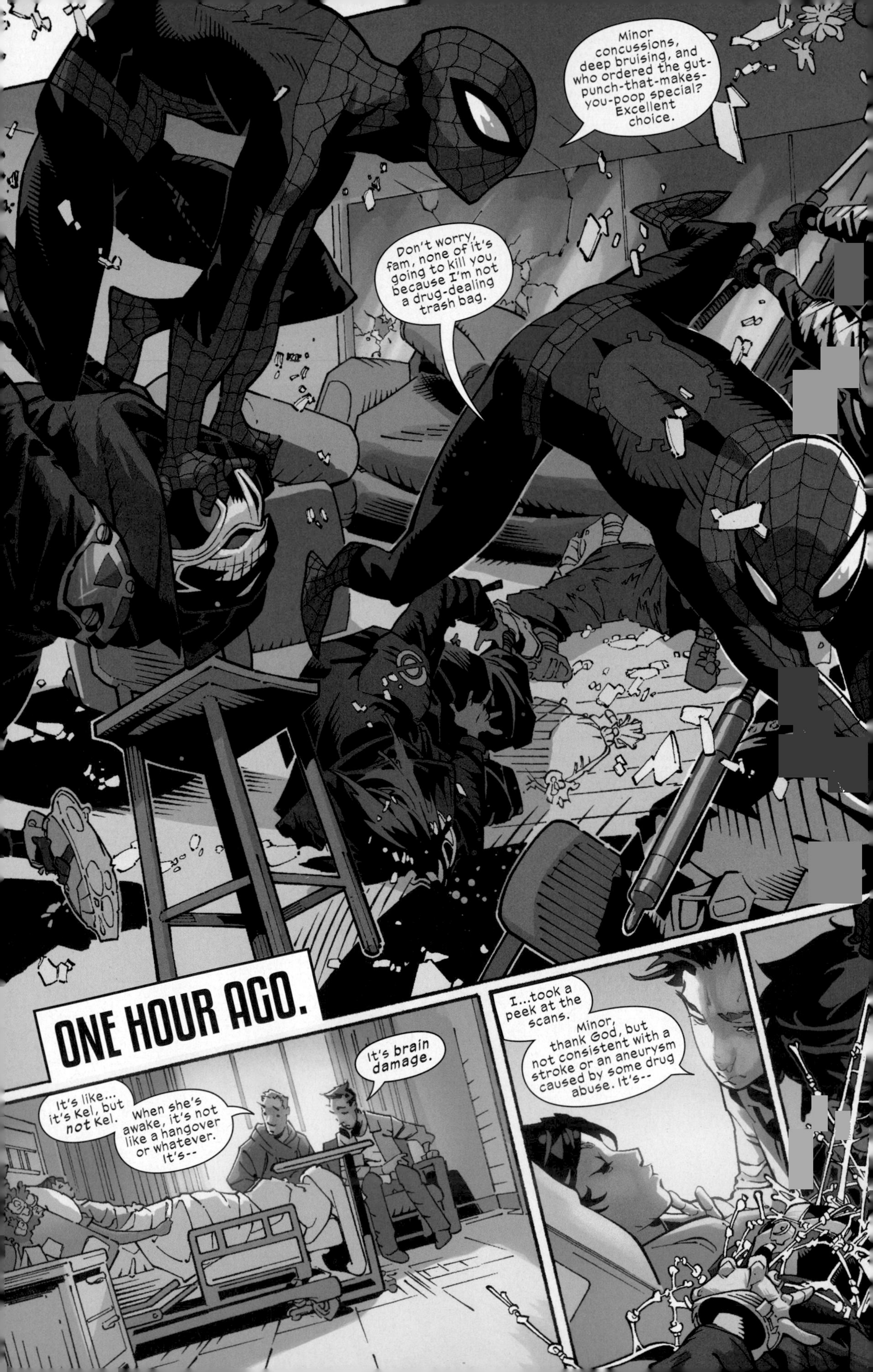
Minor concussions, deep bruising, and who ordered the gut-punch-that-makes-you-poop special? Excellent choice.
Don't worry, fam, none of it's going to kill you, because I'm not a drug-dealing trash bag.
ONE HOUR AGO.
It's like... it's Kel, but not Kel.
When she's awake, it's not like a hangover or whatever. It's--
It's brain damage.
I...took a peek at the scans.
Minor, thank God, but not consistent with a stroke or an aneurysm caused by some drug abuse. It's--

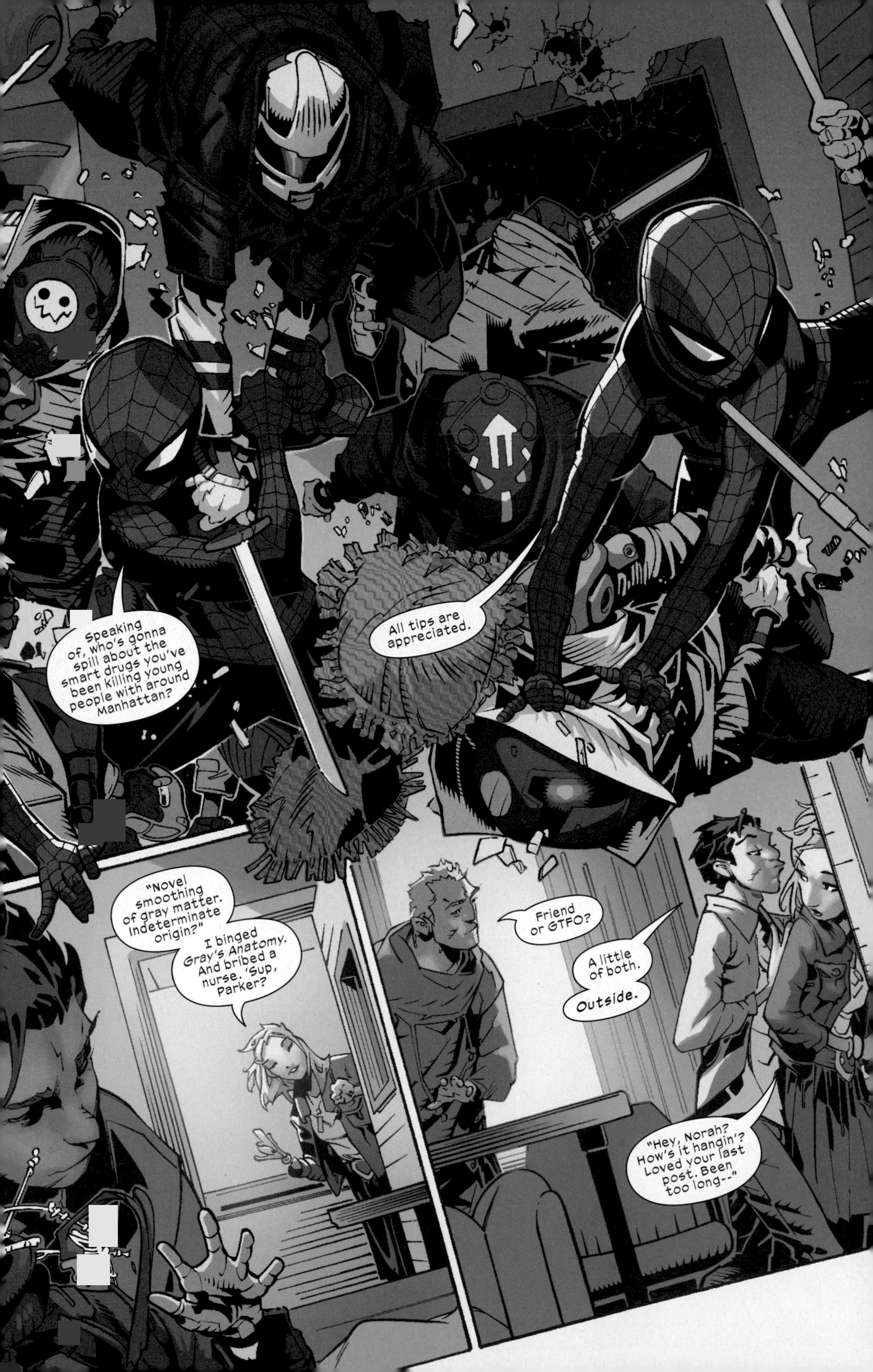
Speaking of, who's gonna spill about the smart drugs you've been killing young people with around Manhattan?
All tips are appreciated.
"Novel smoothing of gray matter. Indeterminate origin?"
I binged Gray's Anatomy. And bribed a nurse. 'Sup, Parker?
Friend or GTFO?
A little of both.
Outside.
"Hey, Norah? How's it hangin'? Loved your last post. Been too long--"

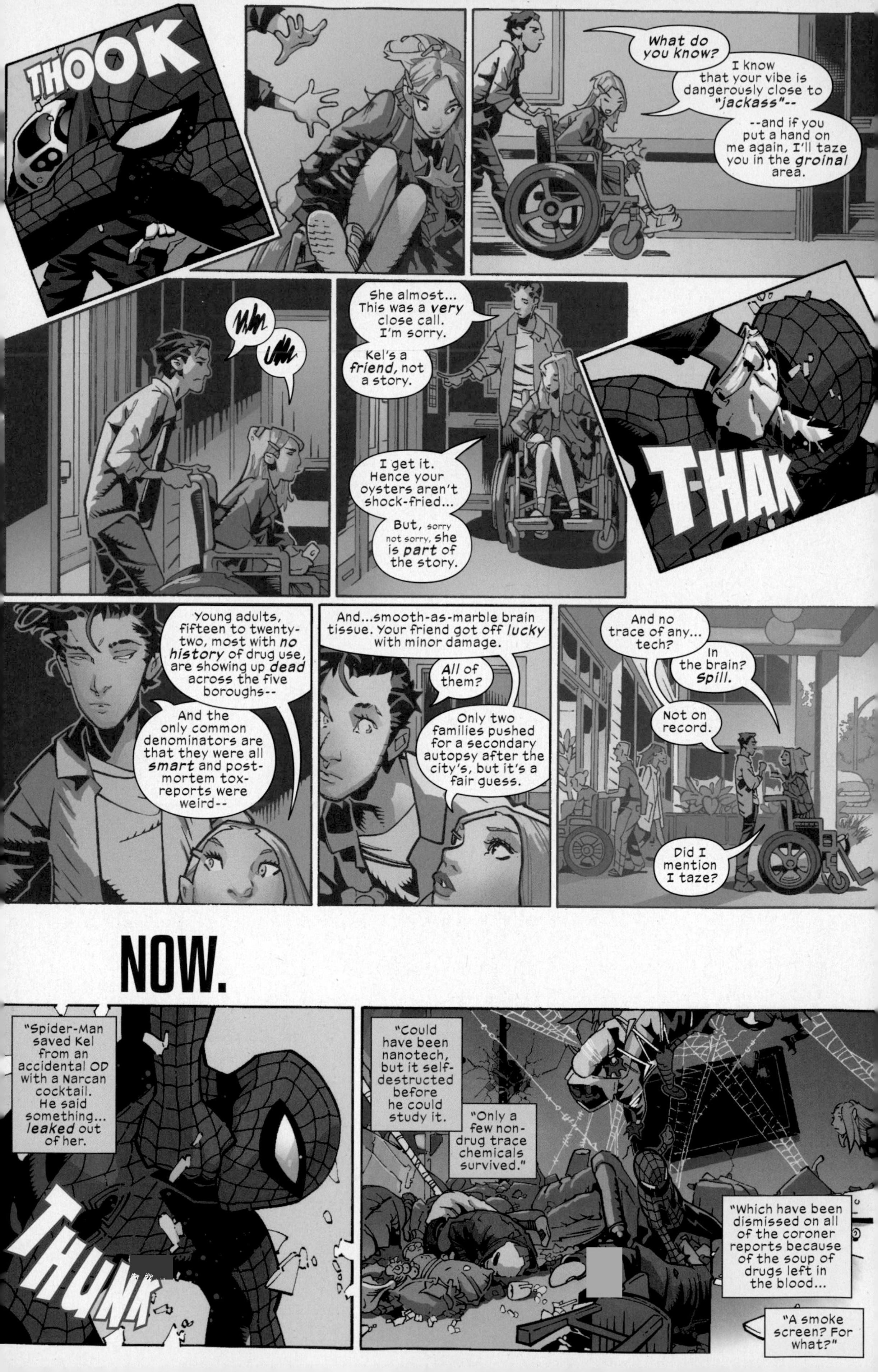
THOOK
What do you know?
I know that your vibe is dangerously close to "jackass"--
--and if you put a hand on me again, I'll taze you in the groinal area.
She almost... This was a very close call. I'm sorry.
Kel's a friend, not a story.
I get it. Hence your oysters aren't shock-fried...
But, sorry not sorry, she is part of the story.
T-HAK
Young adults, fifteen to twenty-two, most with no history of drug use, are showing up dead across the five boroughs--
And the only common denominators are that they were all smart and post-mortem tox-reports were weird--
And...smooth-as-marble brain tissue. Your friend got off lucky with minor damage.
All of them?
Only two families pushed for a secondary autopsy after the city's, but it's a fair guess.
And no trace of any... tech?
In the brain? Spill.
Not on record.
Did I mention I taze?
NOW.
"Spider-Man saved Kel from an accidental OD with a Narcan cocktail. He said something... leaked out of her.
THUNK
"Could have been nanotech, but it self-destructed before he could study it.
"Only a few non-drug trace chemicals survived."
"Which have been dismissed on all of the coroner reports because of the soup of drugs left in the blood...
"A smoke screen? For what?"

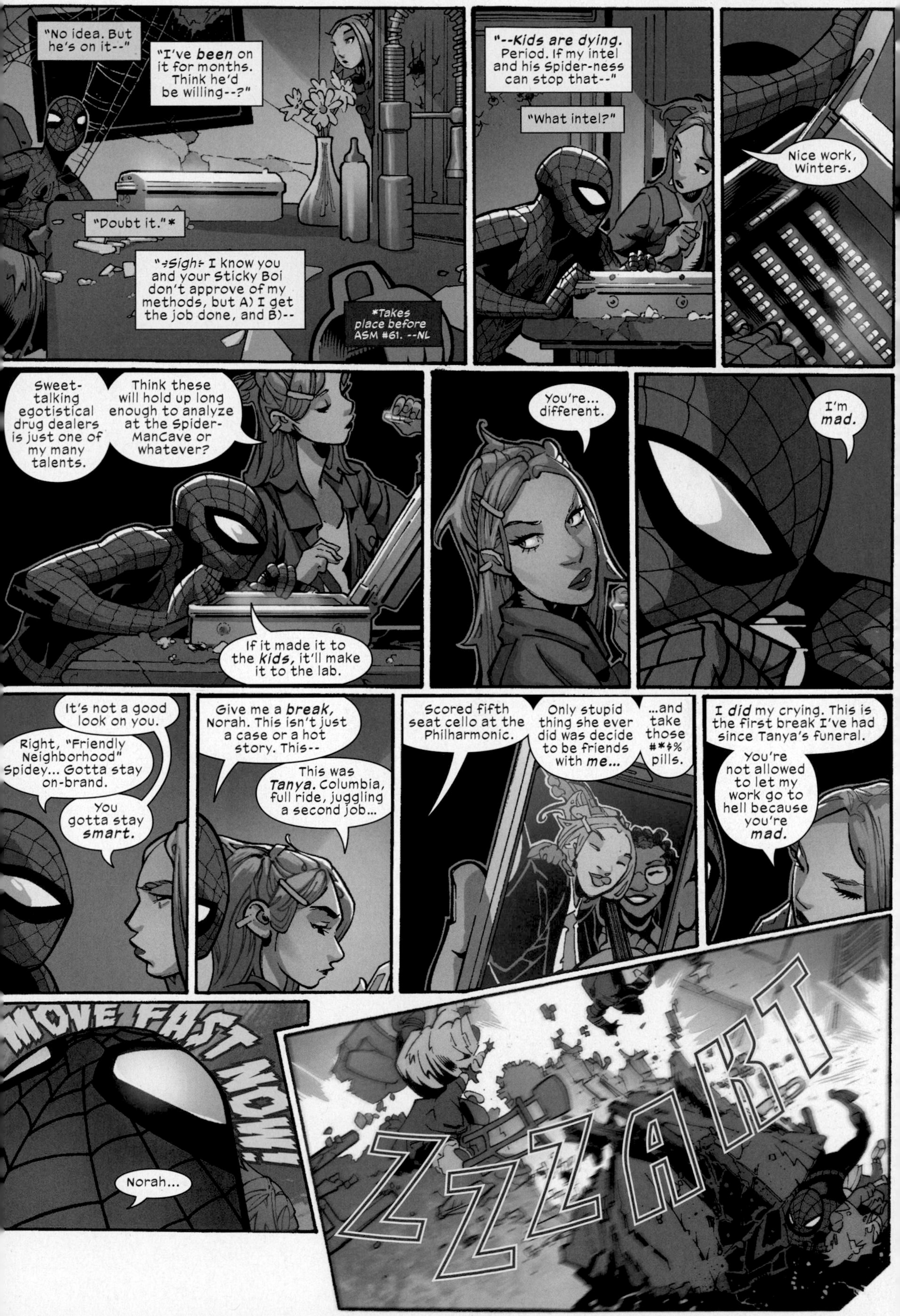
"No idea. But he's on it--"
"I've *been* on it for months. Think he'd be willing--?"
"Doubt it."*
"-Sigh- I know you and your Sticky Boi don't approve of my methods, but A) I get the job done, and B)--
*Takes place before ASM #61. --NL
"--*Kids are dying.* Period. If my intel and his Spider-ness can stop that--"
"What intel?"
Nice work, Winters.
Sweet-talking egotistical drug dealers is just one of my many talents.
Think these will hold up long enough to analyze at the Spider-ManCave or whatever?
If it made it to the *kids,* it'll make it to the lab.
You're... different.
I'm *mad.*
It's not a good look on you.
Right, "Friendly Neighborhood" Spidey... Gotta stay on-brand.
You gotta stay *smart.*
Give me a *break,* Norah. This isn't just a case or a hot story. This--
This was *Tanya.* Columbia, full ride, juggling a second job...
Scored fifth seat cello at the Philharmonic.
Only stupid thing she ever did was decide to be friends with *me*...
...and take those #*$% pills.
I *did* my crying. This is the first break I've had since Tanya's funeral.
You're not allowed to let my work go to hell because you're *mad.*
MOVE! FAST NOW!
Norah...
ZZZAKT

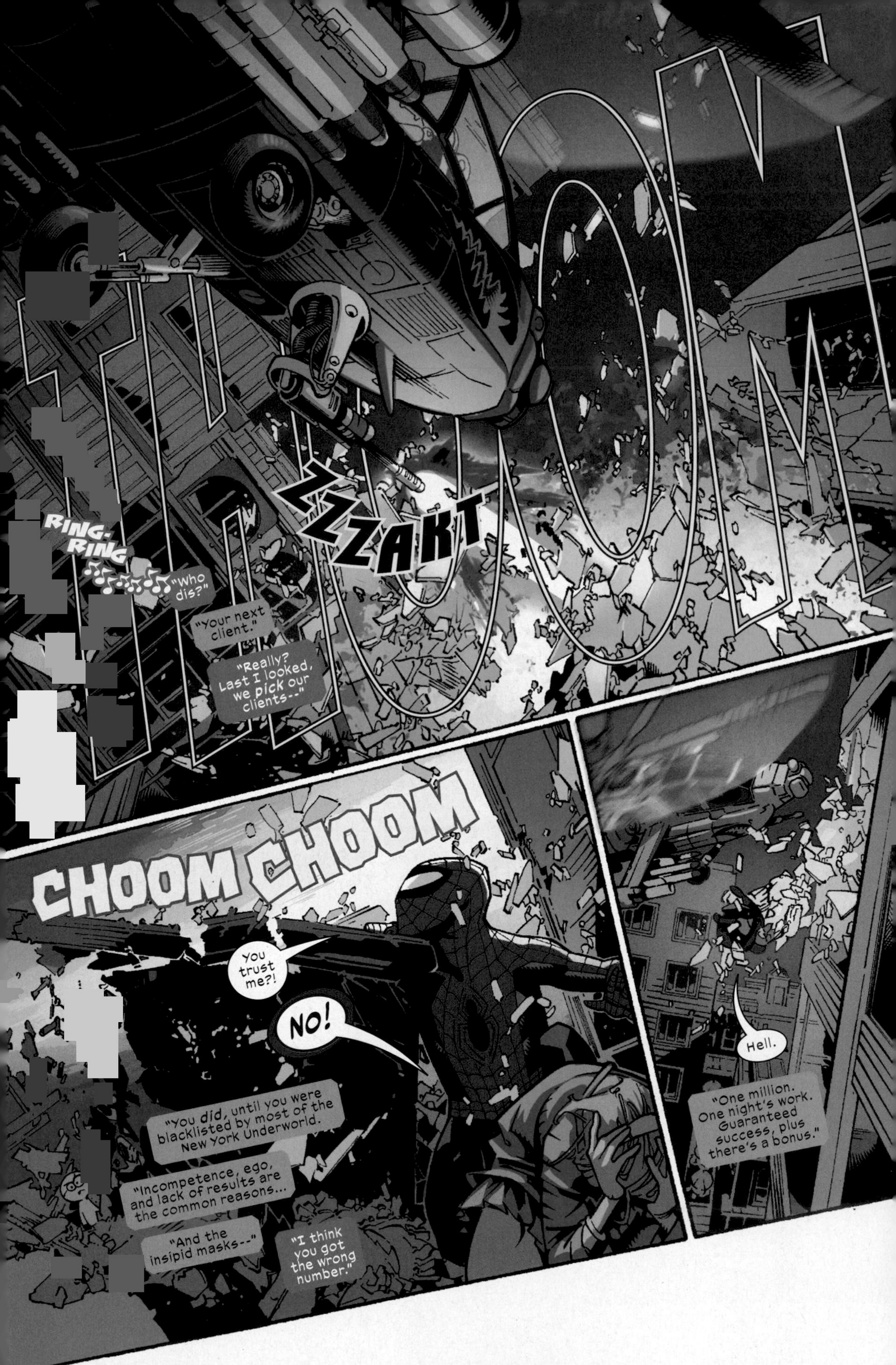
RING-RING
"Who dis?"
"Your next client."
"Really? Last I looked, we pick our clients--"
ZZZAKT
CHOOM CHOOM
You trust me?!
NO!
"You did, until you were blacklisted by most of the New York Underworld.
"Incompetence, ego, and lack of results are the common reasons...
"And the insipid masks--"
"I think you got the wrong number."
Hell.
"One million. One night's work. Guaranteed success, plus there's a bonus."

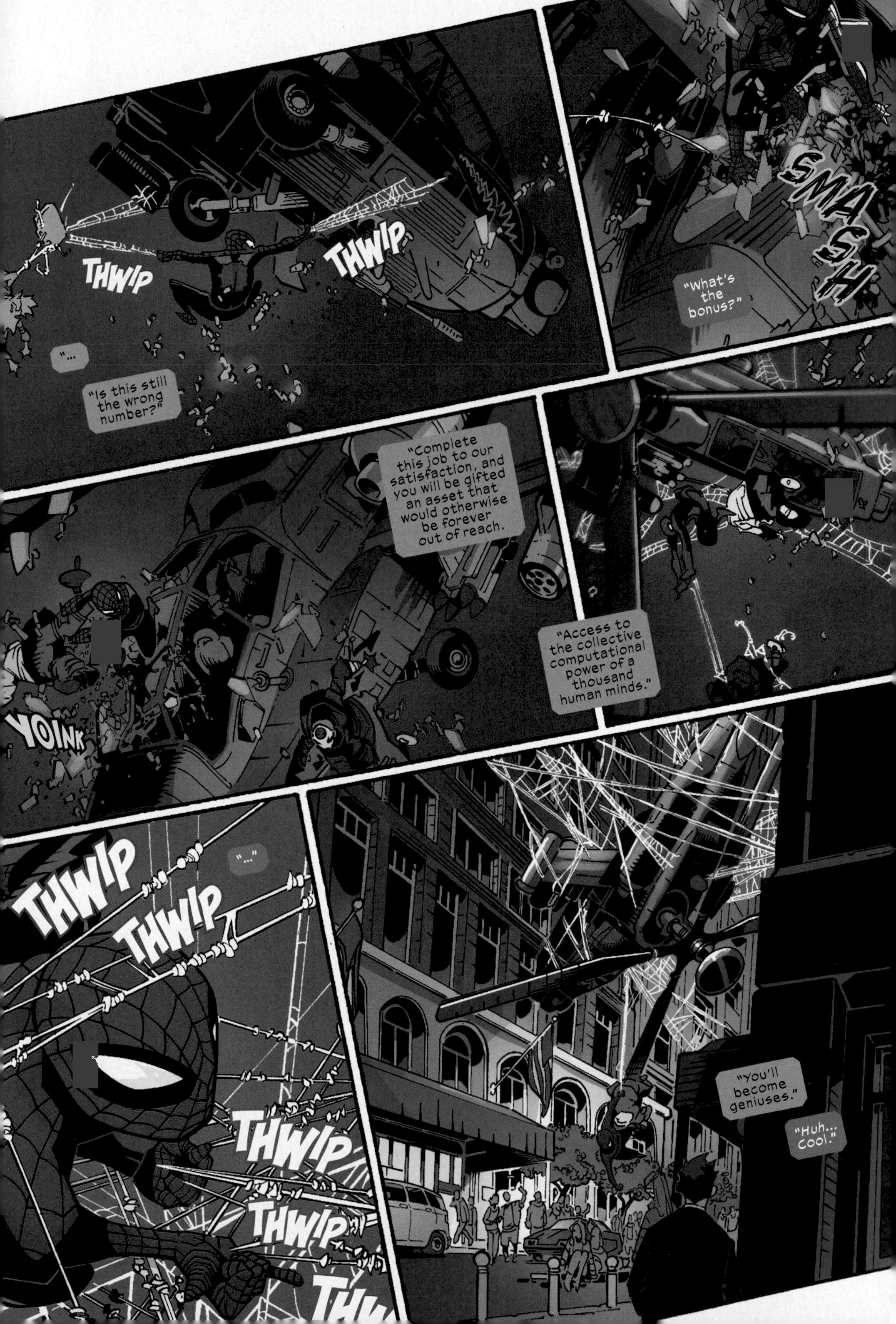
THWIP
THWIP
"..."
"Is this still the wrong number?"
SMASH
"What's the bonus?"
"Complete this job to our satisfaction, and you will be gifted an asset that would otherwise be forever out of reach."
YOINK
"Access to the collective computational power of a thousand human minds."
THWIP
THWIP
"..."
THWIP
THWIP
"You'll become geniuses."
"Huh... Cool."

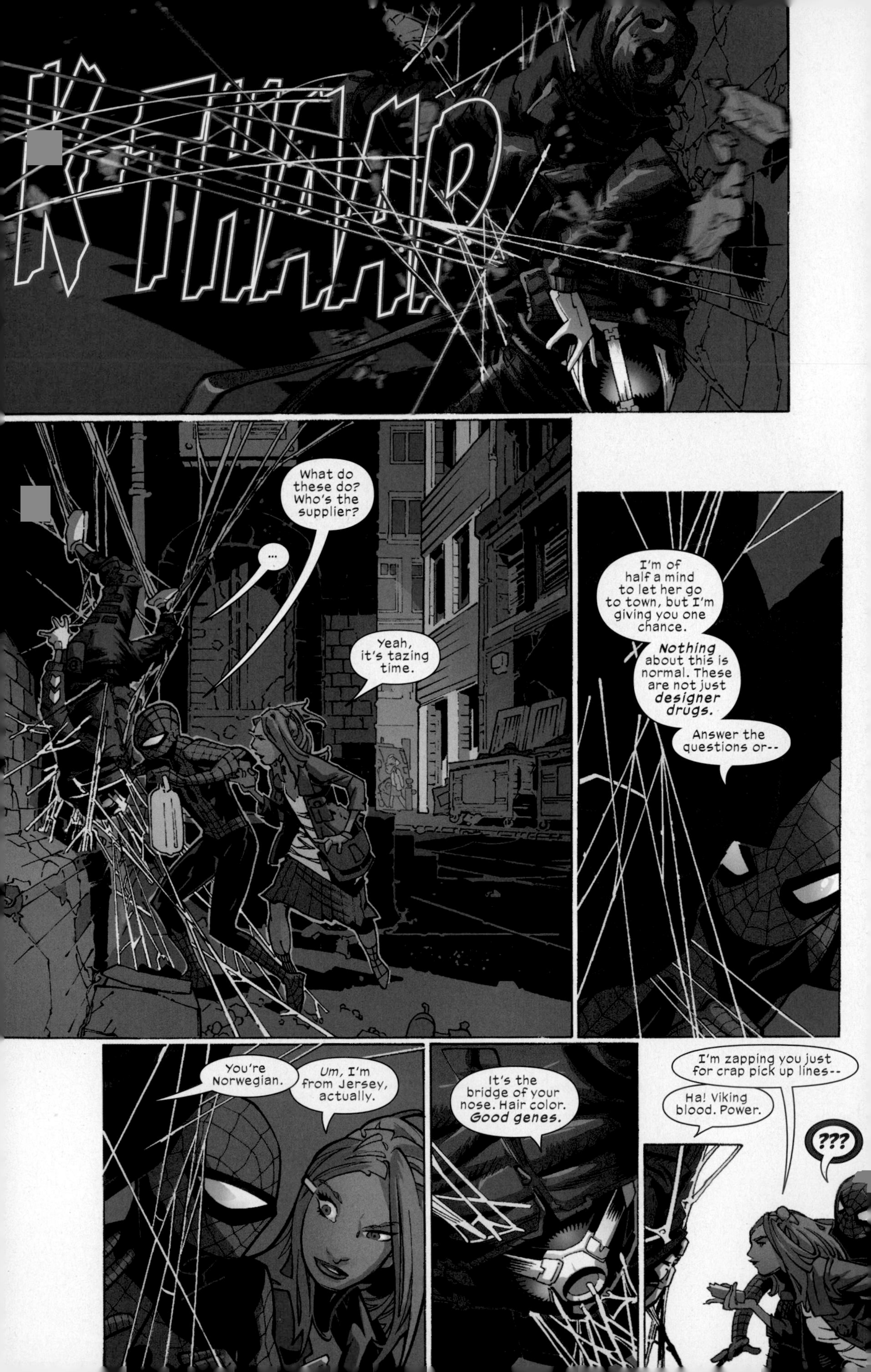

What do these do? Who's the supplier?
...
Yeah, it's tazing time.
I'm of half a mind to let her go to town, but I'm giving you one chance.
Nothing about this is normal. These are not just *designer drugs.*
Answer the questions or--
You're Norwegian.
Um, I'm from Jersey, actually.
It's the bridge of your nose. Hair color. *Good genes.*
I'm zapping you just for crap pick up lines--
Ha! Viking blood. Power.
???

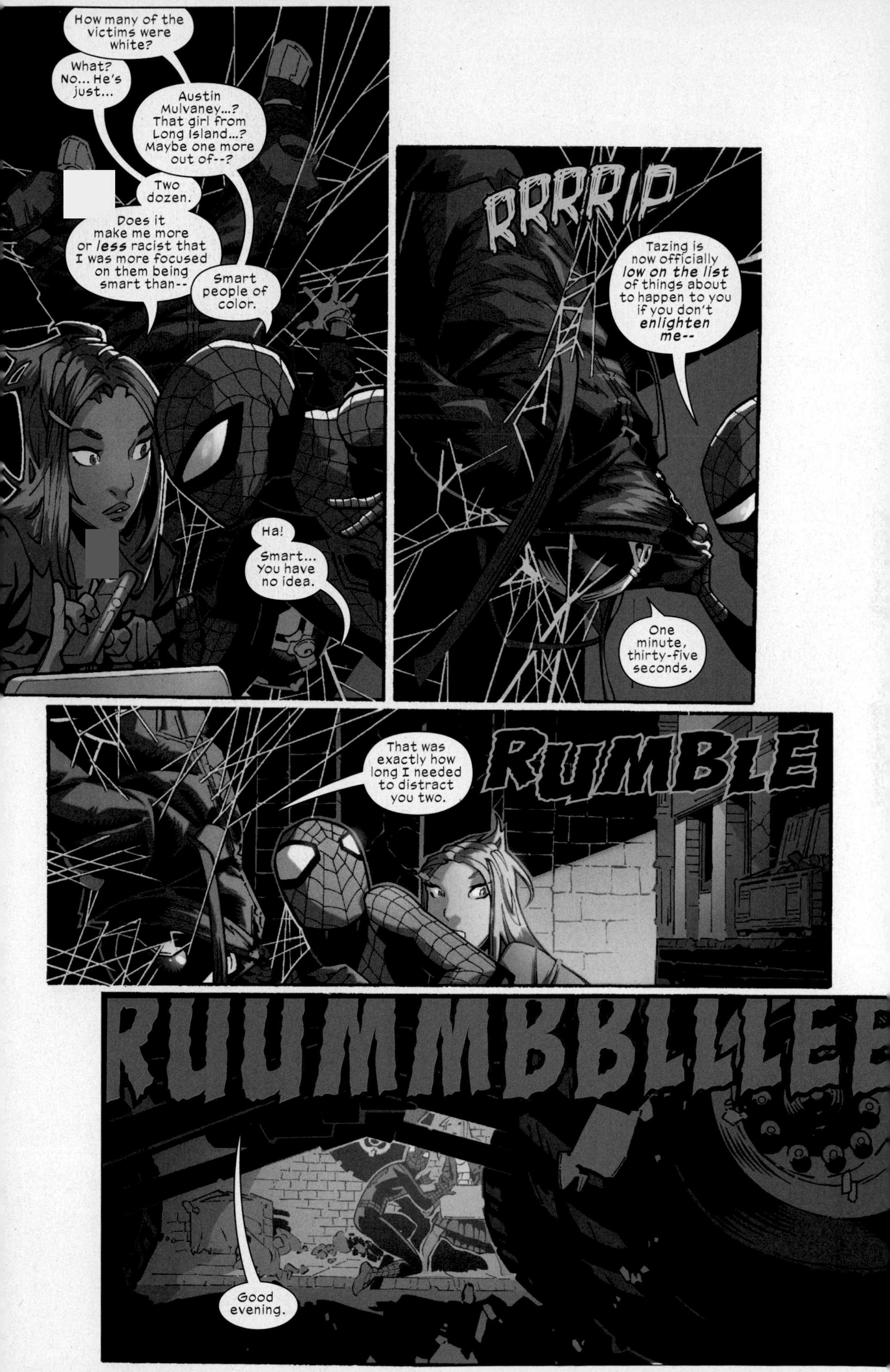
How many of the victims were white?
What? No... He's just...
Austin Mulvaney...? That girl from Long Island...? Maybe one more out of--?
Two dozen.
Does it make me more or *less* racist that I was more focused on them being smart than--
Smart people of color.
Ha! Smart... You have no idea.
RRRRIP
Tazing is now officially *low on the list* of things about to happen to you if you don't *enlighten me--*
One minute, thirty-five seconds.
That was exactly how long I needed to distract you two.
RUMBLE
RUUMMBBLLEE
Good evening.

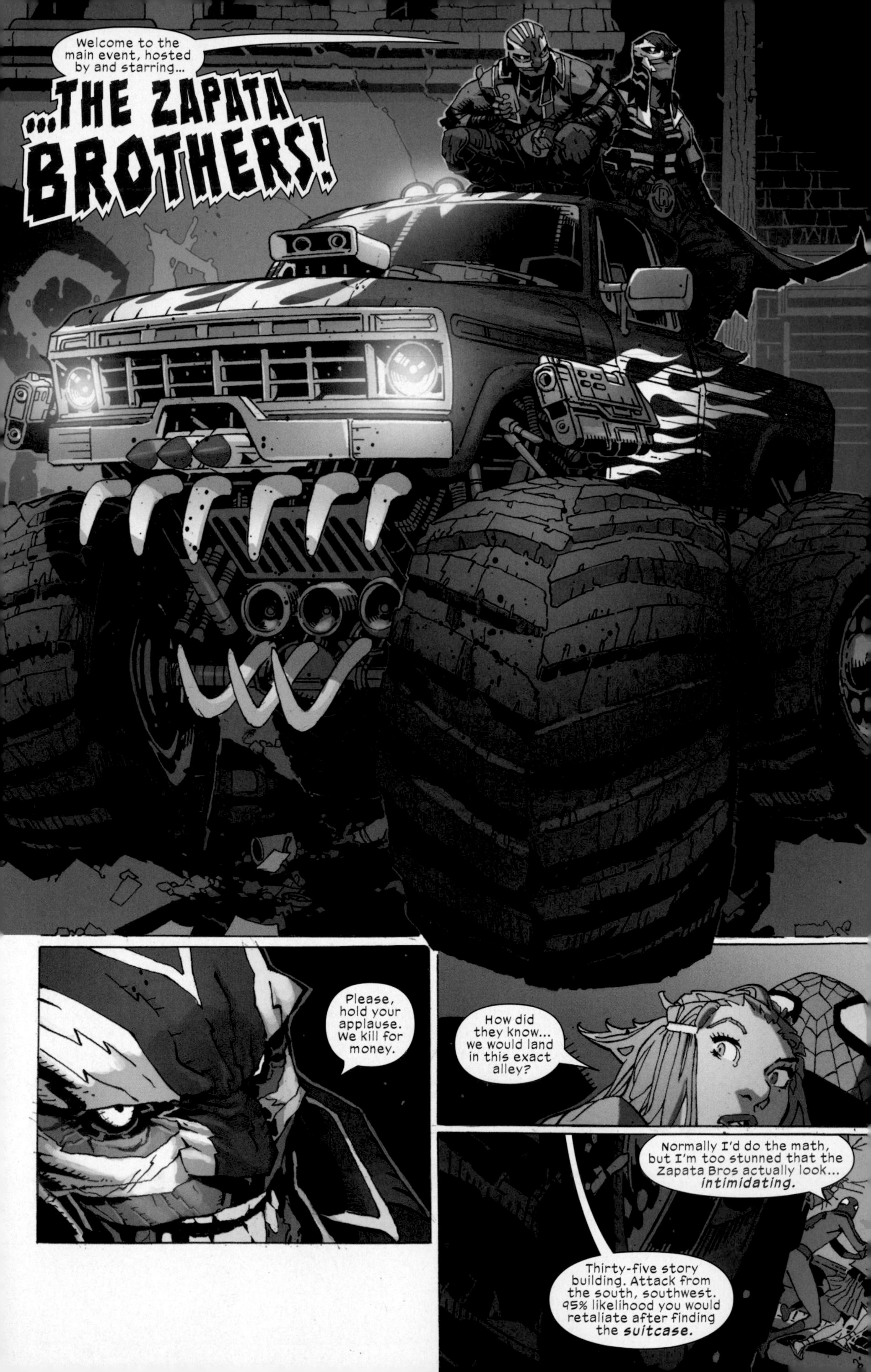
Welcome to the main event, hosted by and starring...
...THE ZAPATA BROTHERS!
Please, hold your applause. We kill for money.
How did they know... we would land in this exact alley?
Normally I'd do the math, but I'm too stunned that the Zapata Bros actually look... intimidating.
Thirty-five story building. Attack from the south, southwest. 95% likelihood you would retaliate after finding the suitcase.

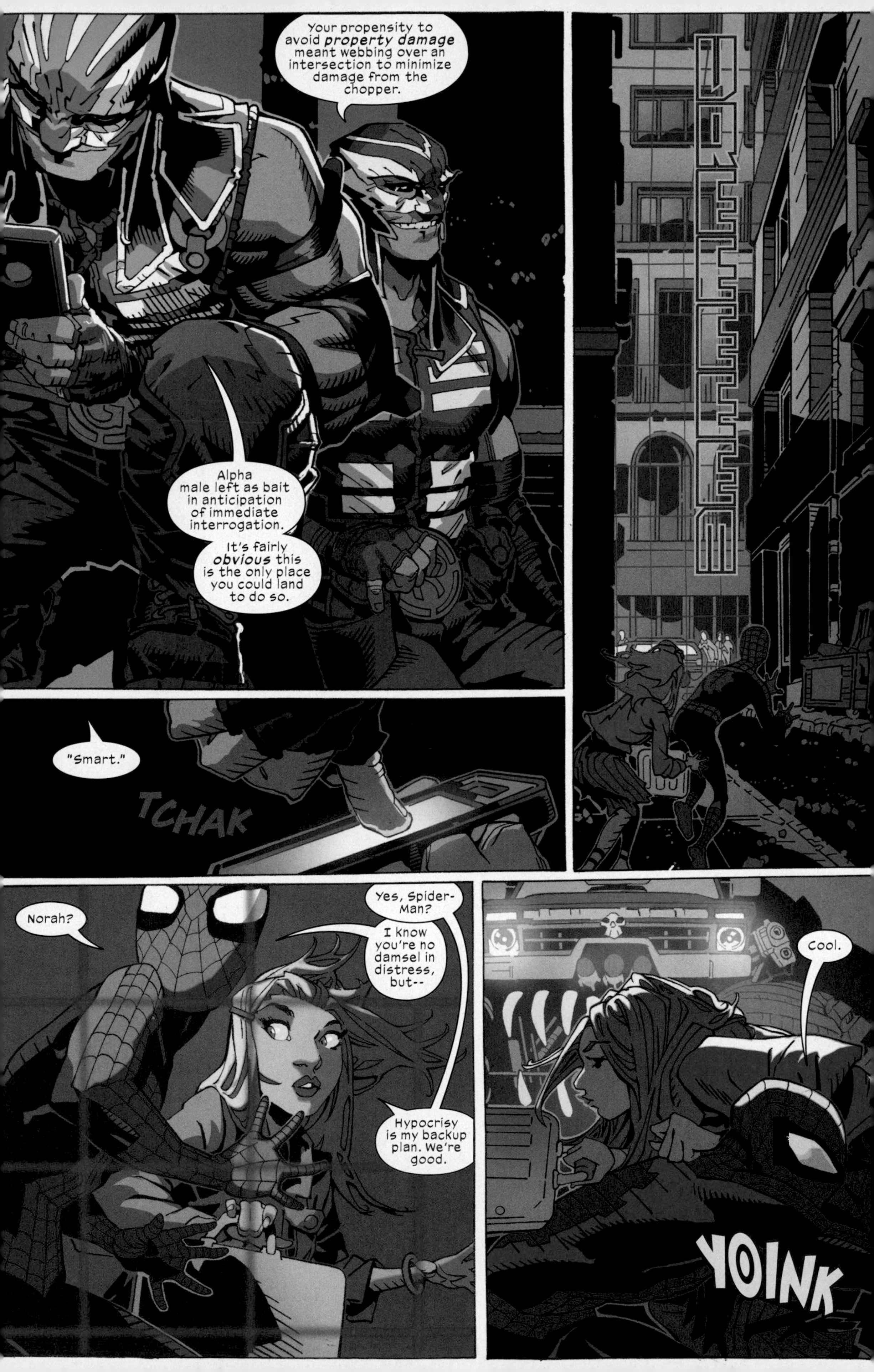

Your propensity to avoid *property damage* meant webbing over an intersection to minimize damage from the chopper.
Alpha male left as bait in anticipation of immediate interrogation.
It's fairly *obvious* this is the only place you could land to do so.
"Smart."
TCHAK
Norah?
Yes, Spider-Man?
I know you're no damsel in distress, but--
Hypocrisy is my backup plan. We're good.
Cool.
YOINK

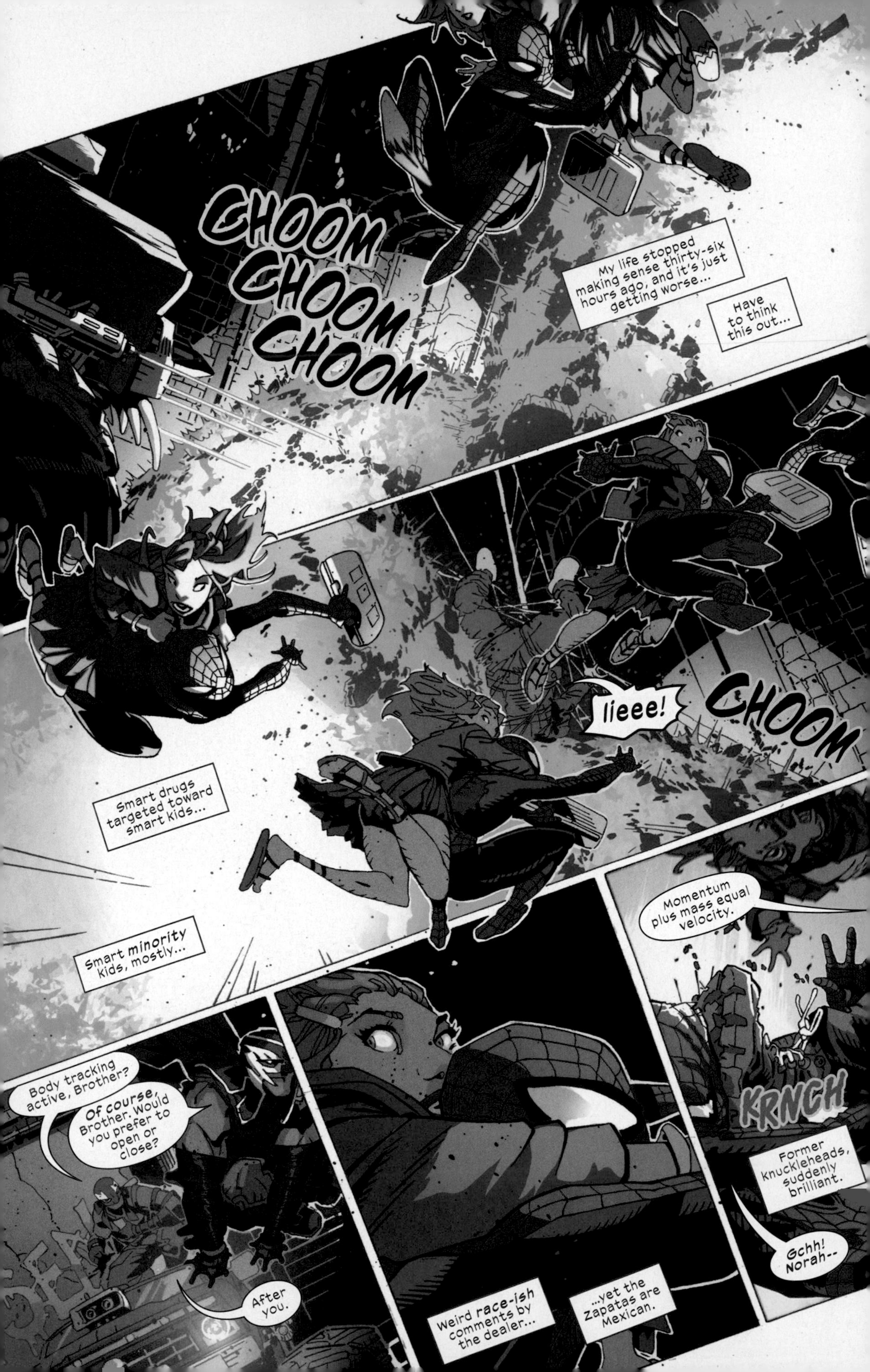
CHOOM CHOOM CHOOM CHOOM
My life stopped making sense thirty-six hours ago, and it's just getting worse...
Have to think this out...
Smart drugs targeted toward smart kids...
Iieee!
CHOOM
Smart minority kids, mostly...
Momentum plus mass equal velocity.
KRNCH
Former knuckleheads, suddenly brilliant.
Gchh! Norah--
Body tracking active, Brother?
Of course, Brother. Would you prefer to open or close?
After you.
Weird race-ish comments by the dealer...
...yet the Zapatas are Mexican.

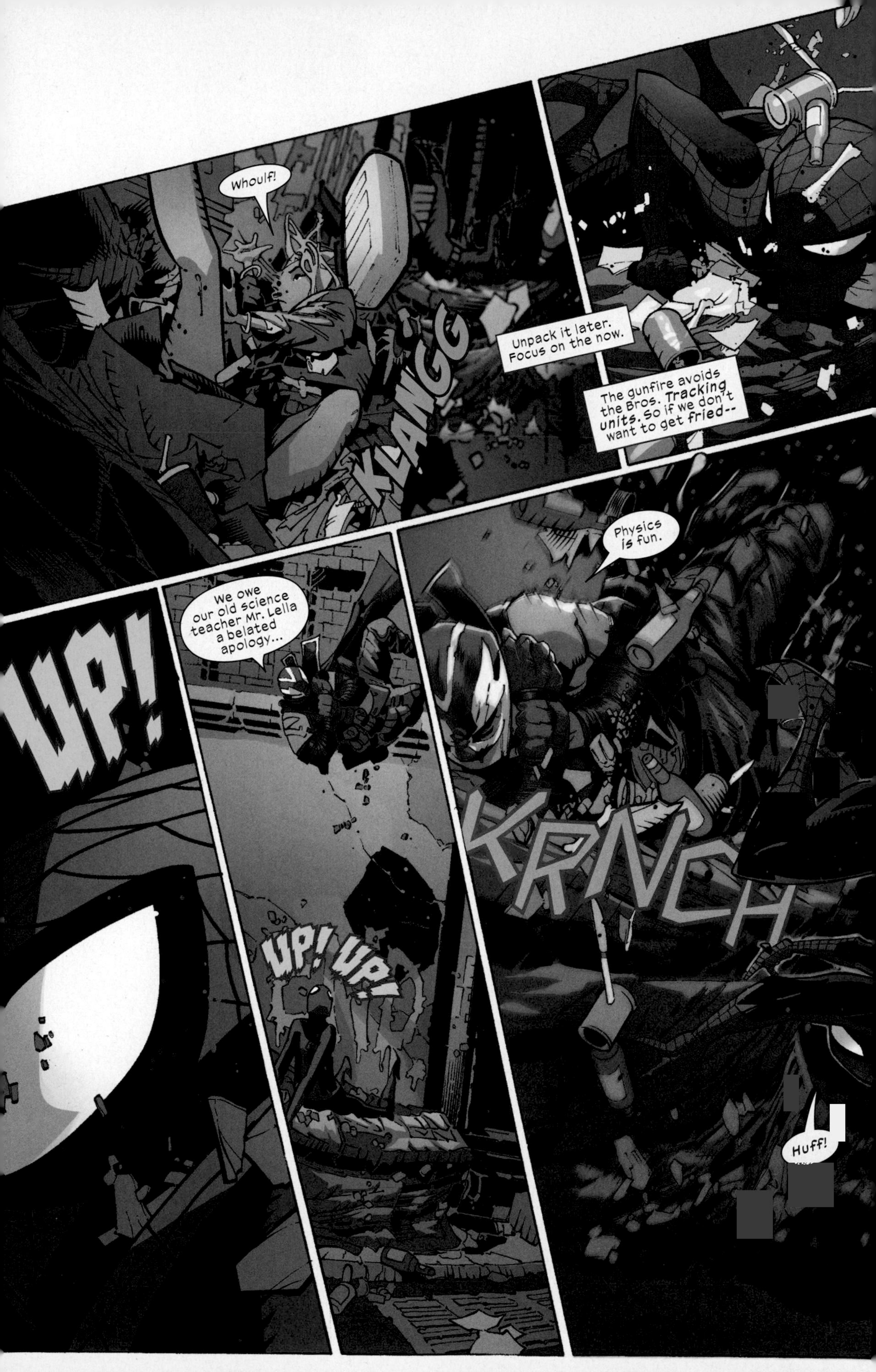

Whoulf!
KLANGG
Unpack it later. Focus on the now.
The gunfire avoids the Bros. Tracking units. So if we don't want to get fried--
Physics is fun.
UP!
We owe our old science teacher Mr. Lella a belated apology...
UP! UP!
KRNCH
Huff!

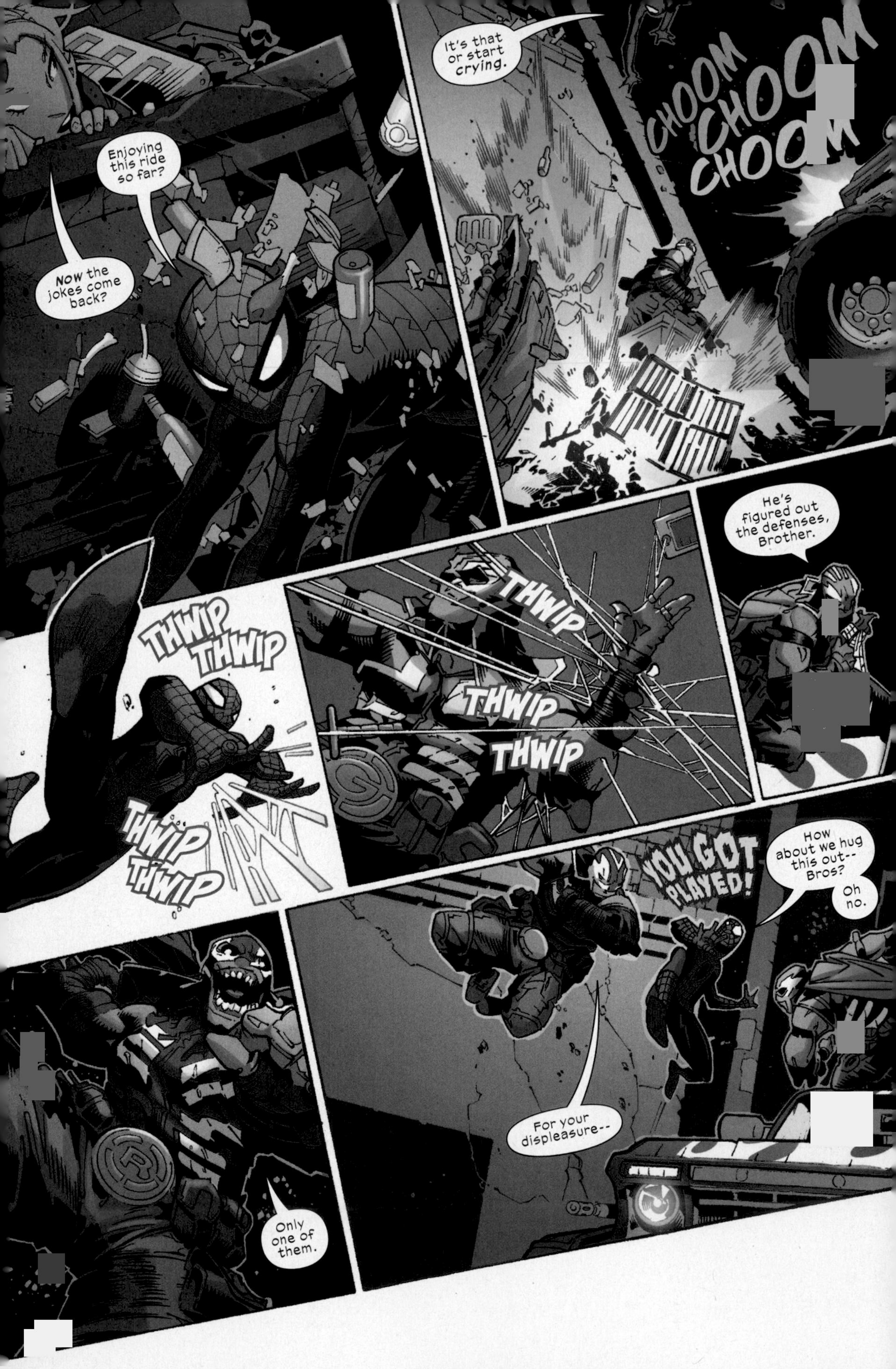
Enjoying this ride so far?
NOW the jokes come back?
It's that or start crying.
CHOOM CHOOM CHOOM
THWIP THWIP
THWIP THWIP
THWIP
THWIP
THWIP
He's figured out the defenses, Brother.
Only one of them.
For your displeasure--
YOU GOT PLAYED!
How about we hug this out-- Bros?
Oh no.

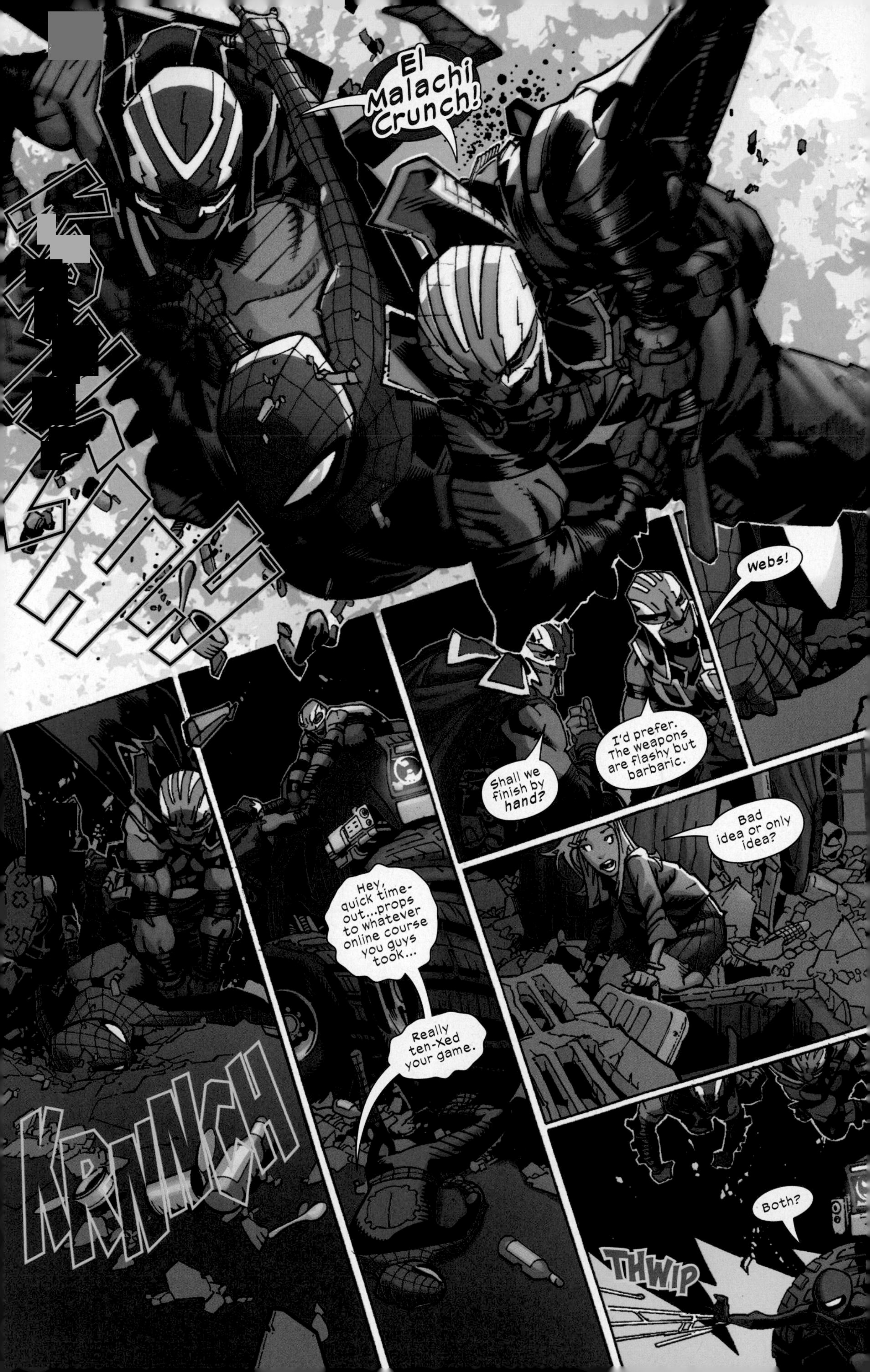

El Malachi Crunch!
[redacted]
Webs!
Shall we finish by hand?
I'd prefer. The weapons are flashy but barbaric.
Bad idea or only idea?
Hey, quick time-out...props to whatever online course you guys took...
Really ten-Xed your game.
[redacted]
Both?
THWIP

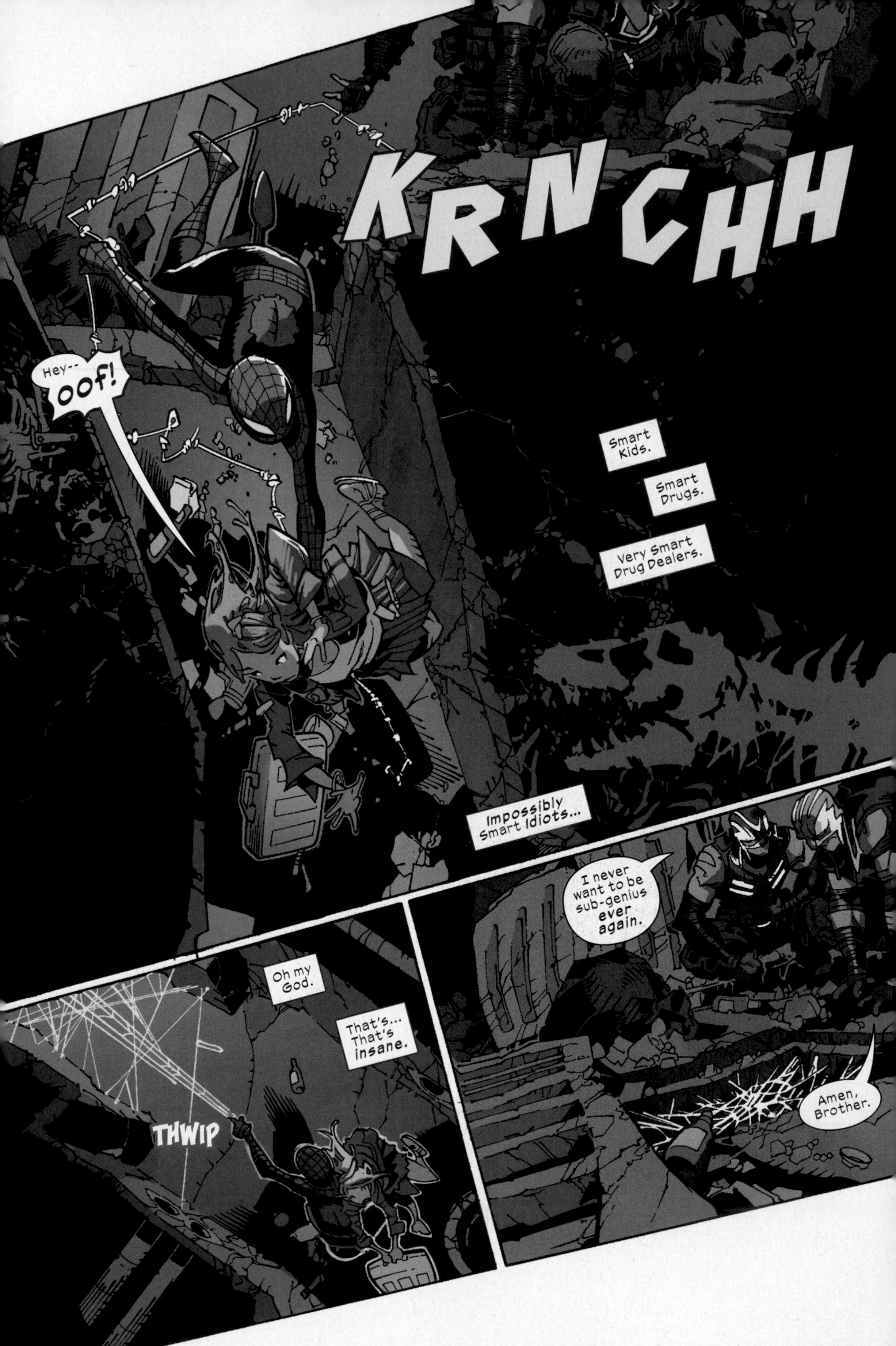
KRNCHH
Hey-- OOF!
Smart Kids.
Smart Drugs.
Very Smart Drug Dealers.
Impossibly Smart Idiots...
I never want to be sub-genius ever again.
Oh my God.
That's... That's insane.
THWIP
Amen, Brother.

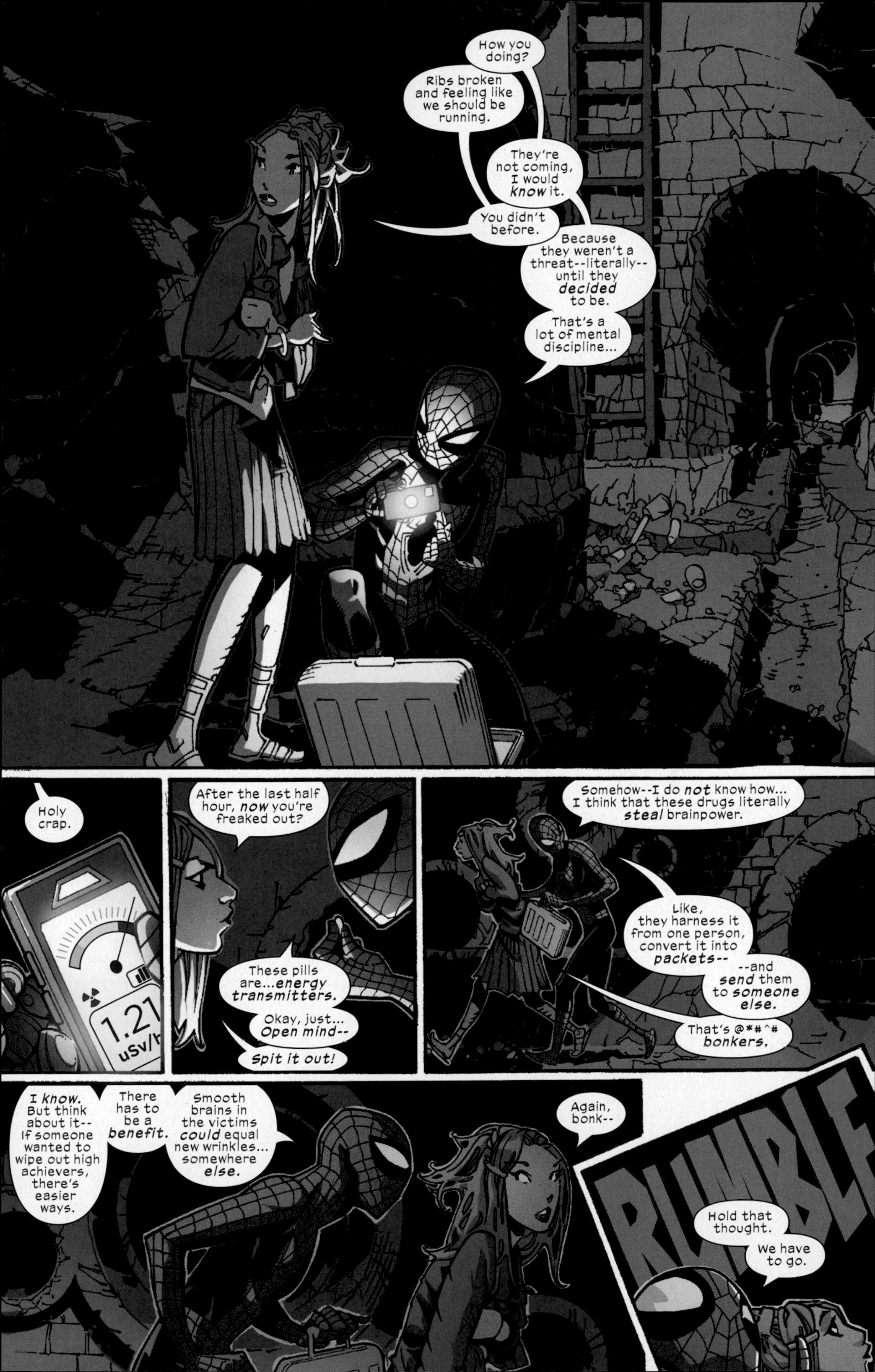
How you doing?
Ribs broken and feeling like we should be running.
They're not coming, I would *know* it.
You didn't before.
Because they weren't a threat--literally--until they *decided* to be.
That's a lot of mental discipline...
Holy crap.
After the last half hour, *now* you're freaked out?
These pills are...*energy transmitters.*
Okay, just... *Open mind--*
Spit it out!
1.21 uSv/h
Somehow--I do *not* know how... I think that these drugs literally *steal* brainpower.
Like, they harness it from one person, convert it into *packets--*
--and *send* them to *someone else.*
That's @*#^# *bonkers.*
I know. But think about it--If someone wanted to wipe out high achievers, there's easier ways.
There has to be a *benefit.*
Smooth brains in the victims *could* equal new wrinkles... somewhere *else.*
Again, bonk--
RUMBLE
Hold that thought.
We have to go.

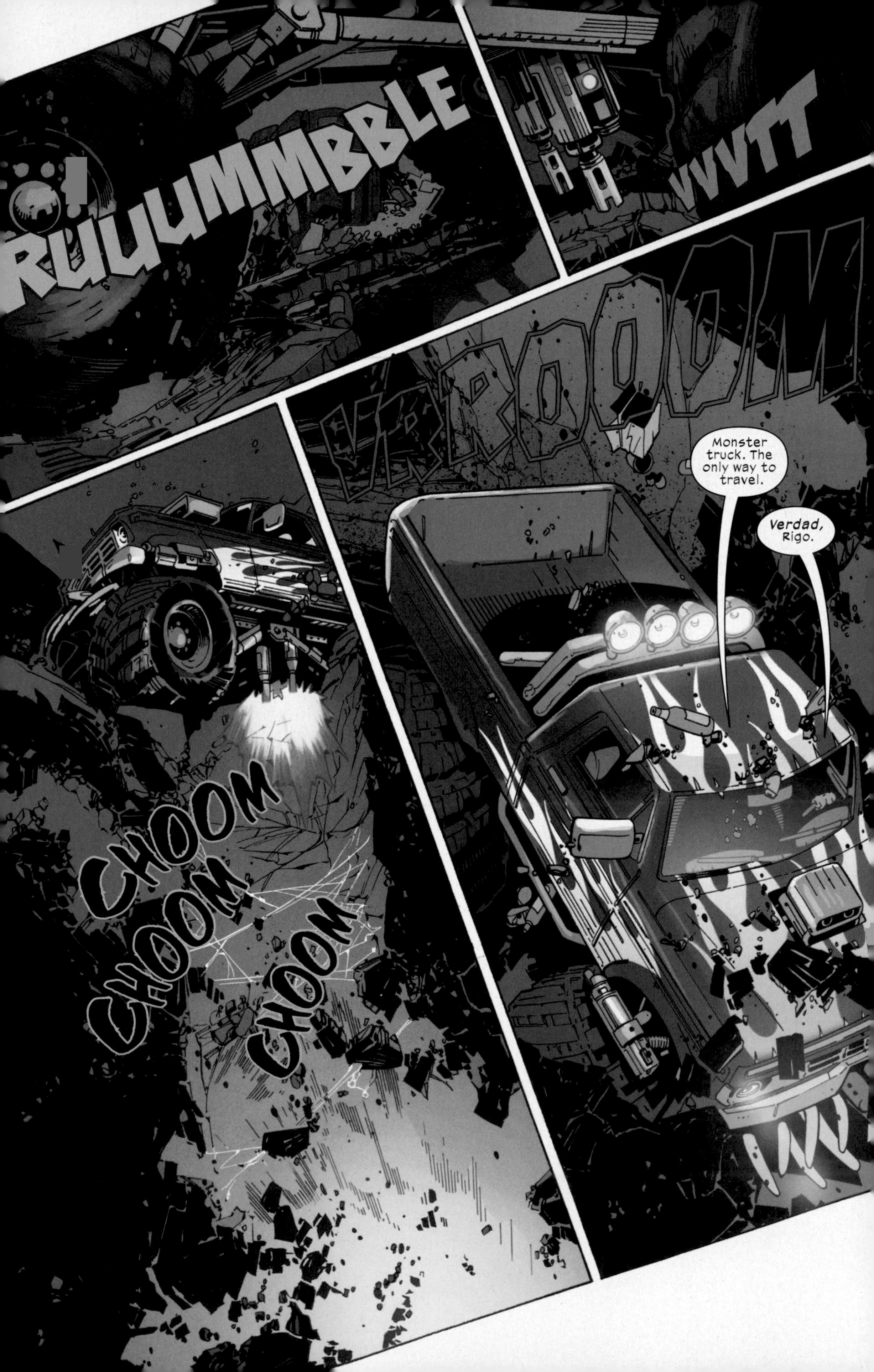
RUUUMMBBLE
VVVTT
VRROOOOM
CHOOM
CHOOM
CHOOM
Monster truck. The only way to travel.
Verdad, Rigo.

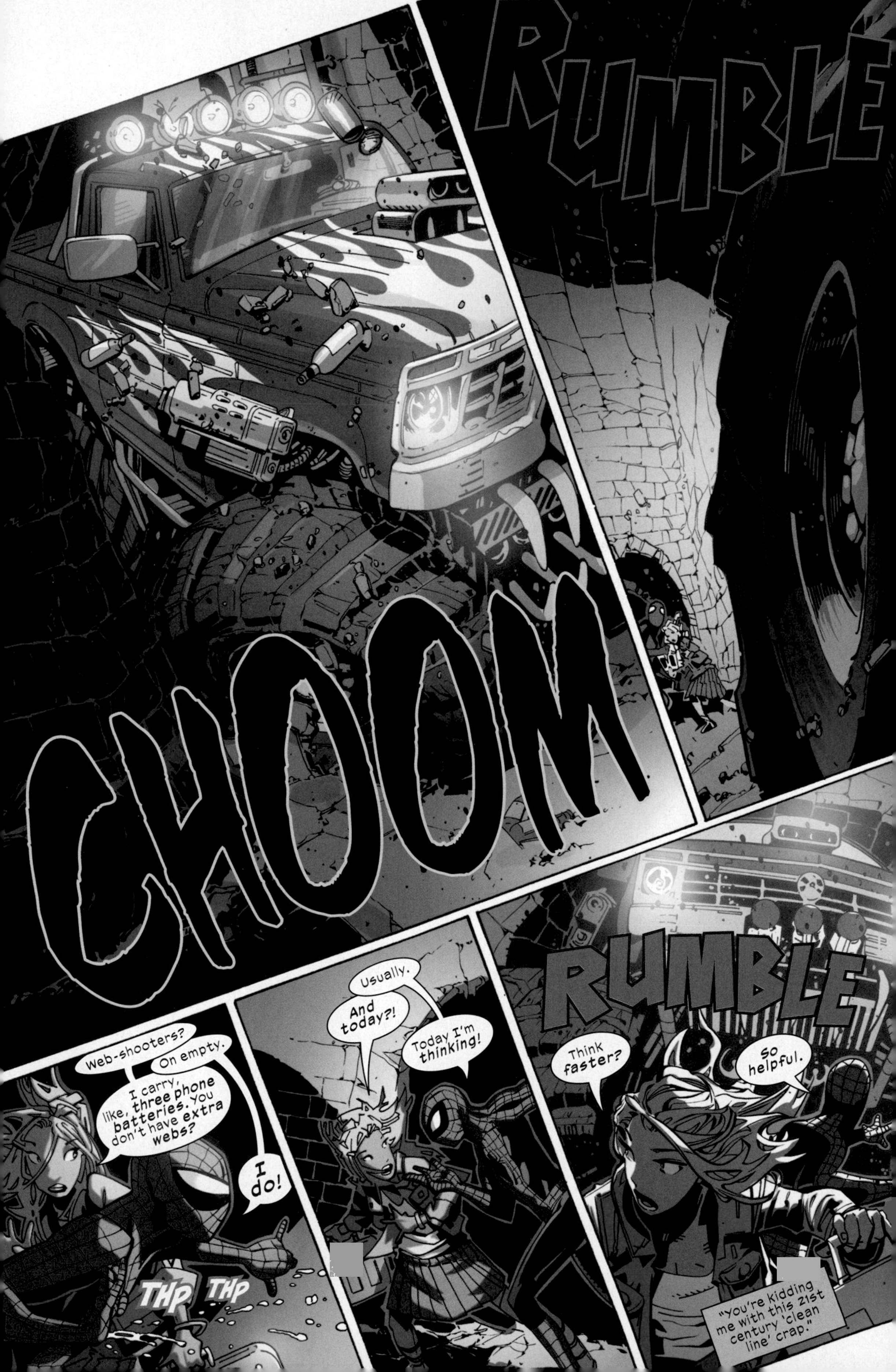

CHOOM
RUMBLE
RUMBLE
Web-shooters?
On empty.
I carry, like, three phone batteries. You don't have extra webs?
I do!
THP THP
Usually.
And today?!
Today I'm thinking!
Think faster?
So helpful.
"You're kidding me with this 21st century 'clean line' crap."

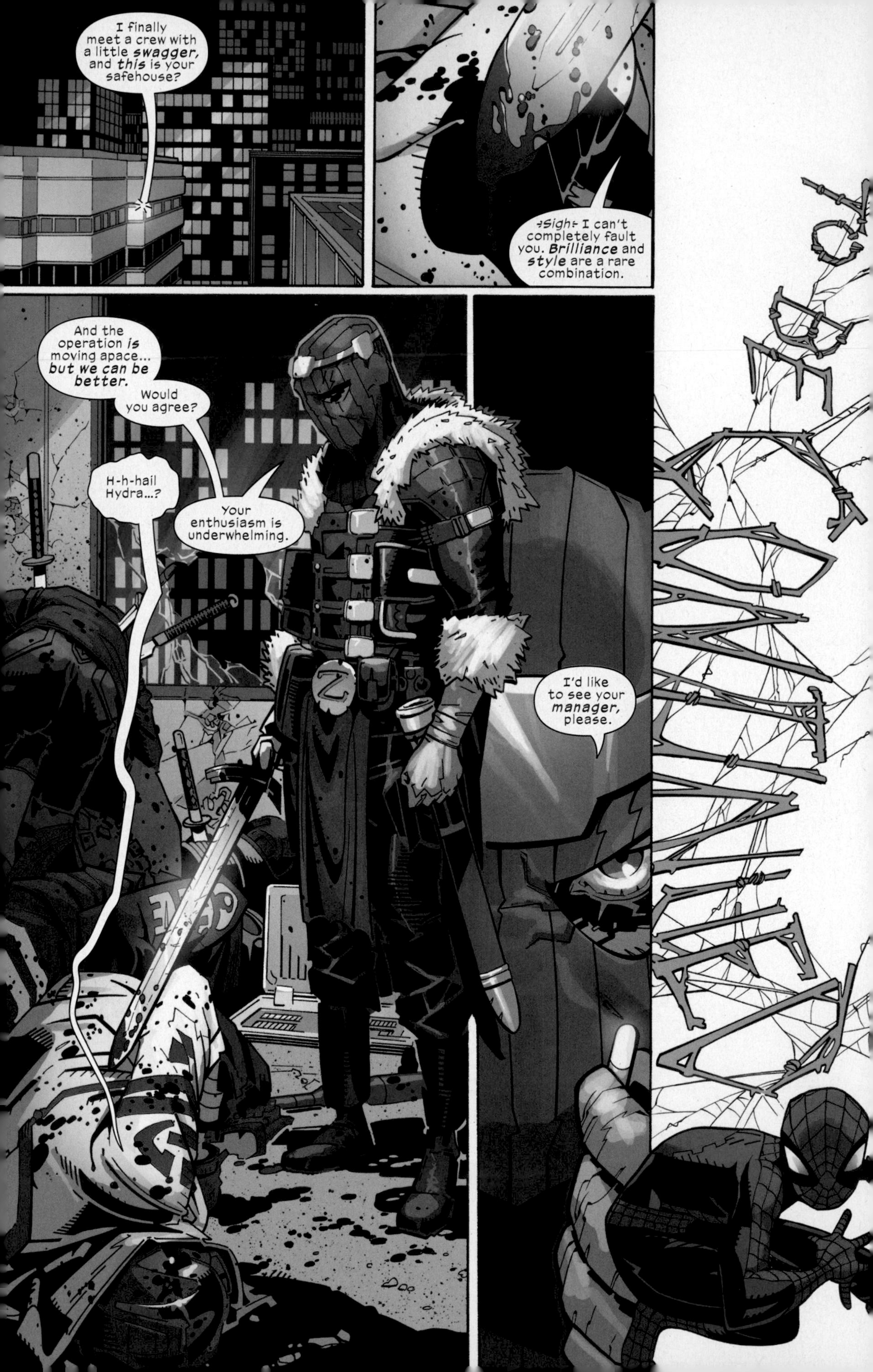
I finally meet a crew with a little swagger, and this is your safehouse?
⸗Sigh⸗ I can't completely fault you. Brilliance and style are a rare combination.
And the operation is moving apace... but we can be better.
Would you agree?
H-h-hail Hydra...?
Your enthusiasm is underwhelming.
I'd like to see your manager, please.

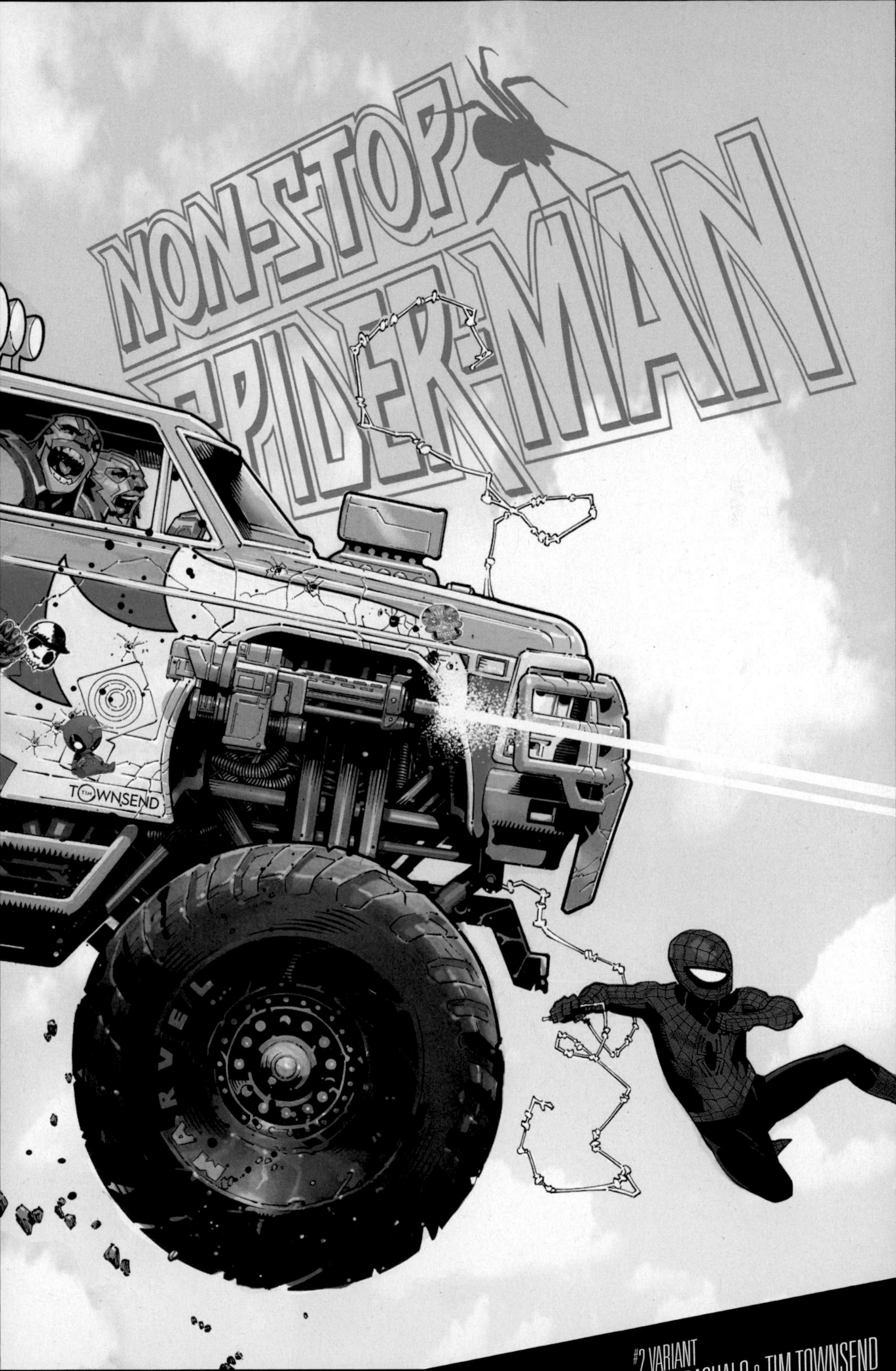
NON-STOP SPIDER-MAN
TOWNSEND
MARVEL

#2 VARIANT
CHRIS BACHALO & TIM TOWNSEND

3. BIG BRAIN PLAY
CHAPTER THREE

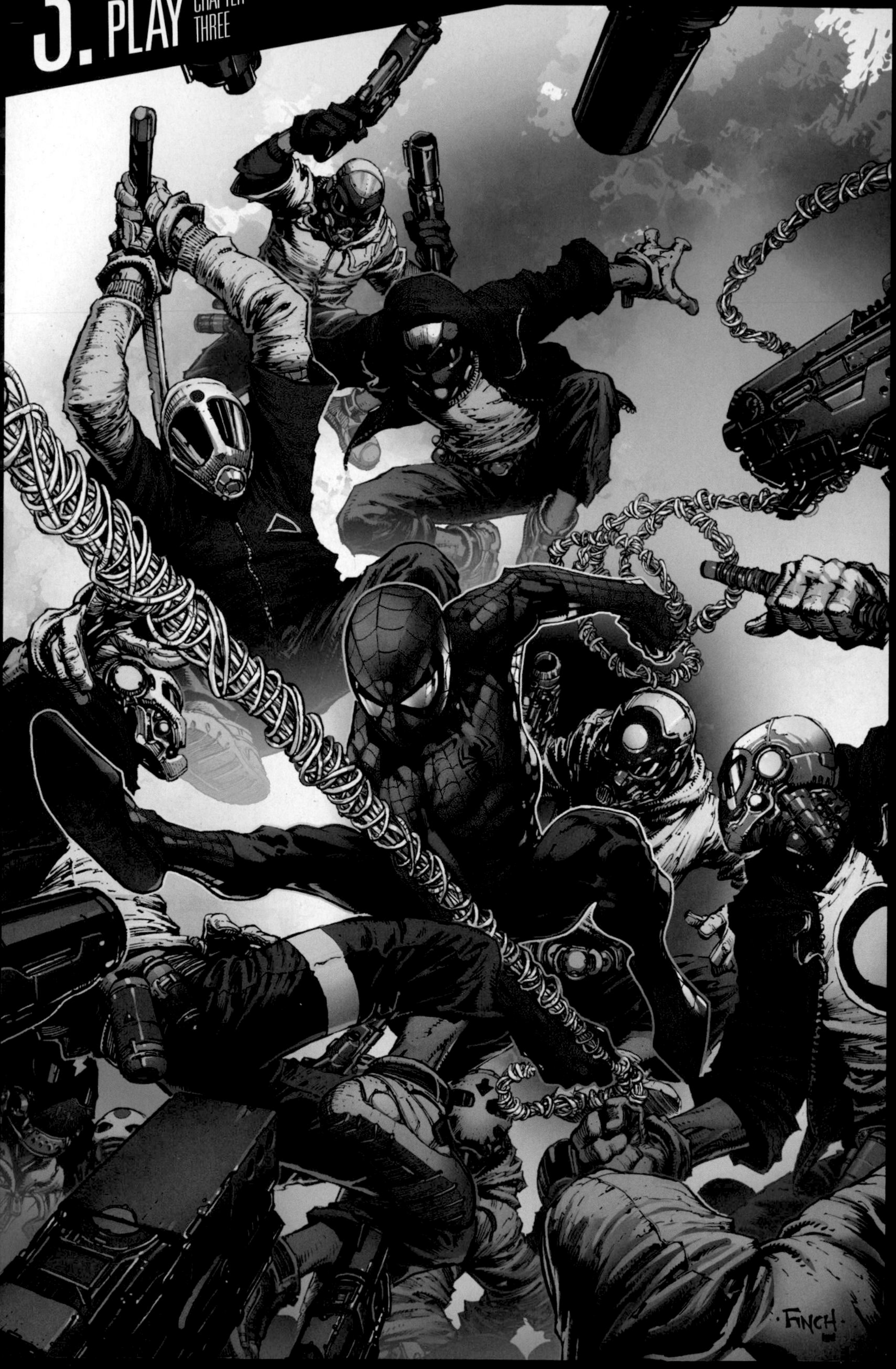
FINCH

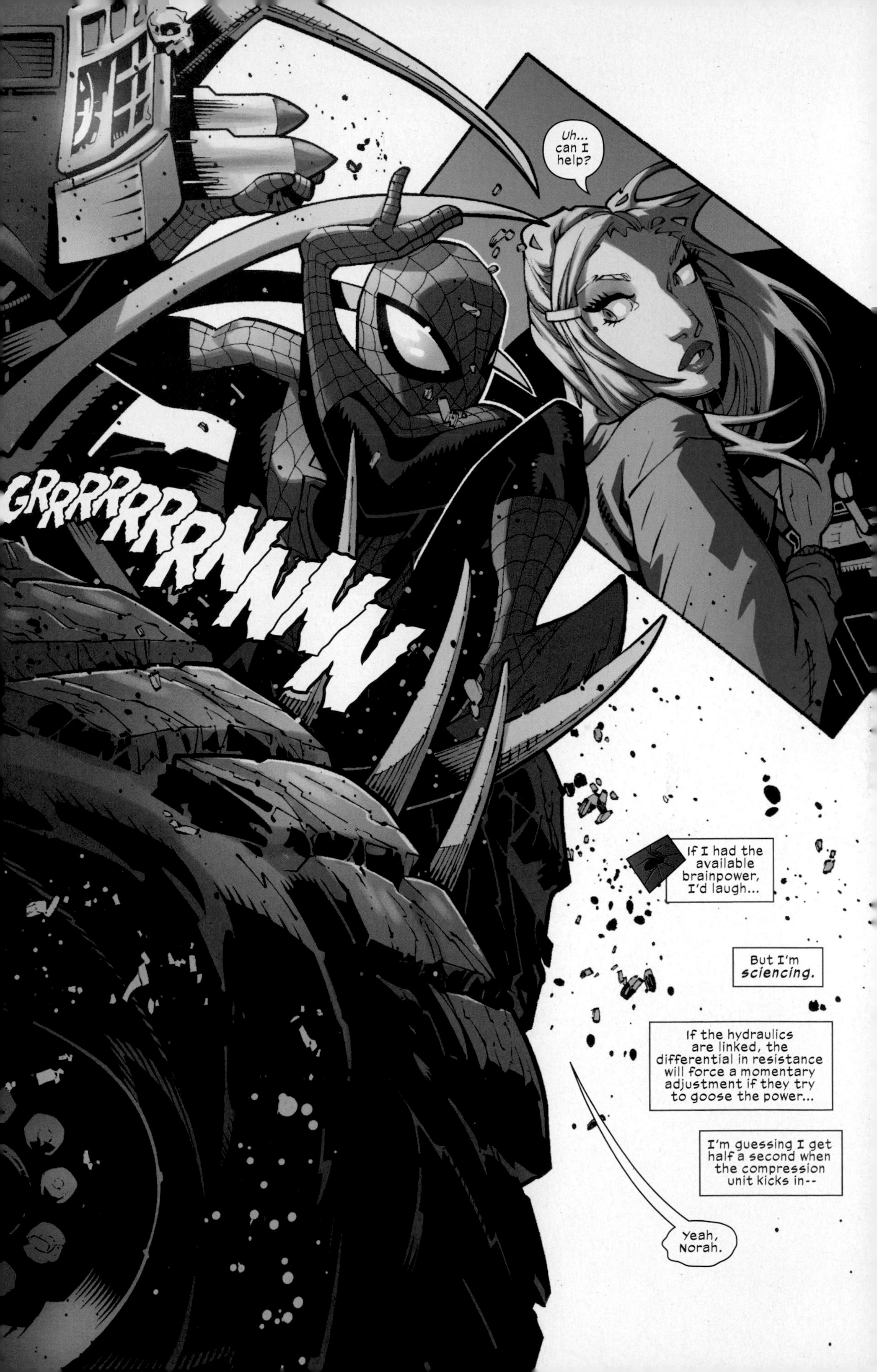
Uh... can I help?
GRRRRRRRRNNNN
If I had the available brainpower, I'd laugh...
But I'm *sciencing.*
If the hydraulics are linked, the differential in resistance will force a momentary adjustment if they try to goose the power...
I'm guessing I get half a second when the compression unit kicks in--
Yeah, Norah.

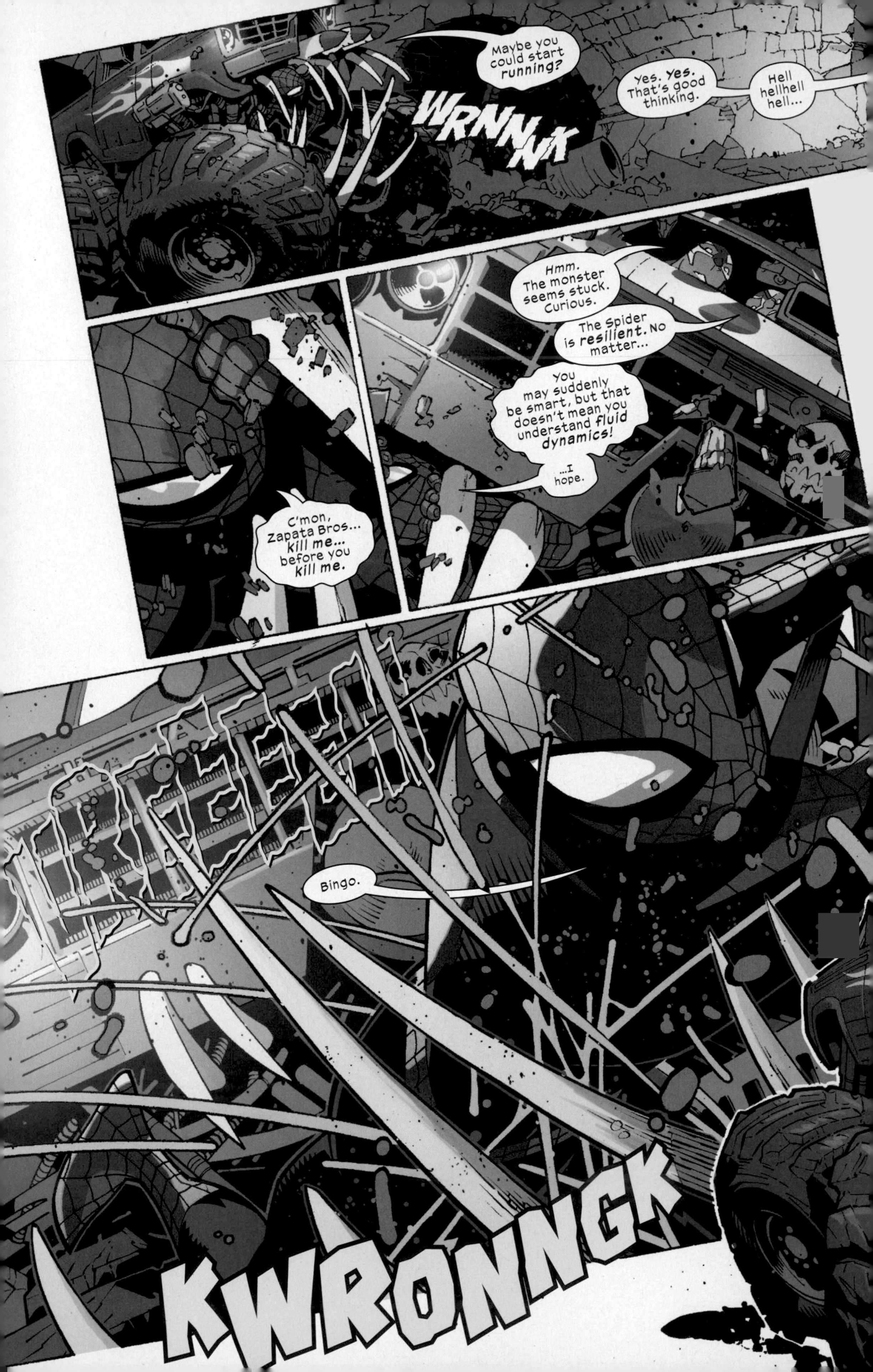
Maybe you could start running?
WRNNNNK
Yes. Yes. That's good thinking.
Hell hellhell hell...
Hmm. The monster seems stuck. Curious.
The Spider is resilient. No matter...
You may suddenly be smart, but that doesn't mean you understand fluid dynamics!
...I hope.
C'mon, Zapata Bros... kill me... before you kill me.
Bingo.
KWRONNGK

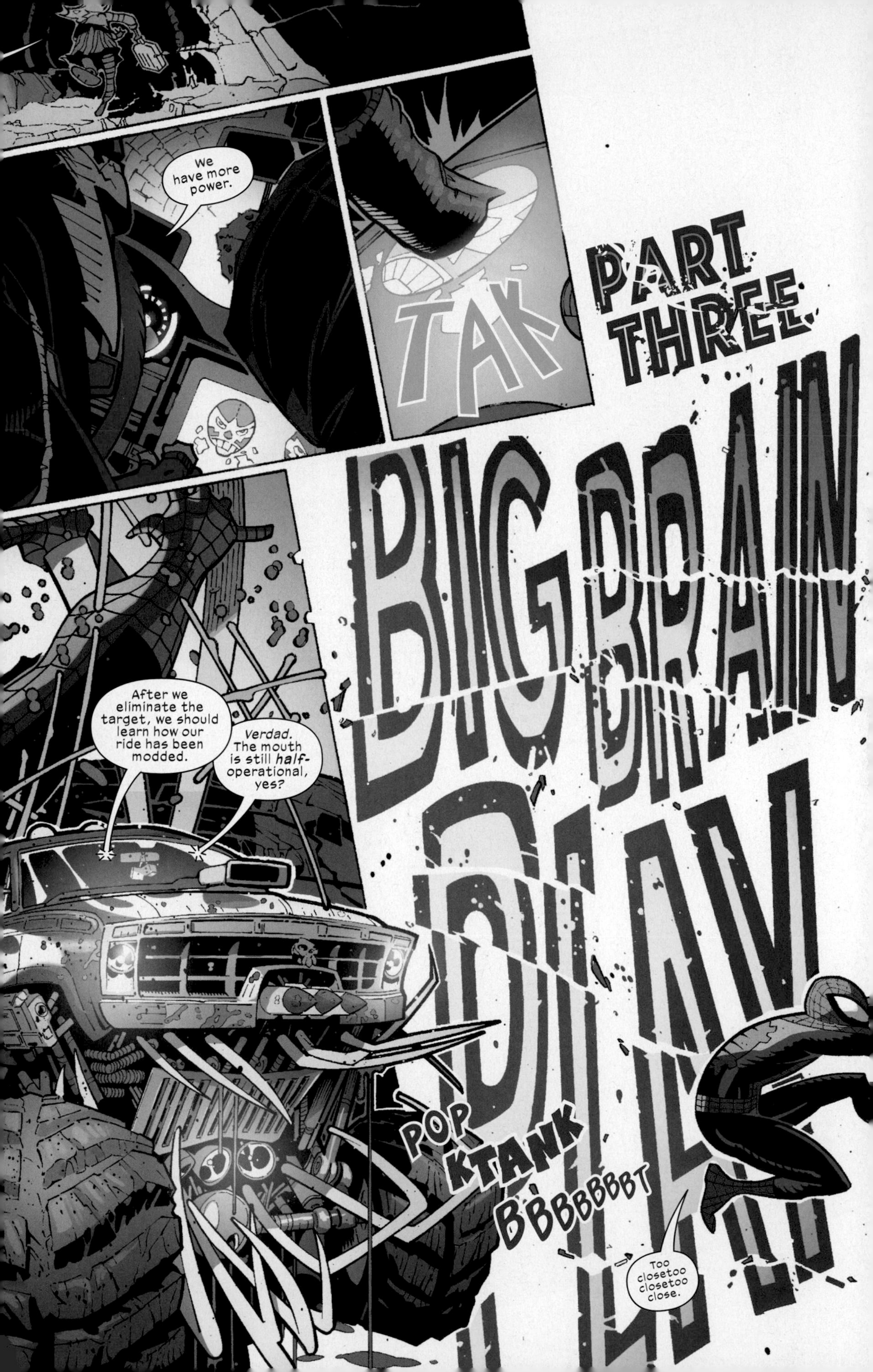
We have more power.
TAK
PART THREE
BIG BRAIN PLAY
After we eliminate the target, we should learn how our ride has been modded.
Verdad. The mouth is still half-operational, yes?
POP
KTANK
BBBBBBBT
Too closetoo closetoo close.

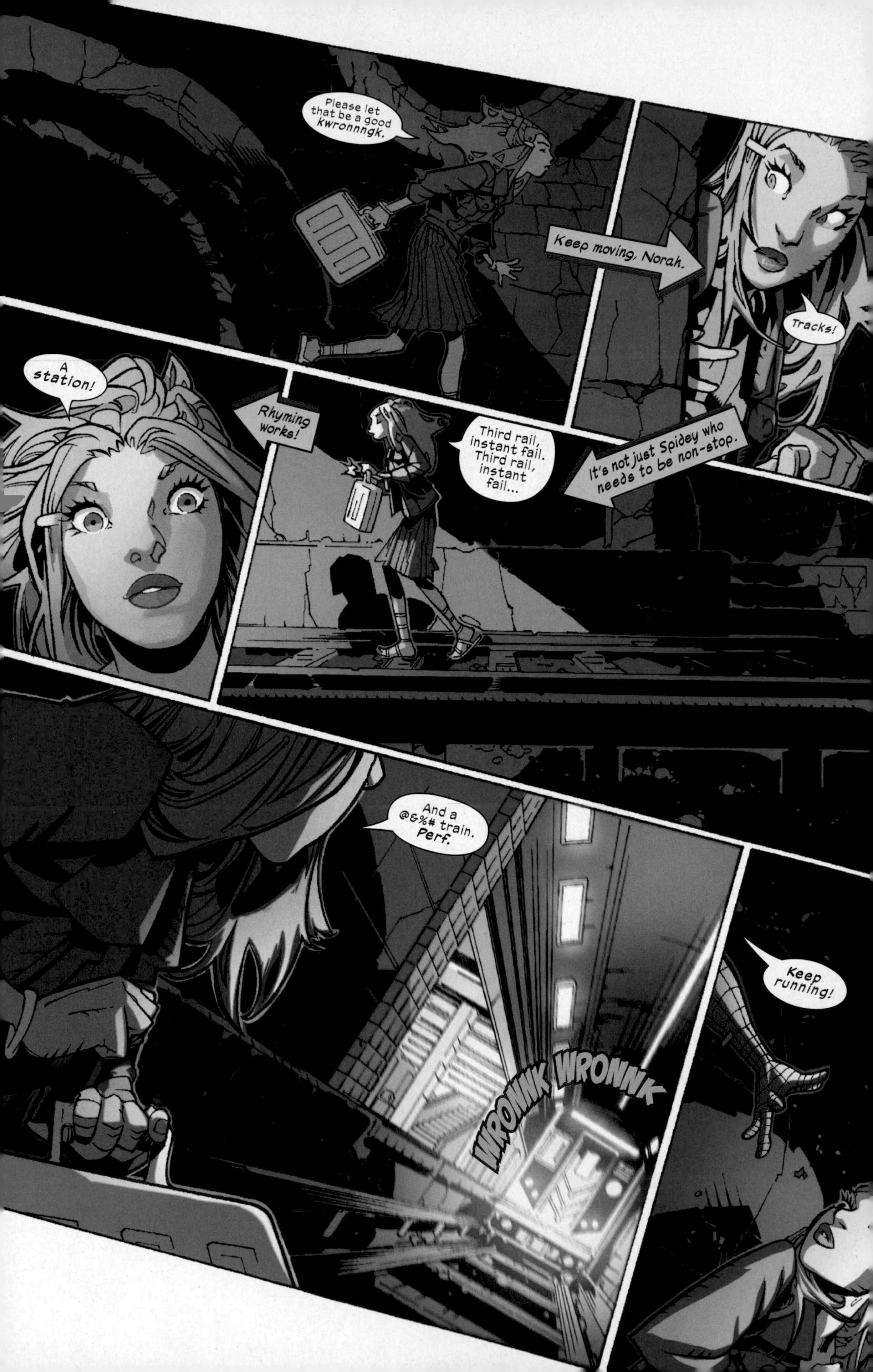
Please let that be a good kwronnngk.
Keep moving, Norah.
Tracks!
A station!
Rhyming works!
Third rail, instant fail. Third rail, instant fail...
It's not just Spidey who needs to be non-stop.
And a @&%# train. Perf.
Keep running!
WRONNK WRONNK

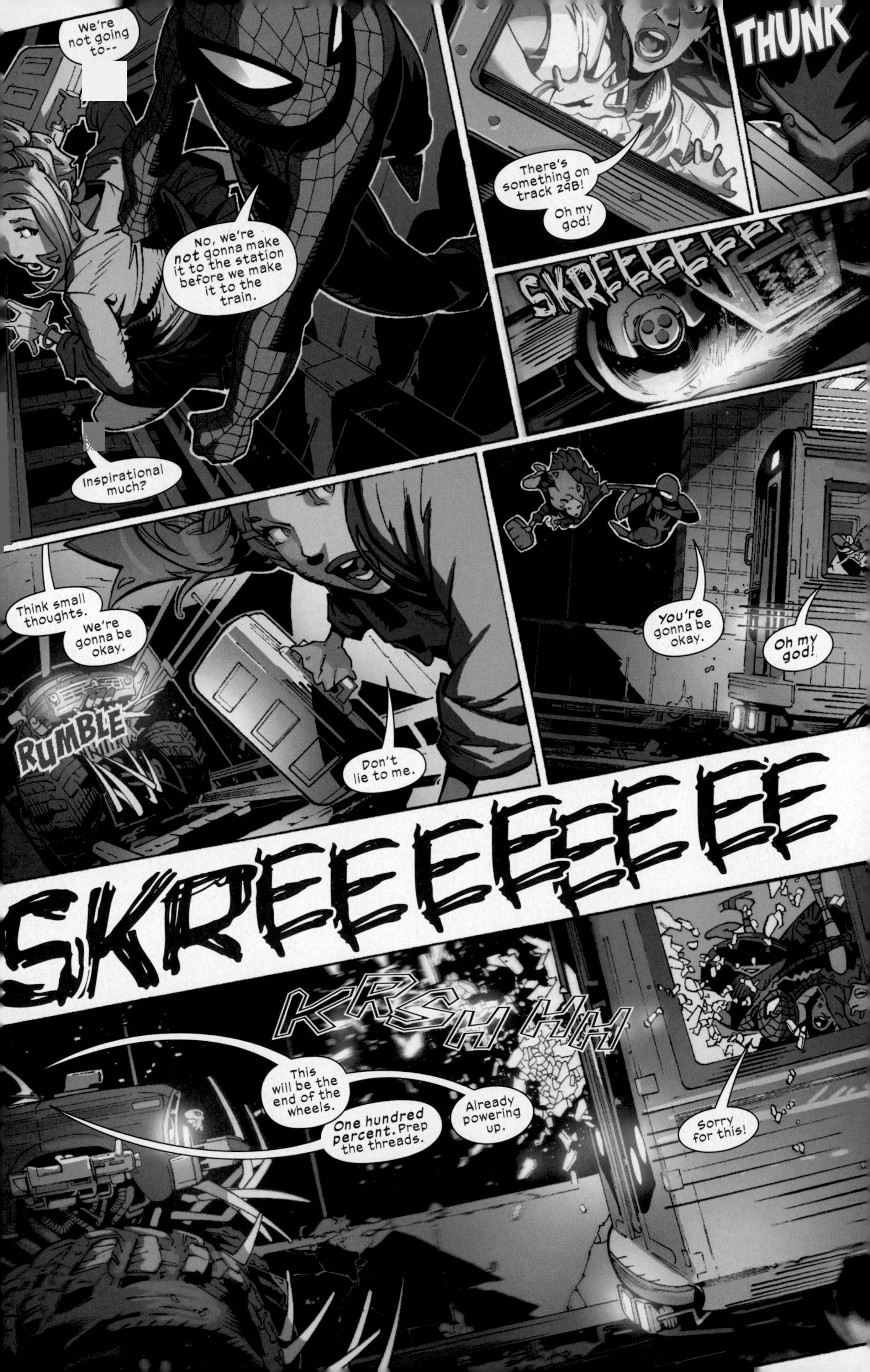

We're not going to--
No, we're *not* gonna make it to the station before we make it to the train.
Inspirational much?
There's something on track 29B!
Oh my god!
THUNK
SKREEEEEEEE
Think small thoughts.
We're gonna be okay.
RUMBLE
Don't lie to me.
You're gonna be okay.
Oh my god!
SKREEEEEEEEEE
KRSHHH
This will be the end of the wheels.
One hundred percent. Prep the threads.
Already powering up.
Sorry for this!

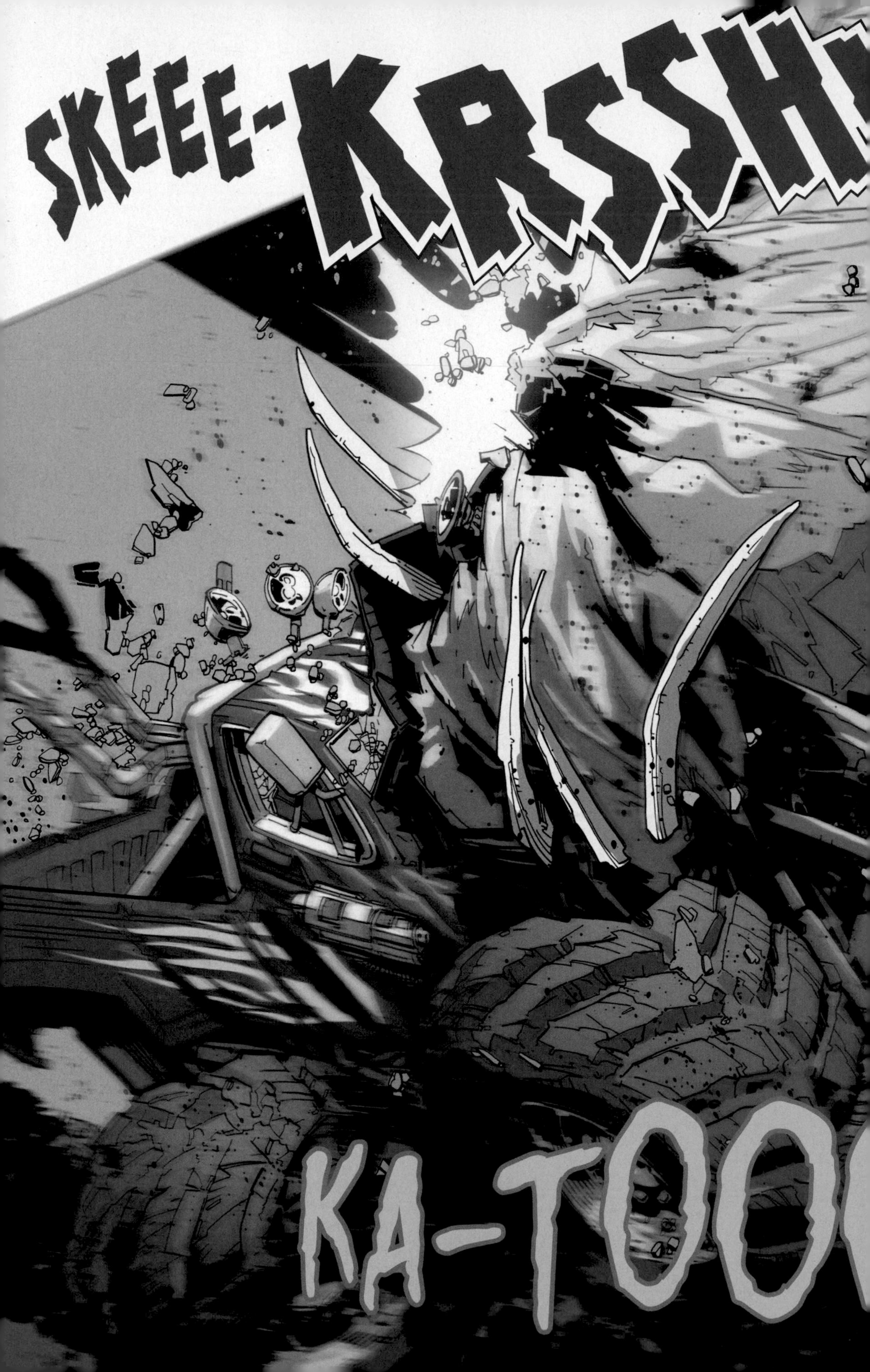

SKEEE-KRSSH
KA-TOO

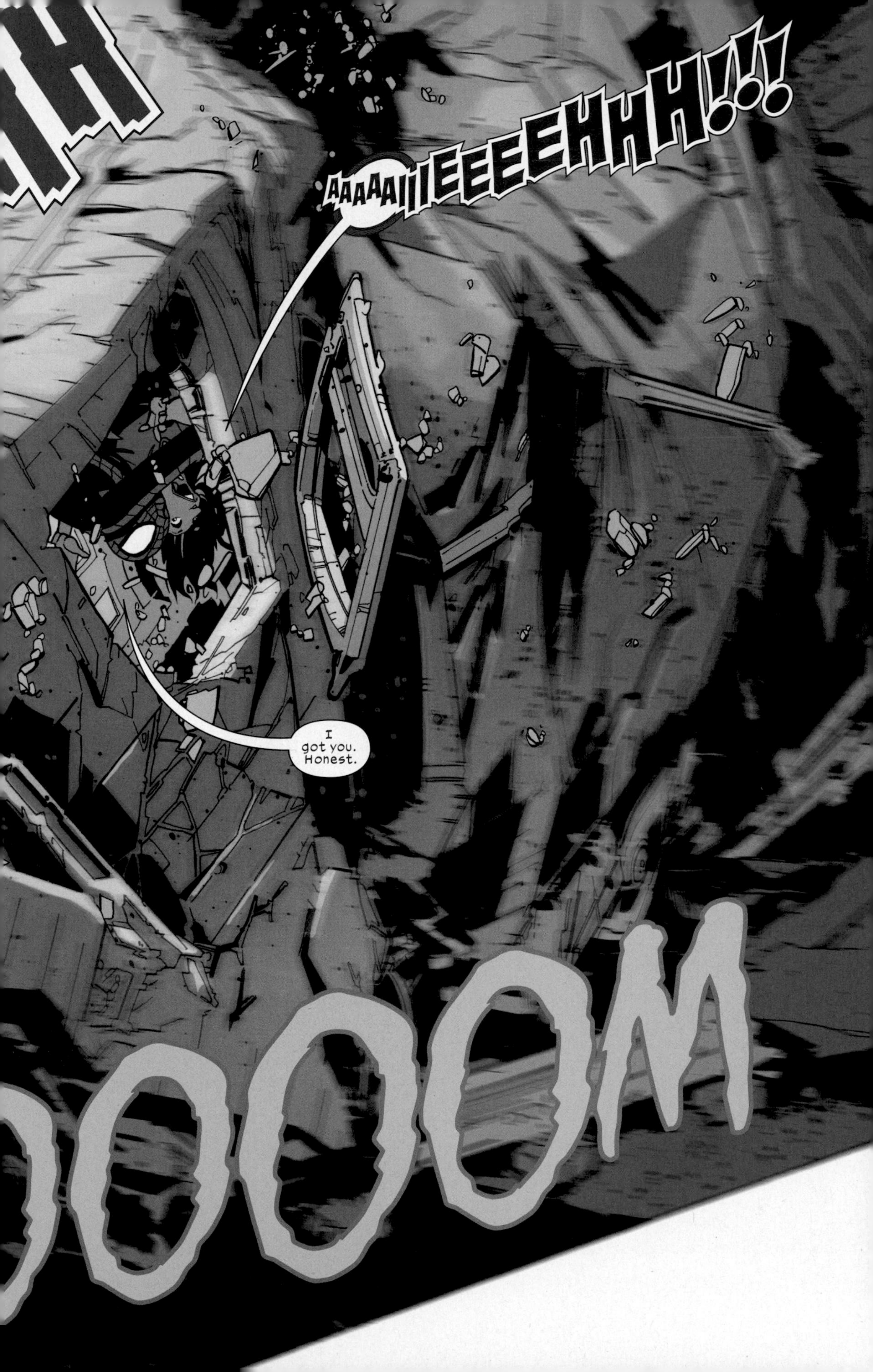
AAAAAIIIIEEEEEHHHH!!!
I got you. Honest.
OOOM

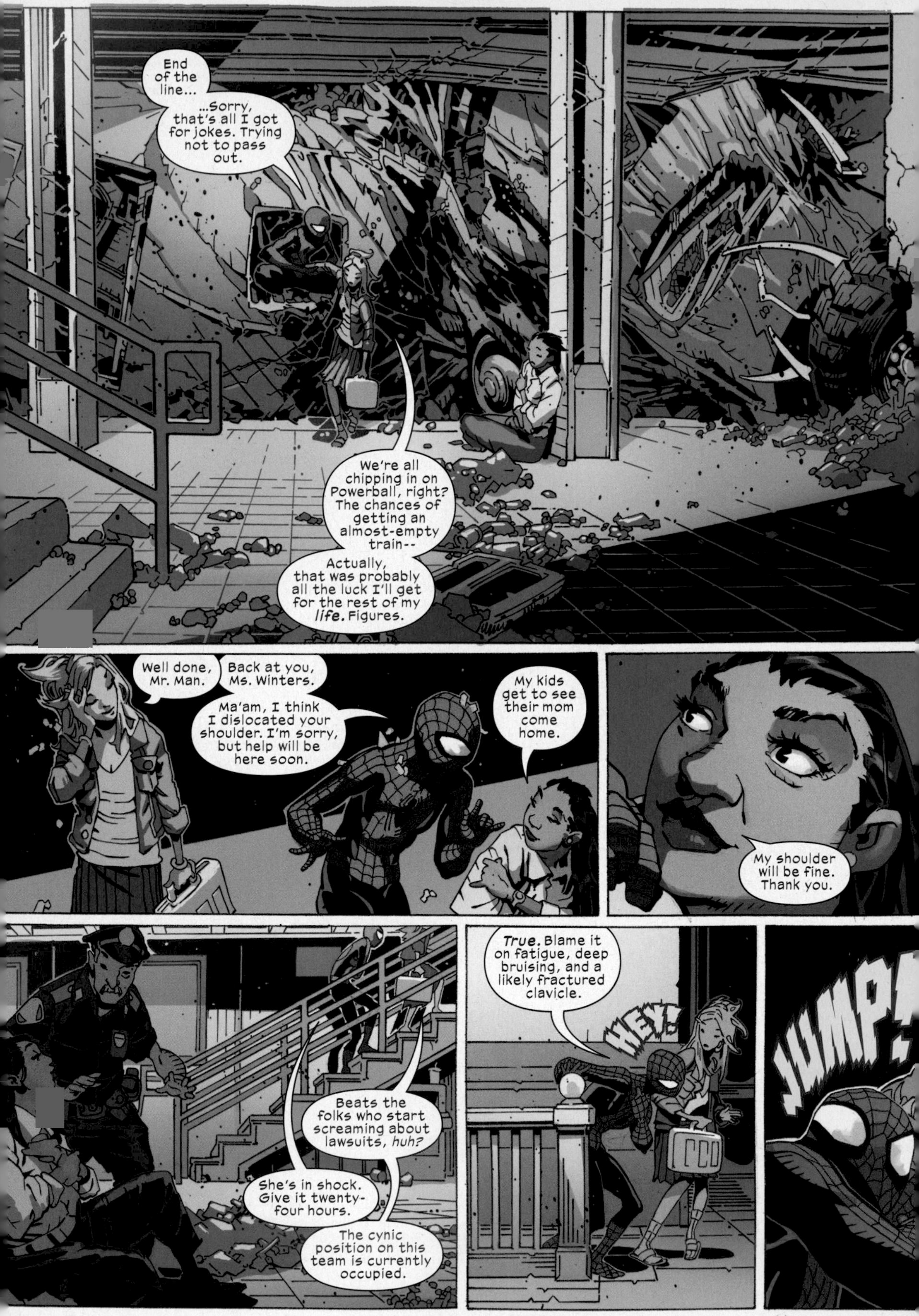
End of the line...
...Sorry, that's all I got for jokes. Trying not to pass out.
We're all chipping in on Powerball, right? The chances of getting an almost-empty train--
Actually, that was probably all the luck I'll get for the rest of my *life.* Figures.
Well done, Mr. Man.
Back at you, Ms. Winters.
Ma'am, I think I dislocated your shoulder. I'm sorry, but help will be here soon.
My kids get to see their mom come home.
My shoulder will be fine. Thank you.
Beats the folks who start screaming about lawsuits, *huh?*
She's in shock. Give it twenty-four hours.
The cynic position on this team is currently occupied.
True. Blame it on fatigue, deep bruising, and a likely fractured clavicle.
HEY!
JUMP!

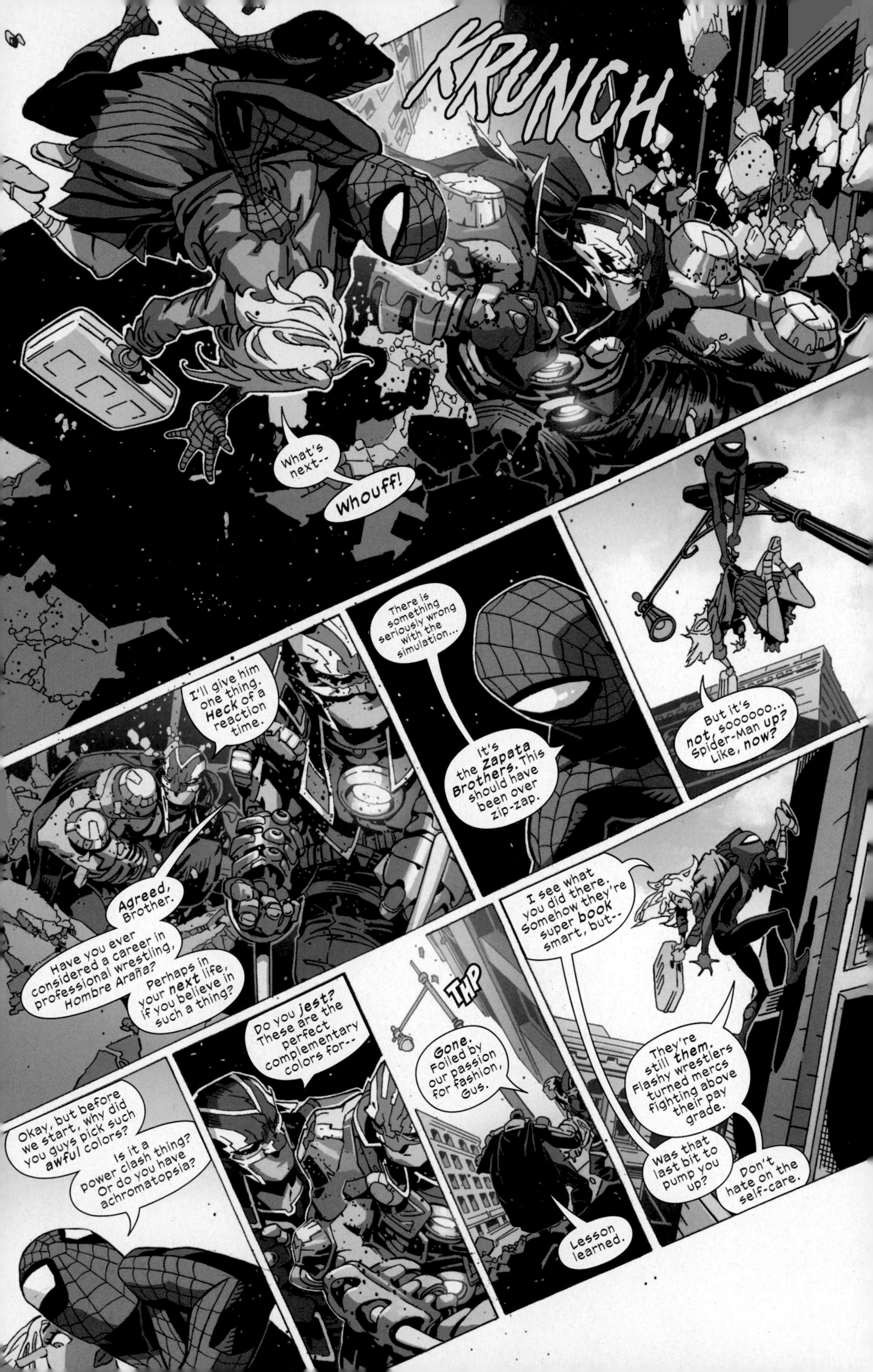

KRUNCH
What's next--
Whouff!
There is something seriously wrong with the simulation...
It's the Zapata Brothers. This should have been over zip-zap.
But it's not, soooooo... Spider-Man up? Like, now?
I'll give him one thing. Heck of a reaction time.
Agreed, Brother.
Have you ever considered a career in professional wrestling, Hombre Araña?
Perhaps in your next life, if you believe in such a thing?
I see what you did there. Somehow they're super book smart, but--
They're still them. Flashy wrestlers turned mercs fighting above their pay grade.
Was that last bit to pump you up?
Don't hate on the self-care.
THP
Okay, but before we start, why did you guys pick such awful colors?
Is it a power clash thing? Or do you have achromatopsia?
Do you jest? These are the perfect complementary colors for--
Gone. Foiled by our passion for fashion, Gus.
Lesson learned.

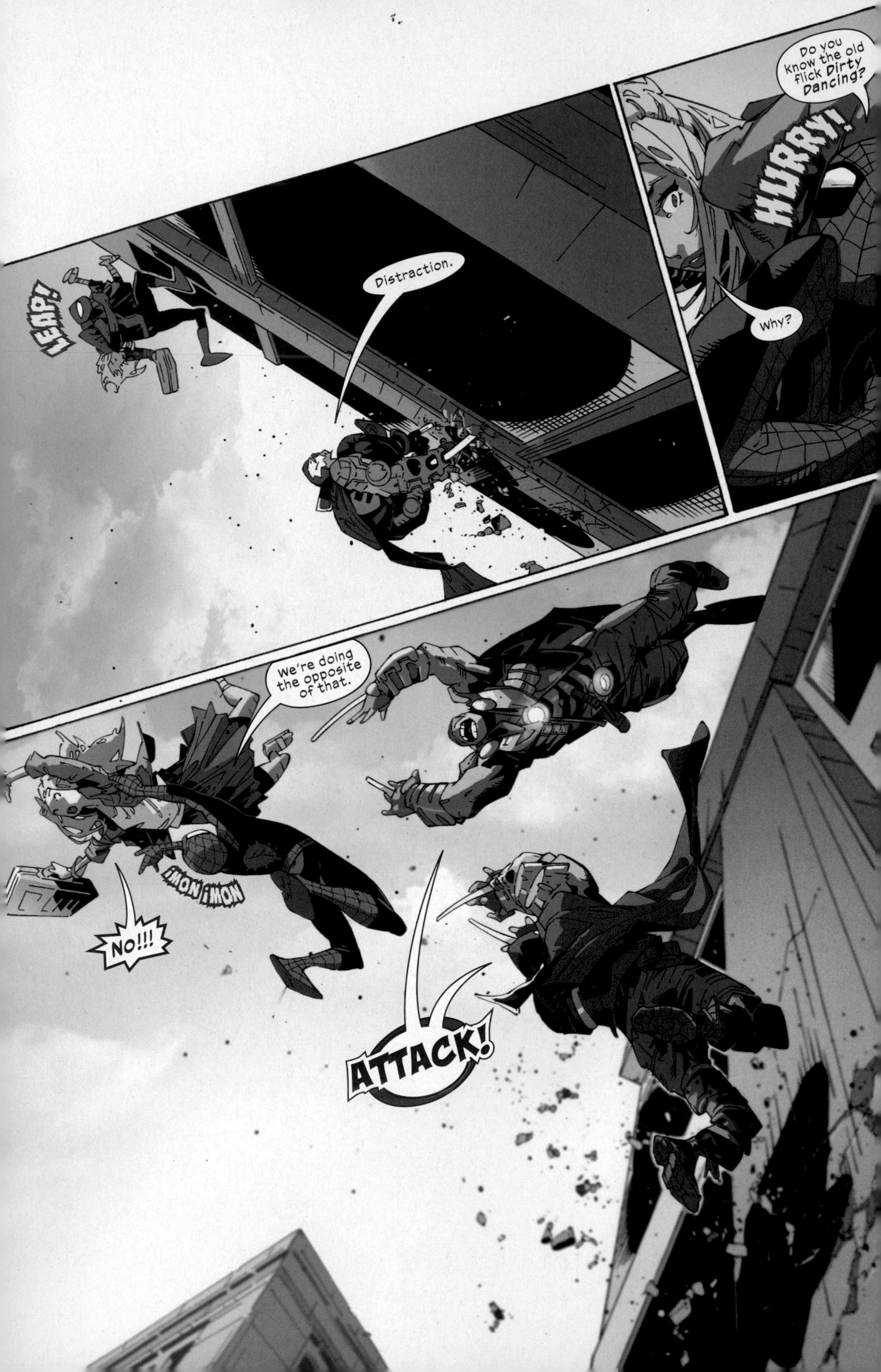
LEAP!
Distraction.
HURRY!
Do you know the old flick Dirty Dancing?
Why?
We're doing the opposite of that.
NOM! NOM!
NO!!!
ATTACK!

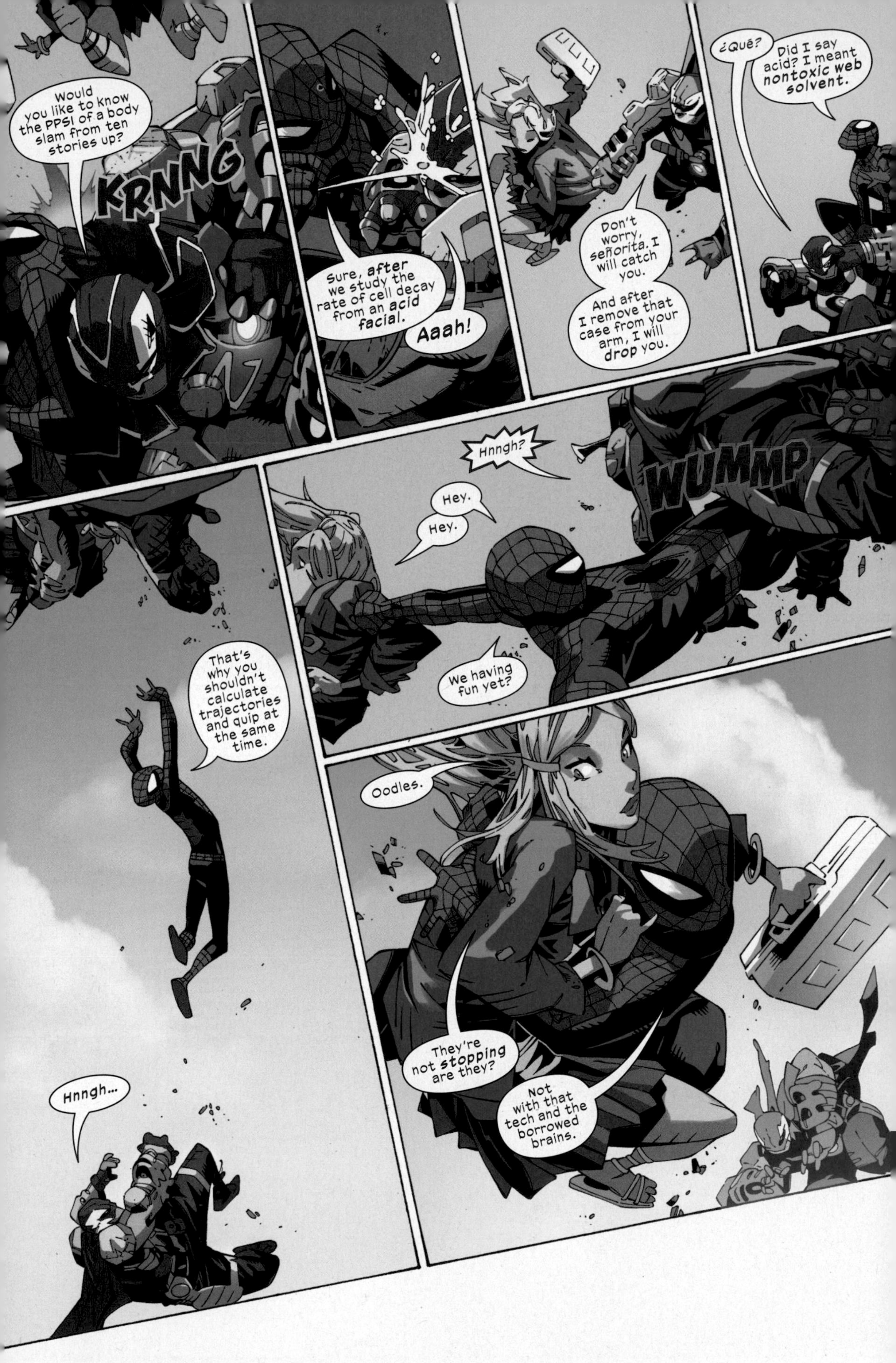
Would you like to know the PPSI of a body slam from ten stories up?
KRNNG
Sure, after we study the rate of cell decay from an acid facial.
Aaah!
Don't worry, señorita. I will catch you.
And after I remove that case from your arm, I will drop you.
¿Qué?
Did I say acid? I meant nontoxic web solvent.
Hnngh?
WUMMP
Hey.
Hey.
We having fun yet?
That's why you shouldn't calculate trajectories and quip at the same time.
Oodles.
They're not stopping are they?
Not with that tech and the borrowed brains.
Hnngh...

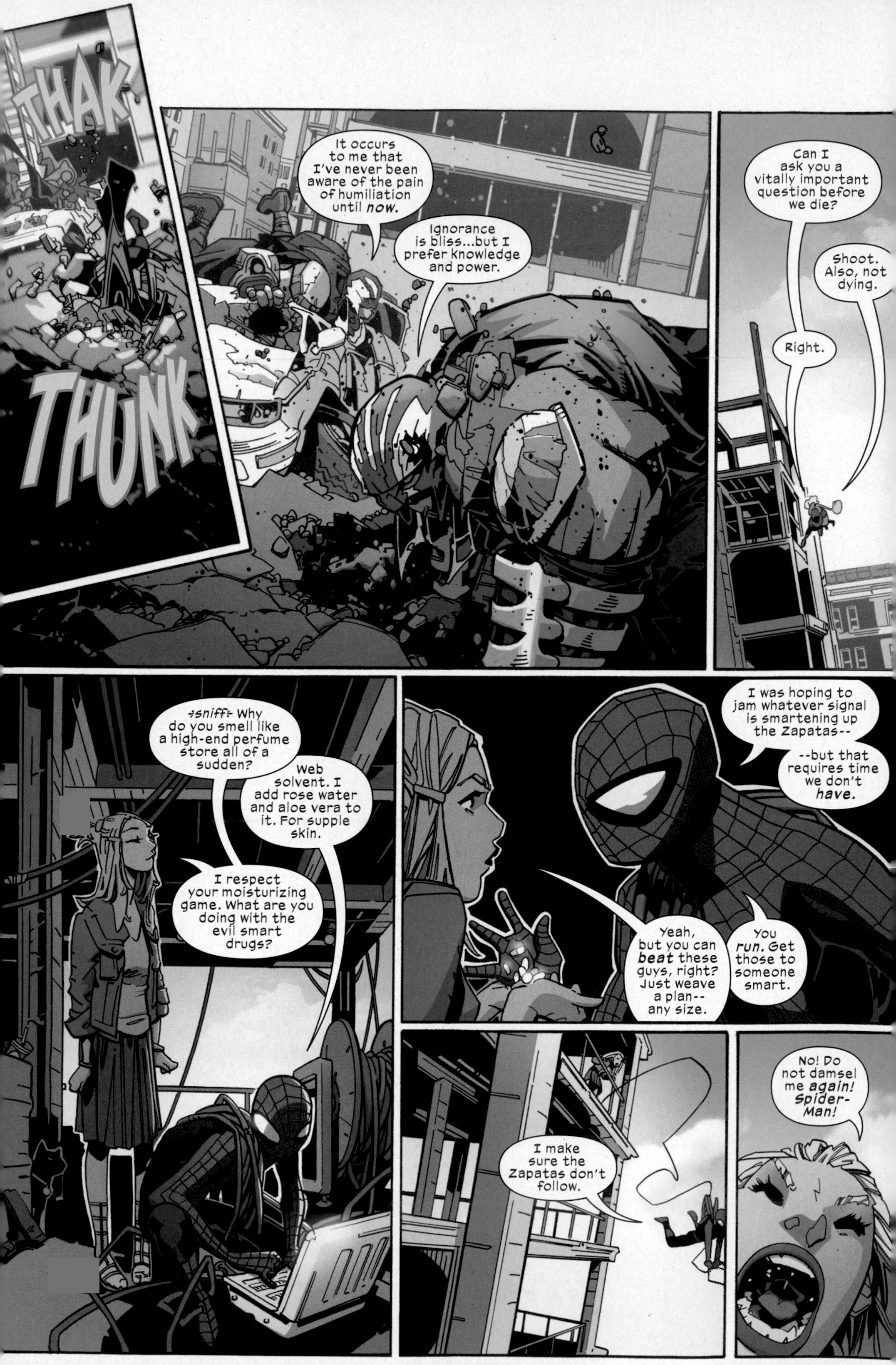
THAK
THUNK
It occurs to me that I've never been aware of the pain of humiliation until *now.*
Ignorance is bliss...but I prefer knowledge and power.
Can I ask you a vitally important question before we die?
Right.
Shoot. Also, not dying.
⇄sniff⇄ Why do you smell like a high-end perfume store all of a sudden?
Web solvent. I add rose water and aloe vera to it. For supple skin.
I respect your moisturizing game. What are you doing with the evil smart drugs?
I was hoping to jam whatever signal is smartening up the Zapatas--
--but that requires time we don't *have.*
Yeah, but you can *beat* these guys, right? Just weave a plan-- any size.
You *run.* Get those to someone smart.
I make sure the Zapatas don't follow.
No! Do not damsel me *again! Spider-Man!*

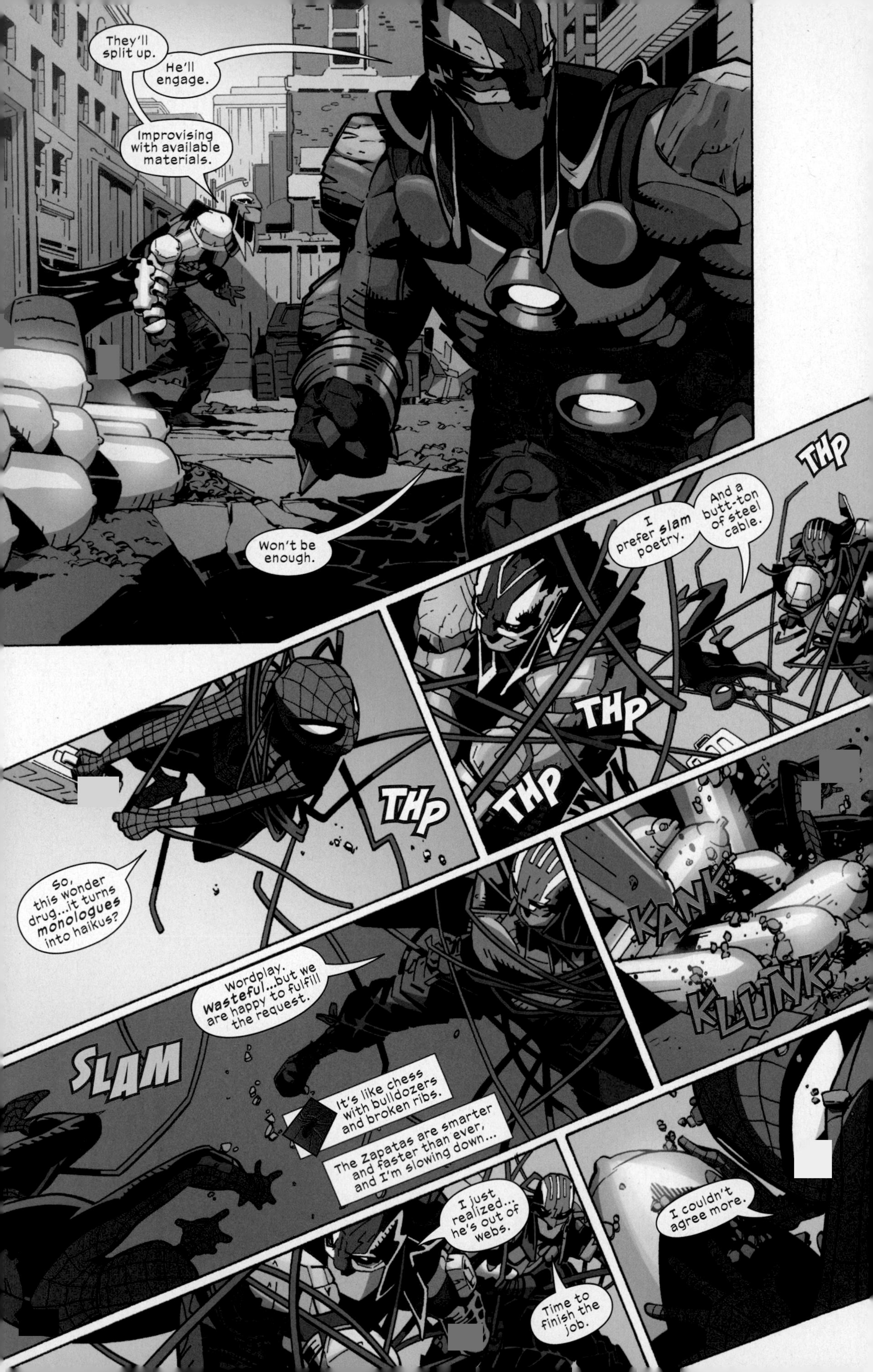

They'll split up.
He'll engage.
Improvising with available materials.
Won't be enough.
I prefer slam poetry.
And a butt-ton of steel cable.
THP
So, this wonder drug...it turns monologues into haikus?
THP
THP
THP
KANK
KLUNK
Wordplay. Wasteful...but we are happy to fulfill the request.
SLAM
It's like chess with bulldozers and broken ribs.
The Zapatas are smarter and faster than ever, and I'm slowing down...
I just realized... he's out of webs.
Time to finish the job.
I couldn't agree more.

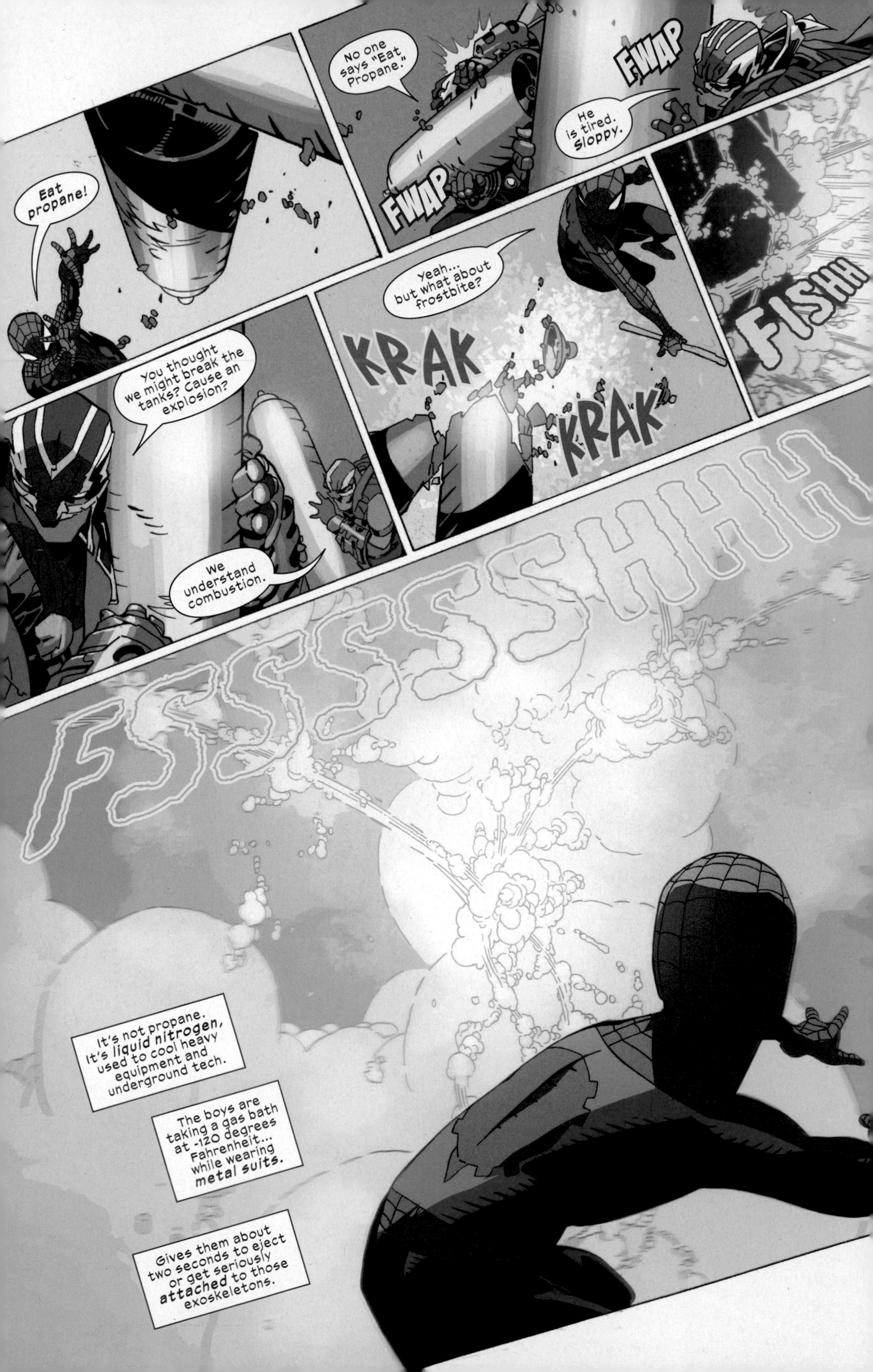
Eat propane!
No one says "Eat Propane."
FWAP
FWAP
He is tired. Sloppy.
You thought we might break the tanks? Cause an explosion?
We understand combustion.
Yeah... but what about frostbite?
KRAK
KRAK
FISHH
FSSSSSHHH
It's not propane. It's liquid nitrogen, used to cool heavy equipment and underground tech.
The boys are taking a gas bath at -120 degrees Fahrenheit... while wearing metal suits.
Gives them about two seconds to eject or get seriously attached to those exoskeletons.

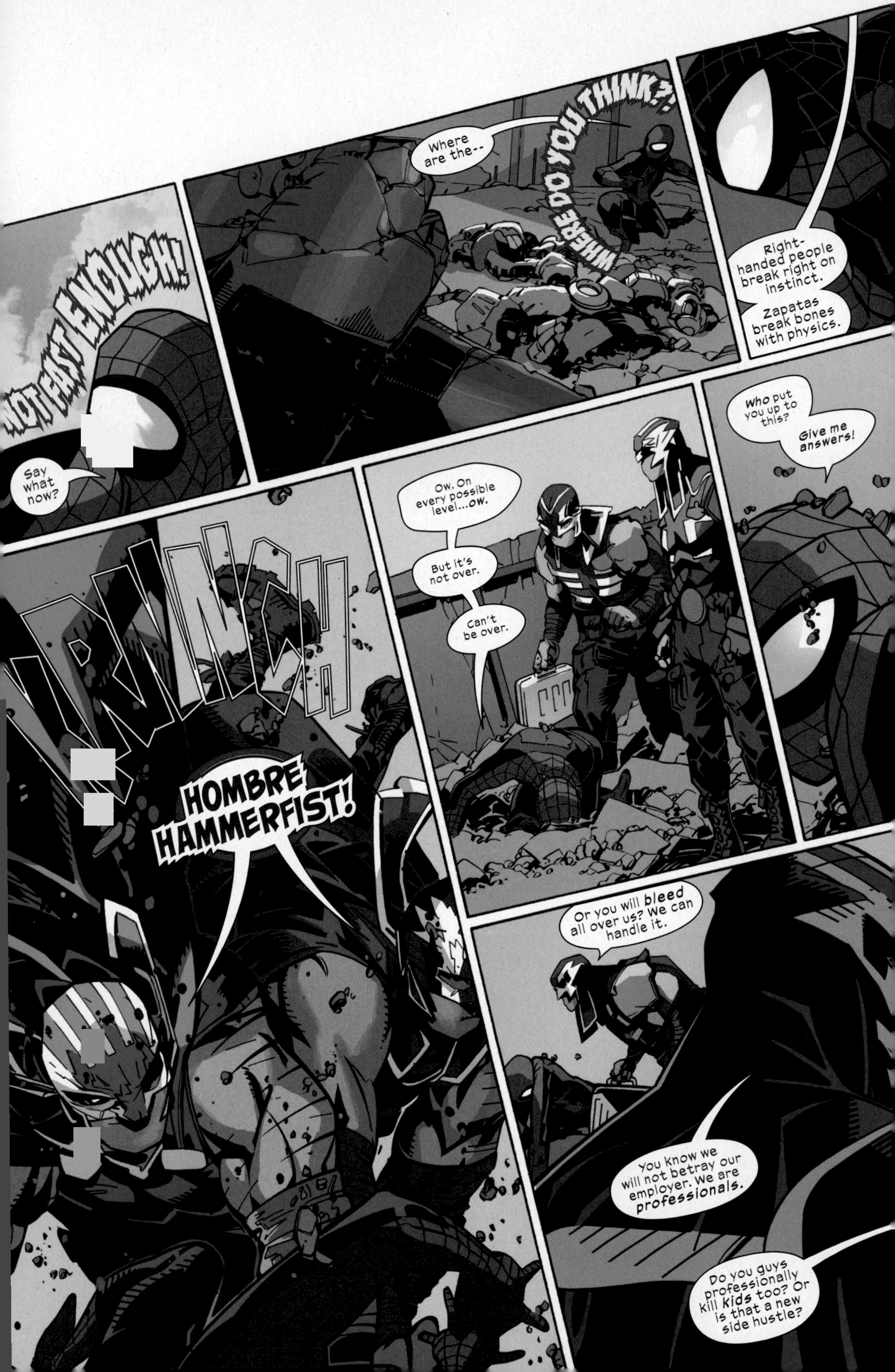
NOT FAST ENOUGH!
Say what now?
Where are the--
WHERE DO YOU THINK?!
Right-handed people break right on instinct.
Zapatas break bones with physics.
KRUNCH
HOMBRE HAMMERFIST!
Ow. On every possible level...ow.
But it's not over.
Can't be over.
Who put you up to this?
Give me answers!
Or you will bleed all over us? We can handle it.
You know we will not betray our employer. We are professionals.
Do you guys professionally kill kids too? Or is that a new side hustle?

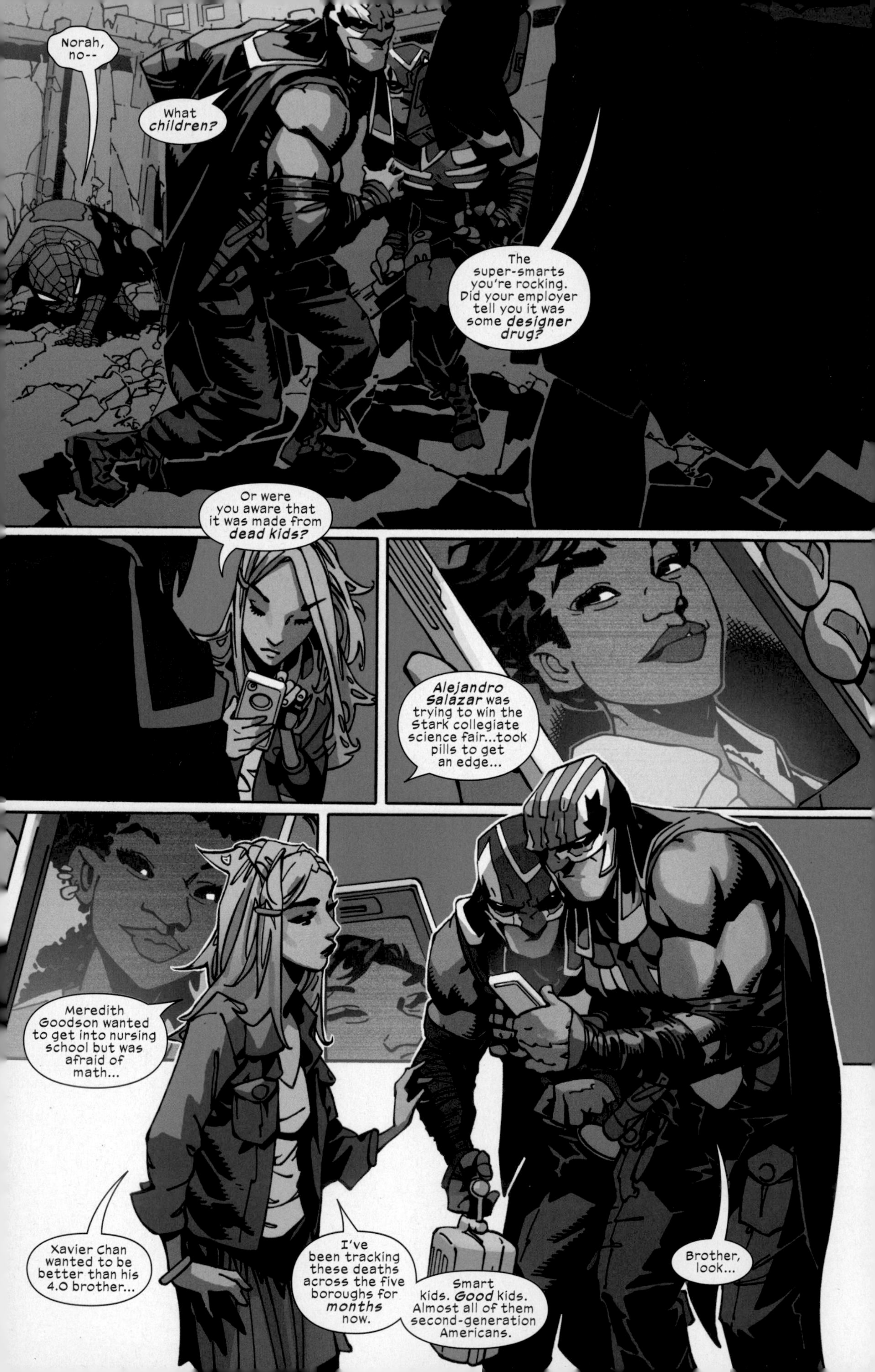
Norah, no--
What children?
The super-smarts you're rocking. Did your employer tell you it was some designer drug?
Or were you aware that it was made from dead kids?
Alejandro Salazar was trying to win the Stark collegiate science fair...took pills to get an edge...
Meredith Goodson wanted to get into nursing school but was afraid of math...
Xavier Chan wanted to be better than his 4.0 brother...
I've been tracking these deaths across the five boroughs for months now.
Smart kids. Good kids. Almost all of them second-generation Americans.
Brother, look...

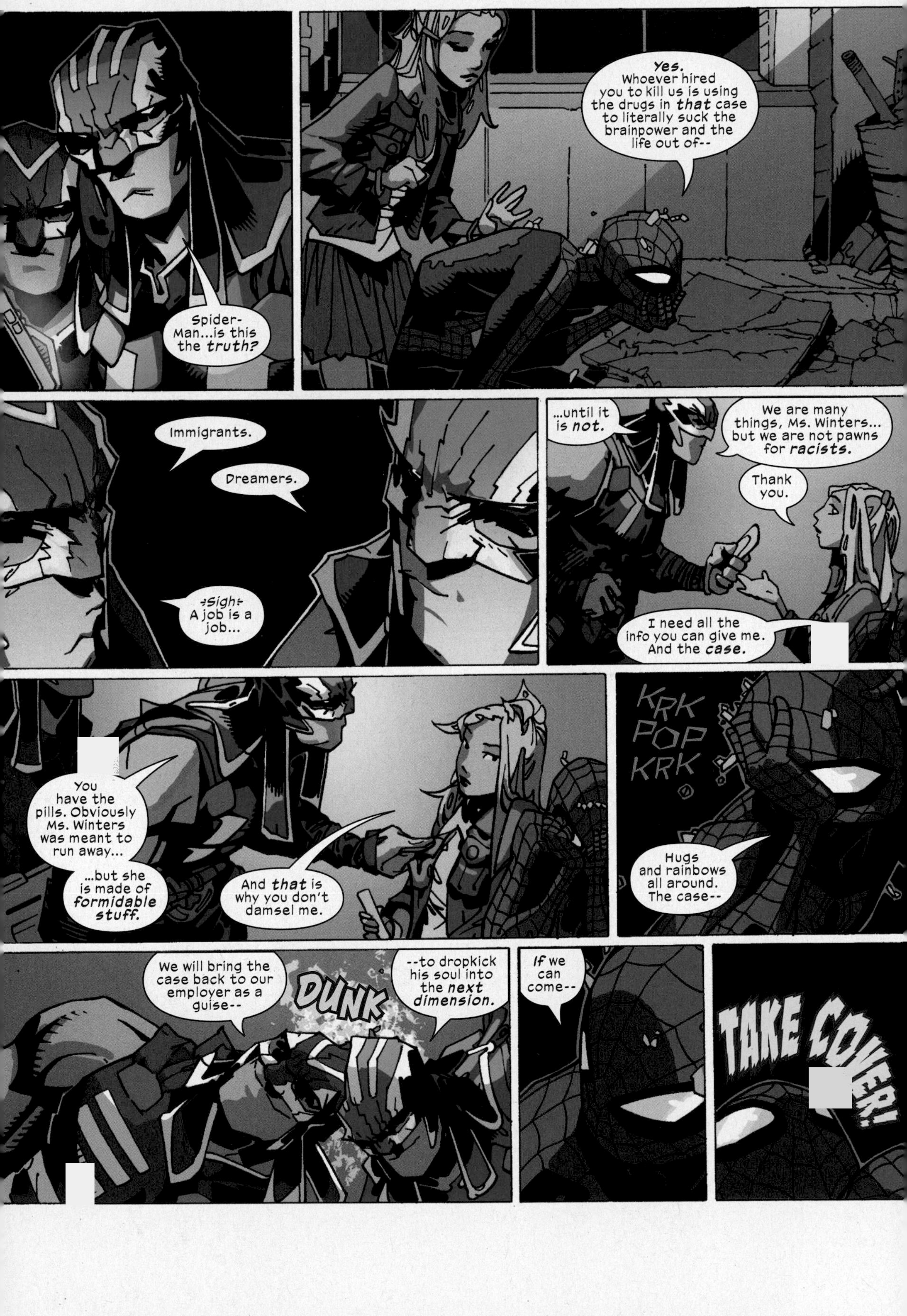

Spider-Man...is this the *truth?*
Yes. Whoever hired you to kill us is using the drugs in *that* case to literally suck the brainpower and the life out of--
Immigrants.
Dreamers.
⋮Sigh⋮ A job is a job...
...until it is *not.*
We are many things, Ms. Winters... but we are not pawns for *racists.*
Thank you.
I need all the info you can give me. And the *case.*
You have the pills. Obviously Ms. Winters was meant to run away...
...but she is made of *formidable stuff.*
And *that* is why you don't damsel me.
KRK POP KRK
Hugs and rainbows all around. The case--
We will bring the case back to our employer as a guise--
DUNK
--to dropkick his soul into the *next dimension.*
If we can come--
TAKE COVER!

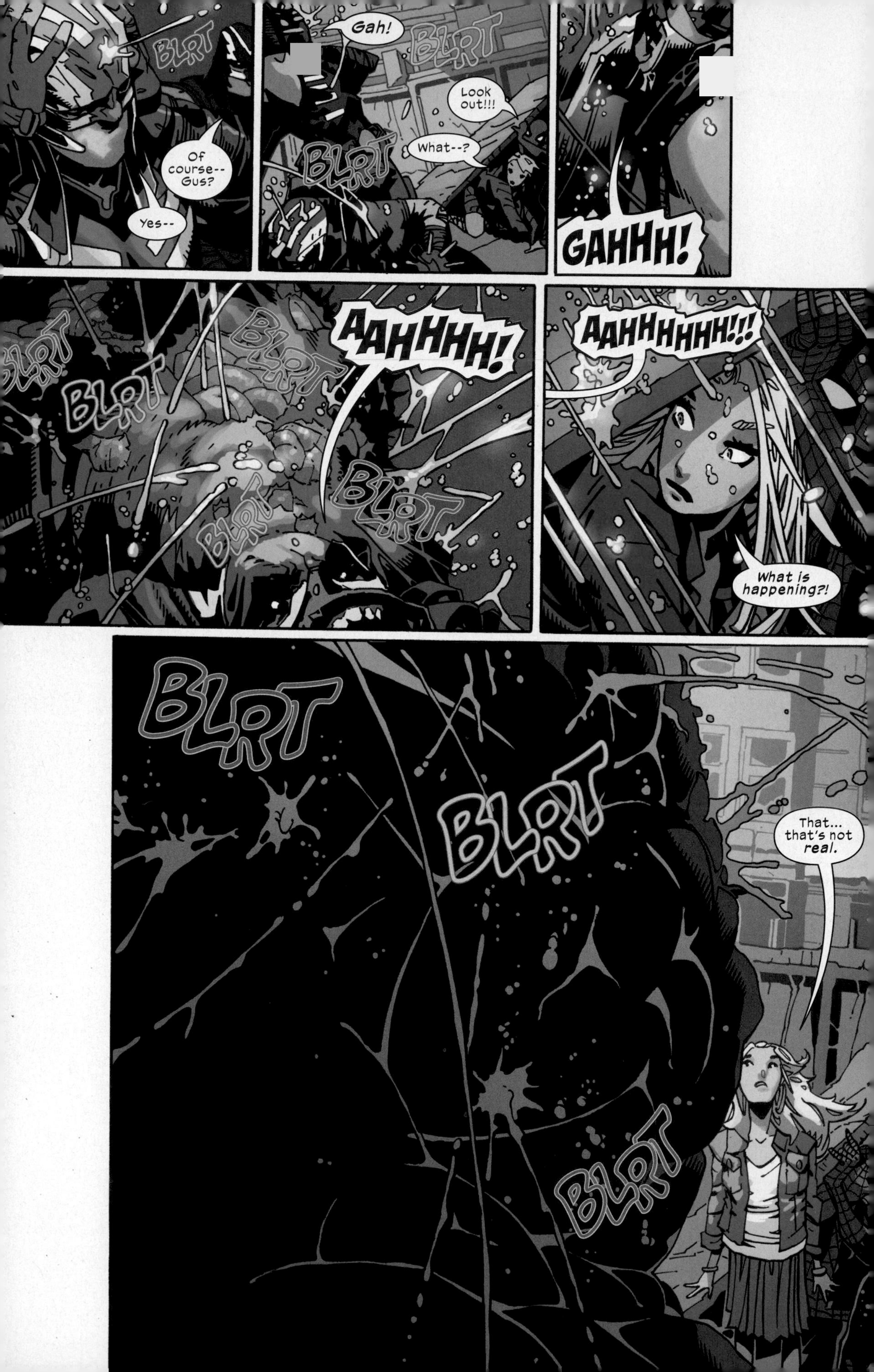
BLRT
Of course-- Gus?
Yes--
Gah!
BLRT
Look out!!!
What--?
BLRT
GAHHH!
BLRT
BLRT
BLRT
AAHHHH!
BLRT
BLRT
AAHHHHHH!!!
What is happening?!
BLRT
BLRT
That... that's not real.
BLRT

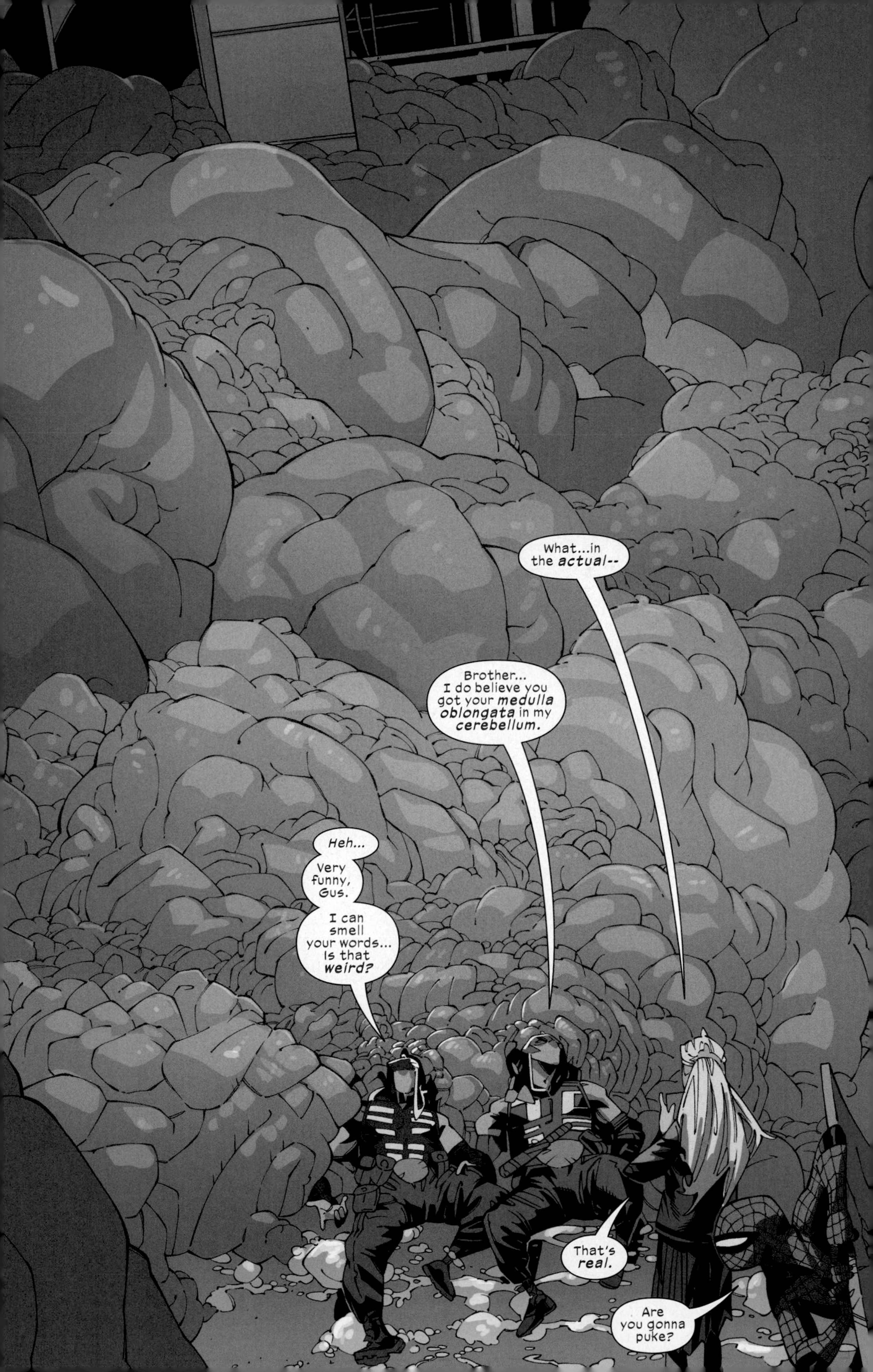
What...in the *actual*--
Brother... I do believe you got your *medulla oblongata* in my *cerebellum.*
Heh...
Very funny, Gus.
I can smell your words... Is that *weird?*
That's *real.*
Are you gonna puke?

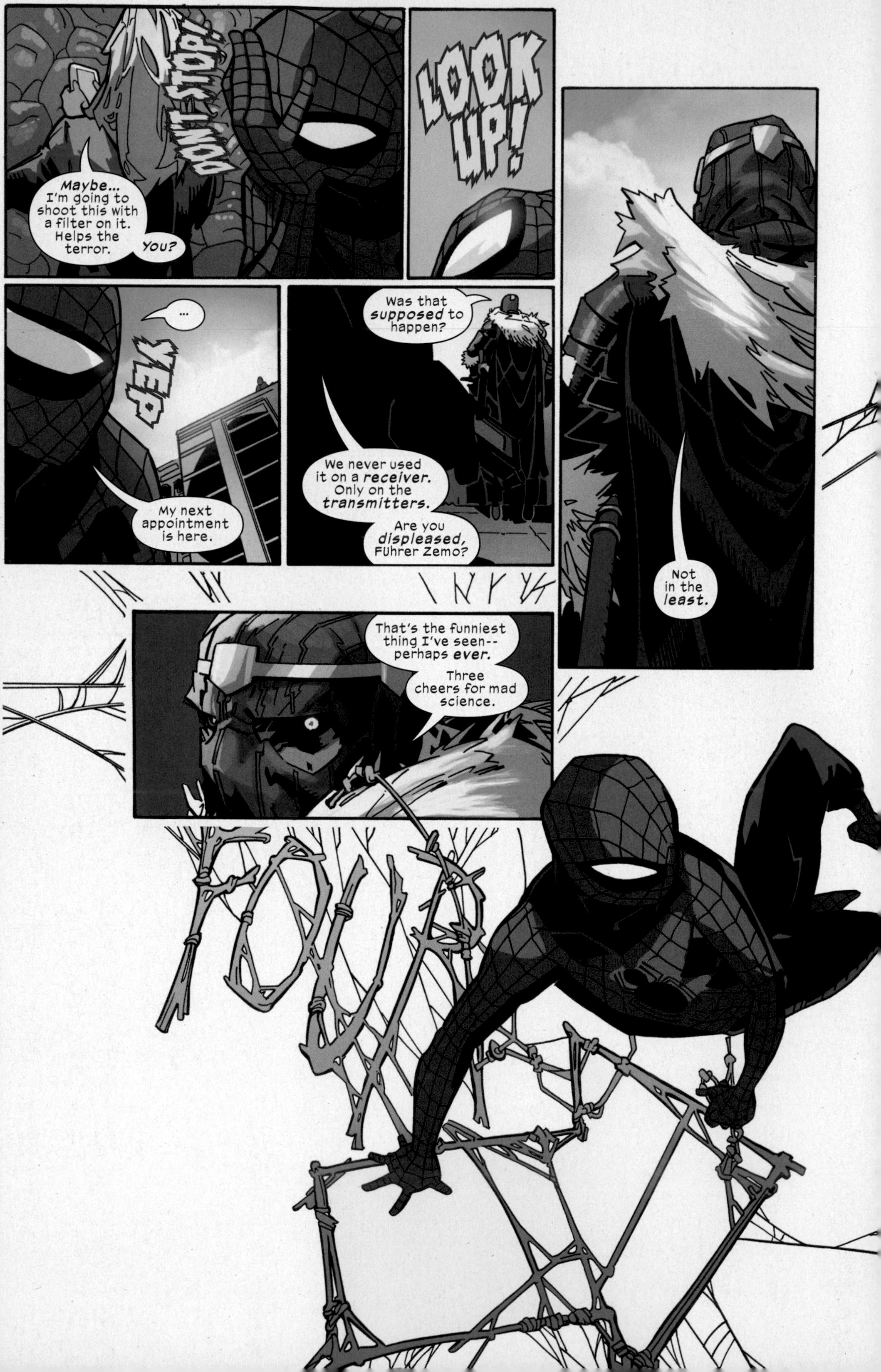
DON'T STOP!
Maybe... I'm going to shoot this with a filter on it. Helps the terror.
You?
LOOK UP!
...
YEP
My next appointment is here.
Was that supposed to happen?
We never used it on a receiver. Only on the transmitters.
Are you displeased, Führer Zemo?
Not in the least.
That's the funniest thing I've seen--perhaps ever.
Three cheers for mad science.

4. THE SECRET LIVES OF SAVAGES CHAPTER ONE

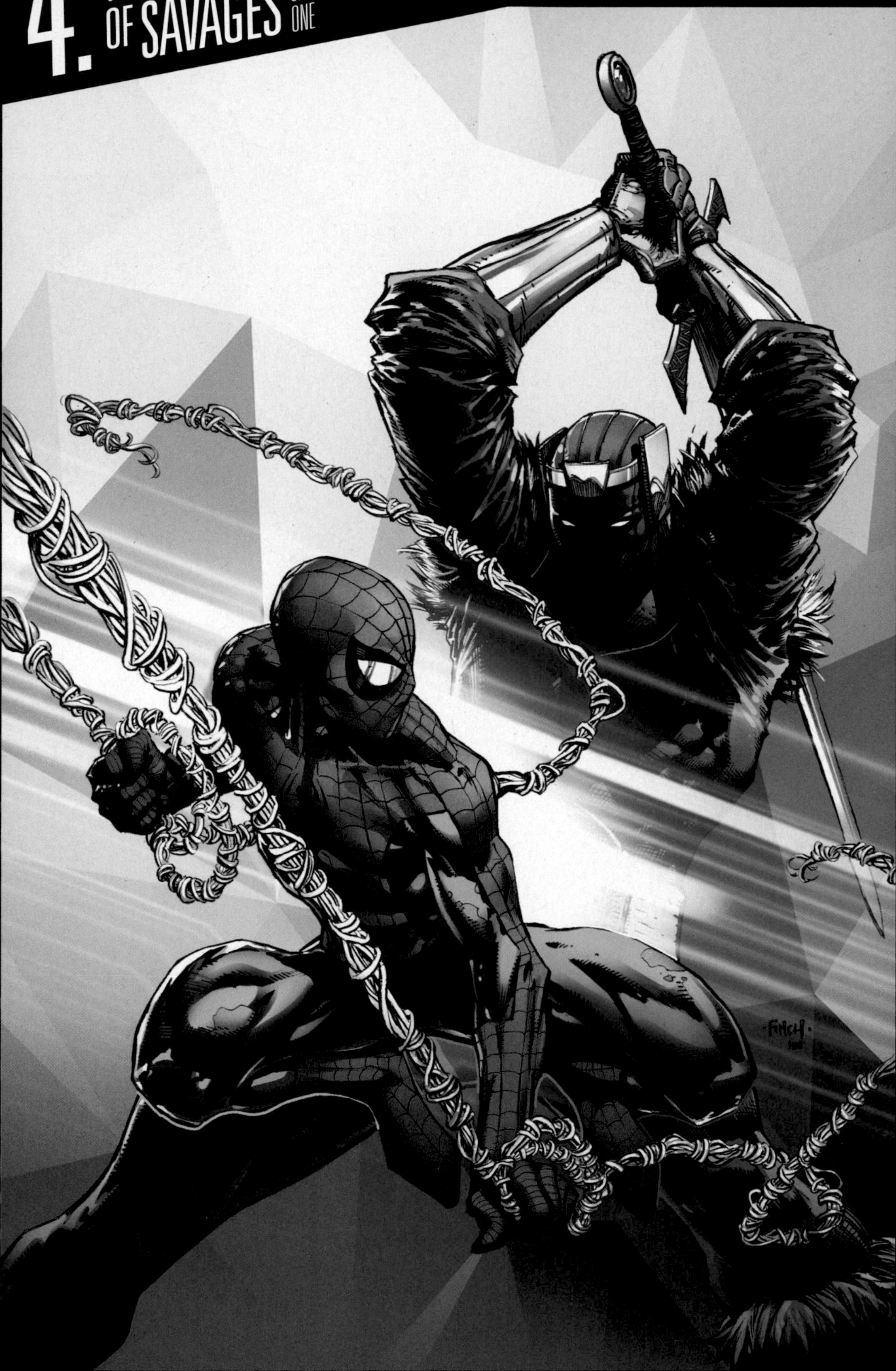

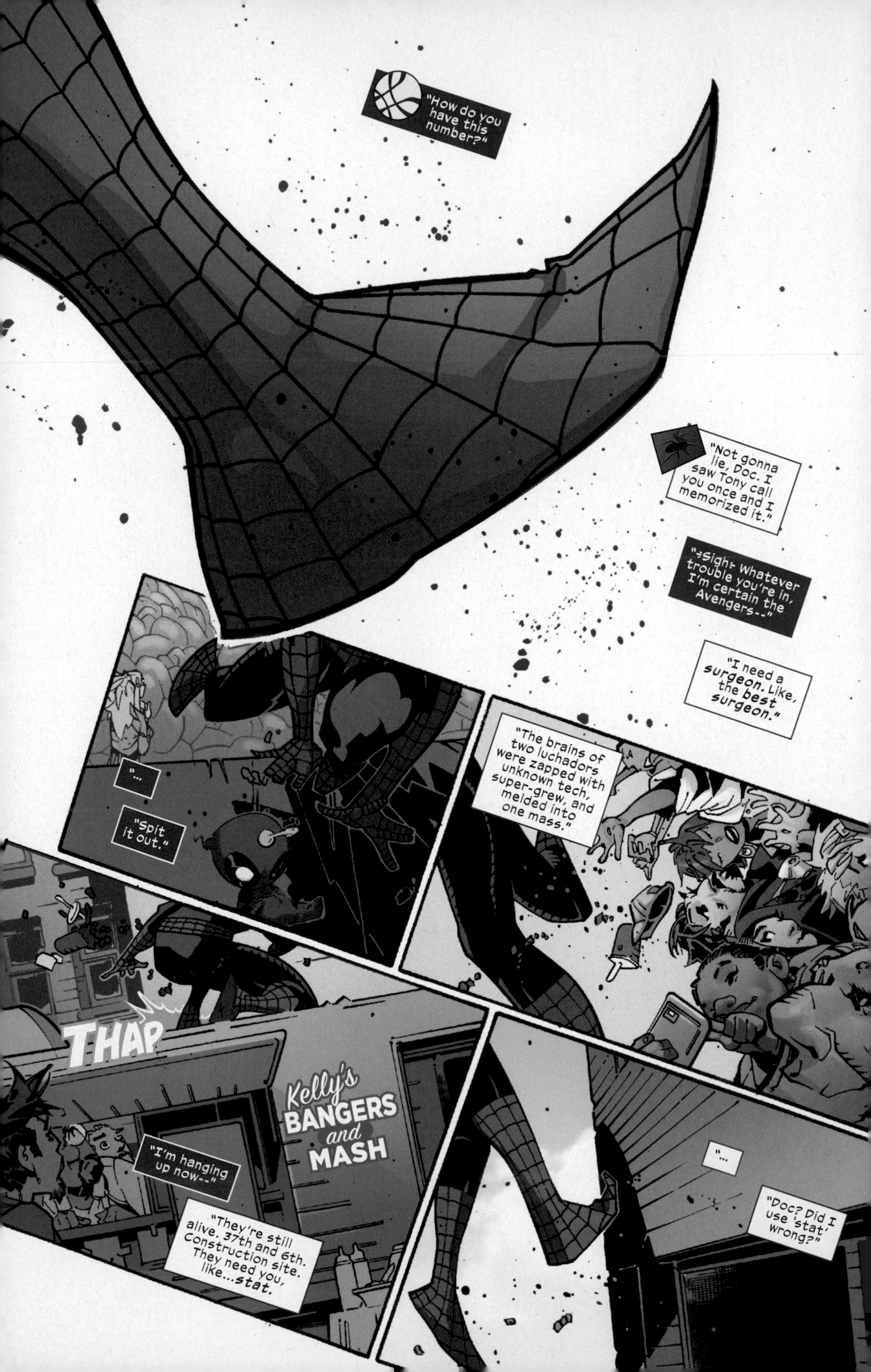

"How do you have this number?"
"Not gonna lie, Doc. I saw Tony call you once and I memorized it."
"*Sigh* Whatever trouble you're in, I'm certain the Avengers--"
"I need a surgeon. Like, the best surgeon."
"...
"Spit it out."
"The brains of two luchadors were zapped with unknown tech, super-grew, and melded into one mass."
THAP
Kelly's BANGERS and MASH
"I'm hanging up now--"
"They're still alive. 37th and 6th. Construction site. They need you, like...stat.
"...
"Doc? Did I use 'stat' wrong?"

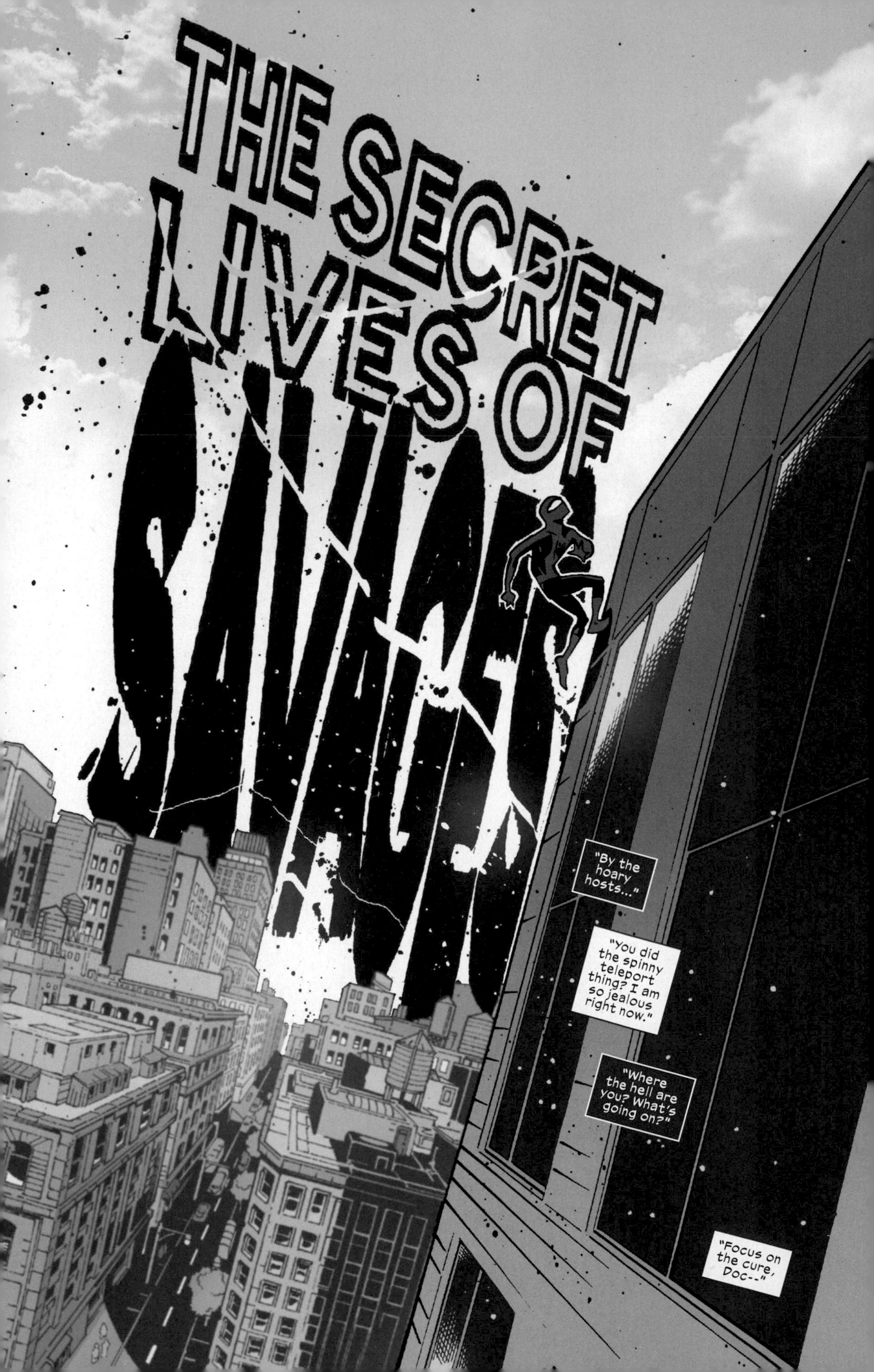
THE SECRET LIVES OF SAVAGES
"By the hoary hosts..."
"You did the spinny teleport thing? I am so jealous right now."
"Where the hell are you? What's going on?"
"Focus on the cure, Doc--"

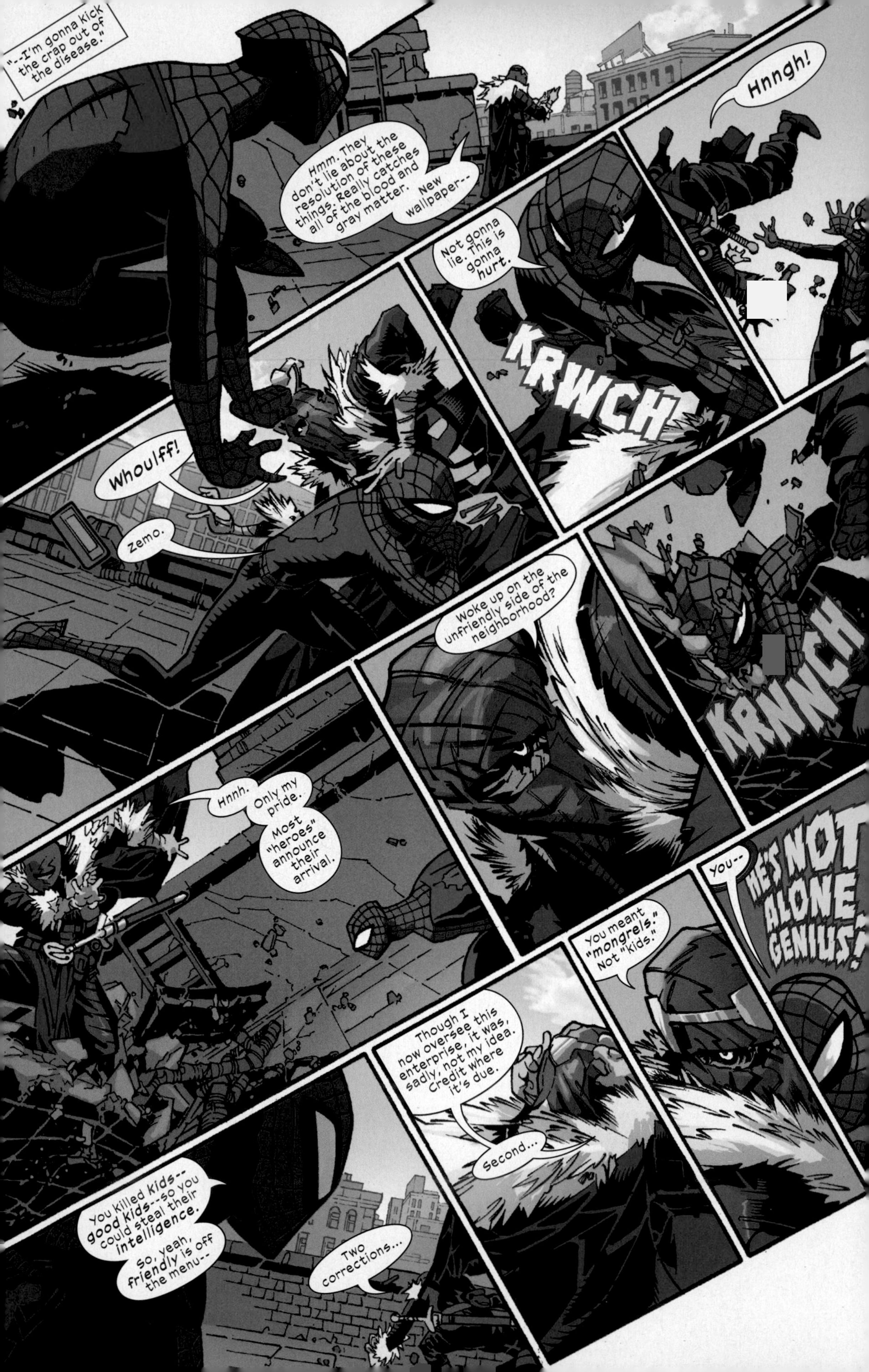
"--I'm gonna kick the crap out of the disease."
Hmm. They don't lie about the resolution of these things. Really catches all of the blood and gray matter.
New wallpaper--
Hnngh!
Not gonna lie. This is gonna hurt.
KRWCH
Whoulff!
Zemo.
Woke up on the unfriendly side of the neighborhood?
KRNNCH
Hnnh.
Only my pride.
Most "heroes" announce their arrival.
You--
HE'S NOT ALONE, GENIUS!
You meant "mongrels." Not "kids."
Though I now oversee this enterprise, it was, sadly, not my idea. Credit where it's due.
Second...
You killed kids--good kids--so you could steal their intelligence.
So, yeah, friendly is off the menu--
Two corrections...

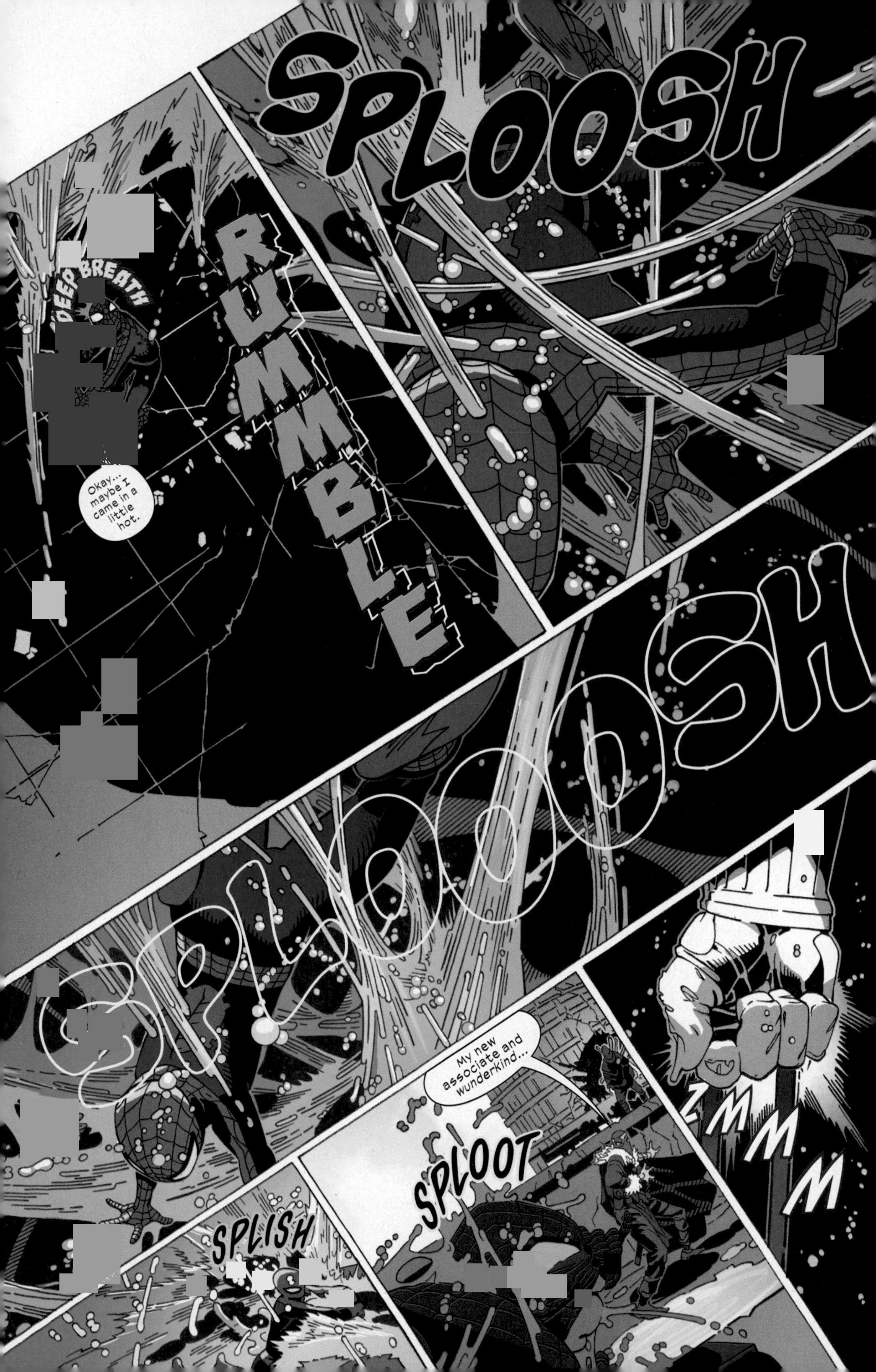
DEEP BREATH
RUMMBLE
Okay... maybe I came in a little hot.
SPLOOSH
SPLOOOOSH
ZMMMM
My new associate and wunderkind...
SPLOOT
SPLISH

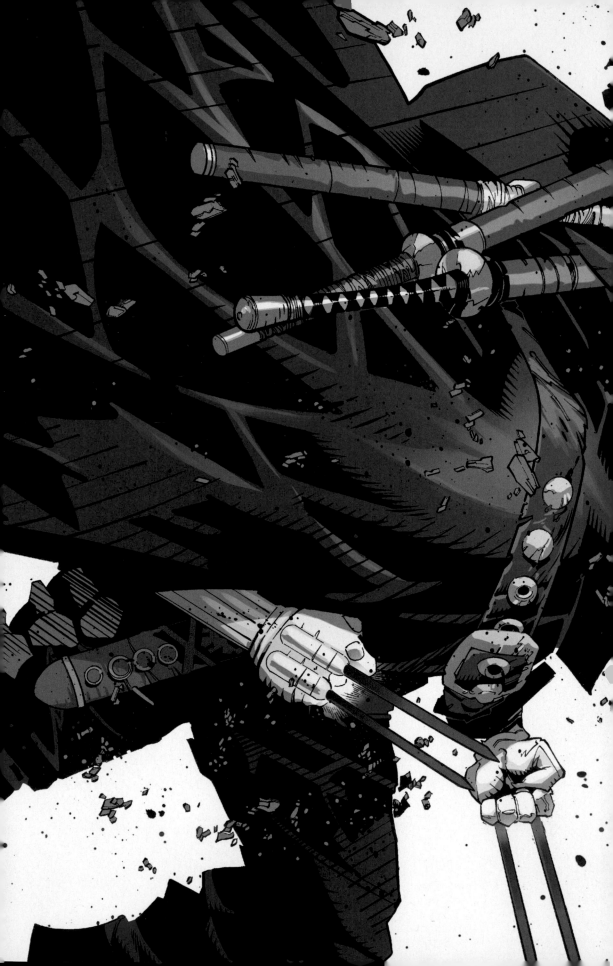

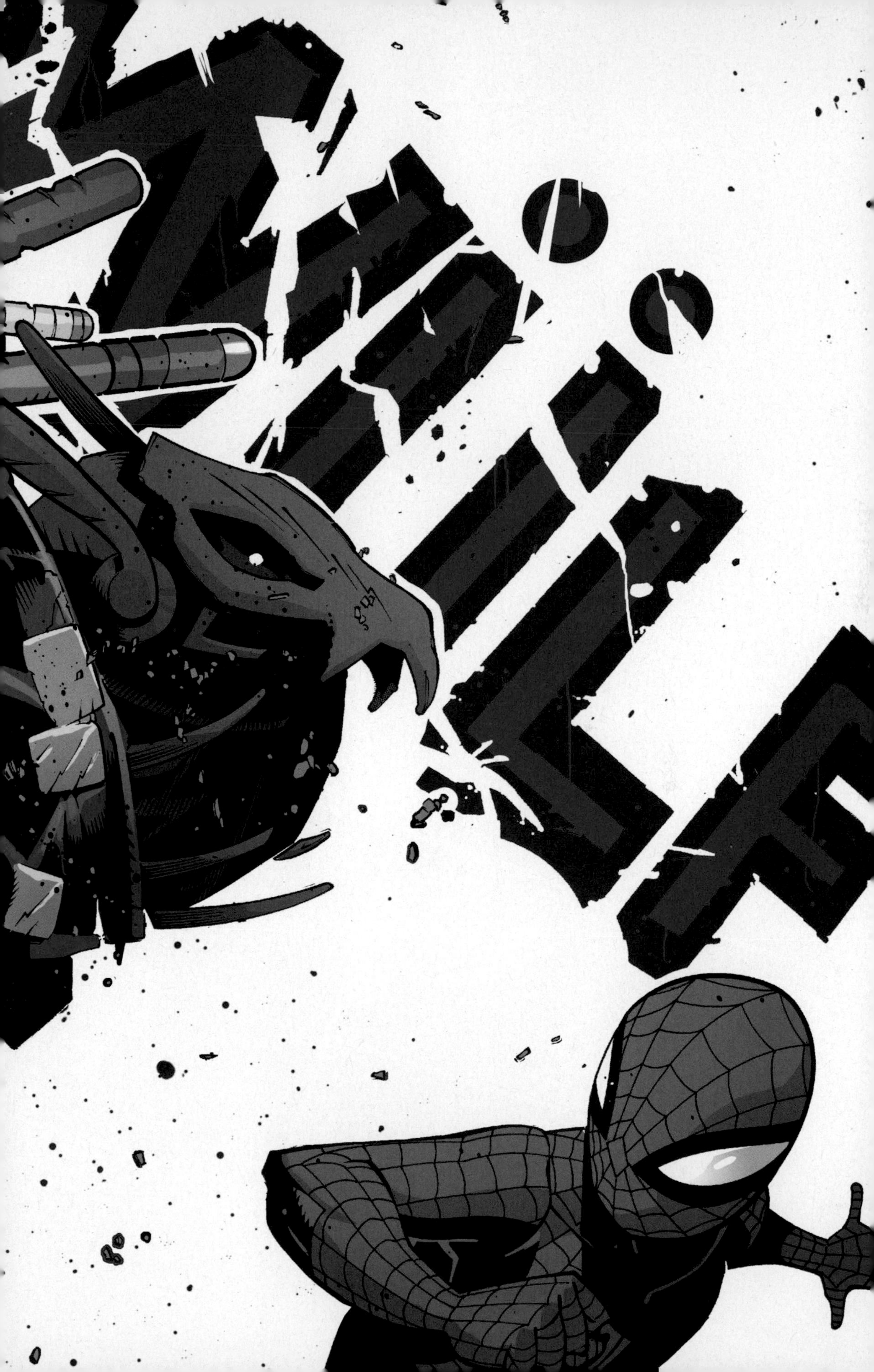

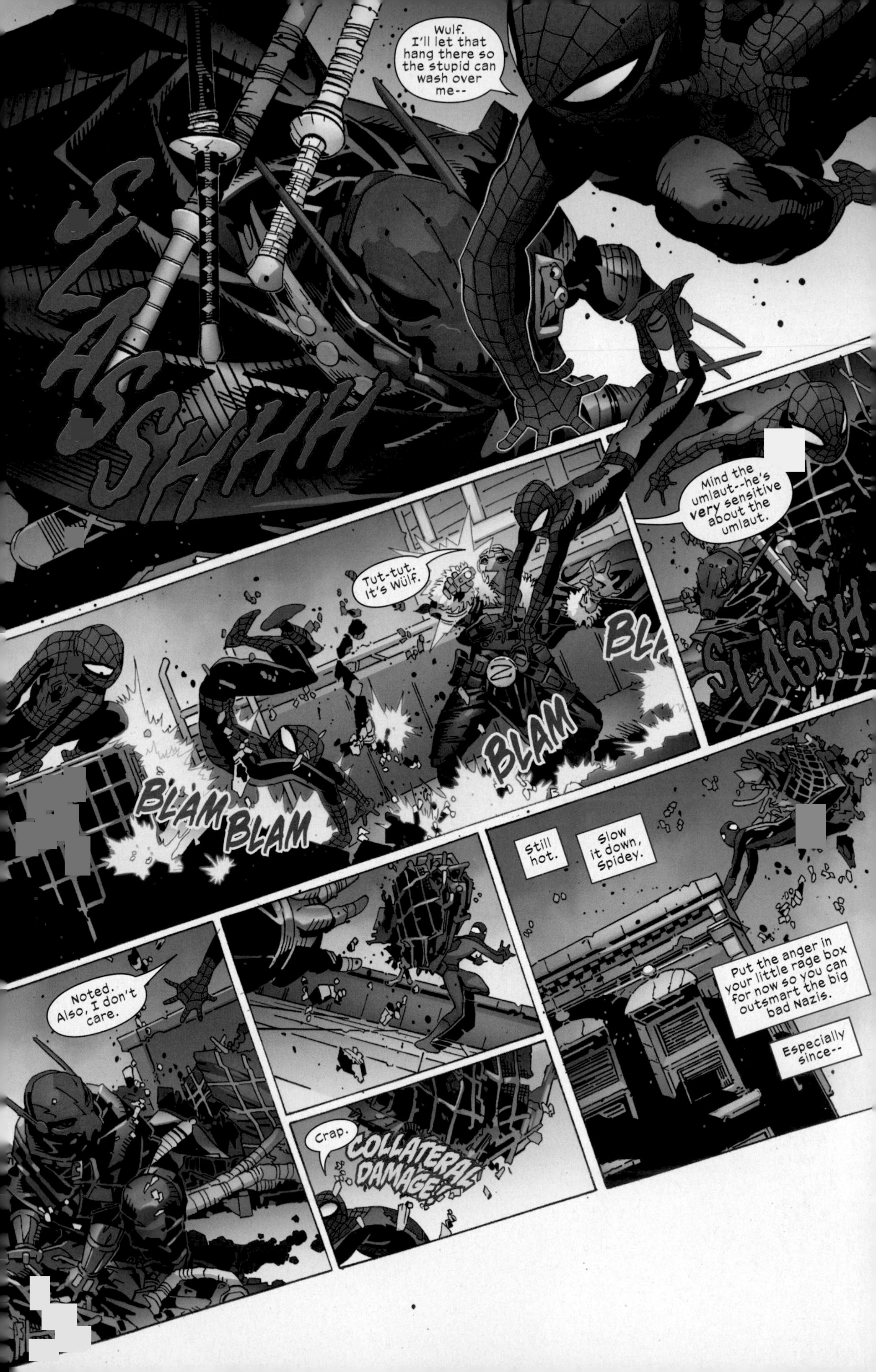
Wulf. I'll let that hang there so the stupid can wash over me--
SLASSHHH
Tut-tut. It's Wülf.
Mind the umlaut--he's very sensitive about the umlaut.
BLAM BLAM
BLAM
BLA
SLASSH
Still hot.
Slow it down, Spidey.
Put the anger in your little rage box for now so you can outsmart the big bad Nazis.
Especially since--
Noted. Also, I don't care.
Crap.
COLLATERAL DAMAGE!

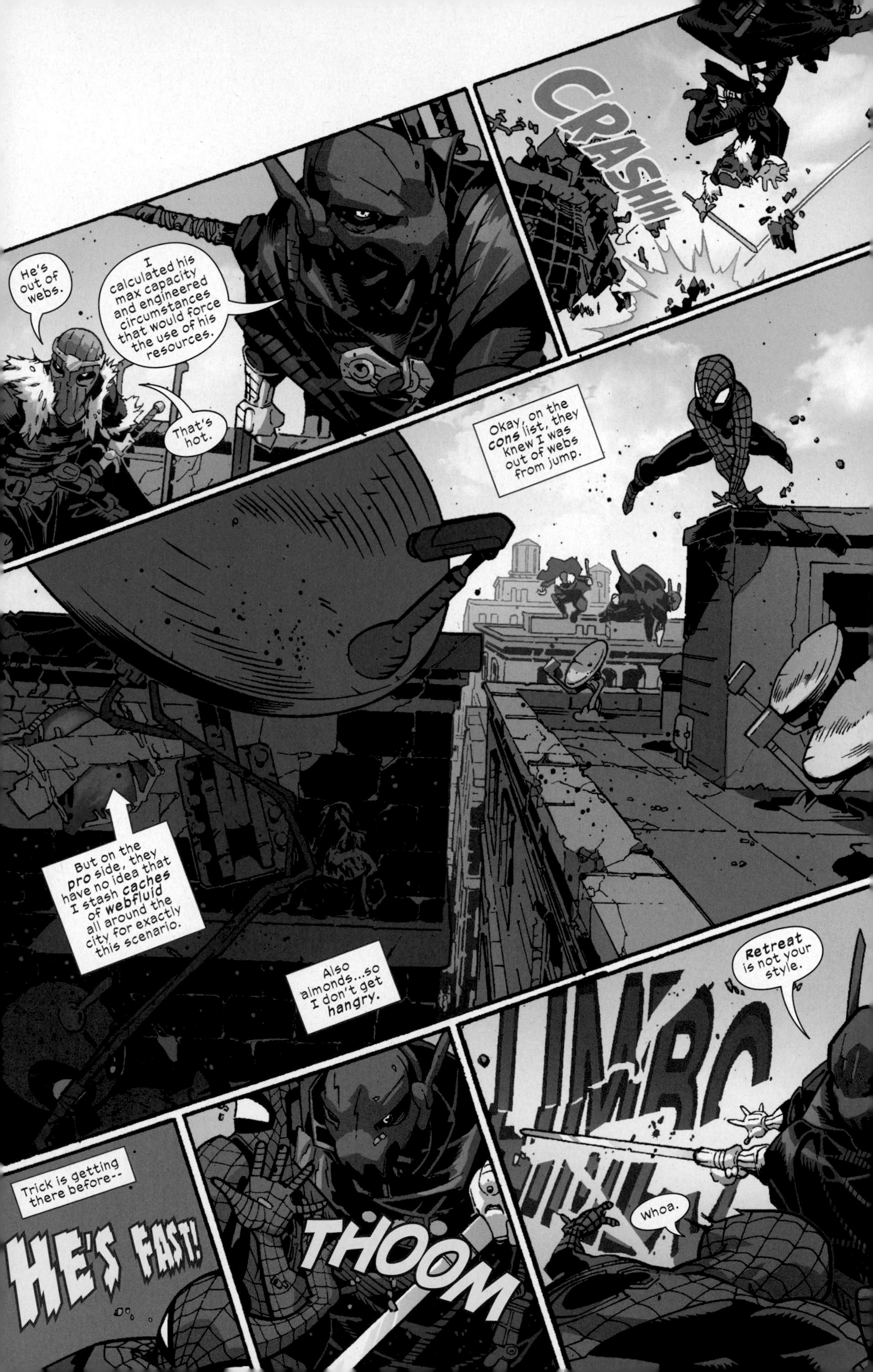
CRASHH
He's out of webs.
I calculated his max capacity and engineered circumstances that would force the use of his resources.
That's hot.
Okay, on the cons list, they knew I was out of webs from jump.
But on the pro side, they have no idea that I stash caches of webfluid all around the city for exactly this scenario.
Also almonds...so I don't get hangry.
Trick is getting there before--
HE'S FAST!
THOOM
Retreat is not your style.
Whoa.

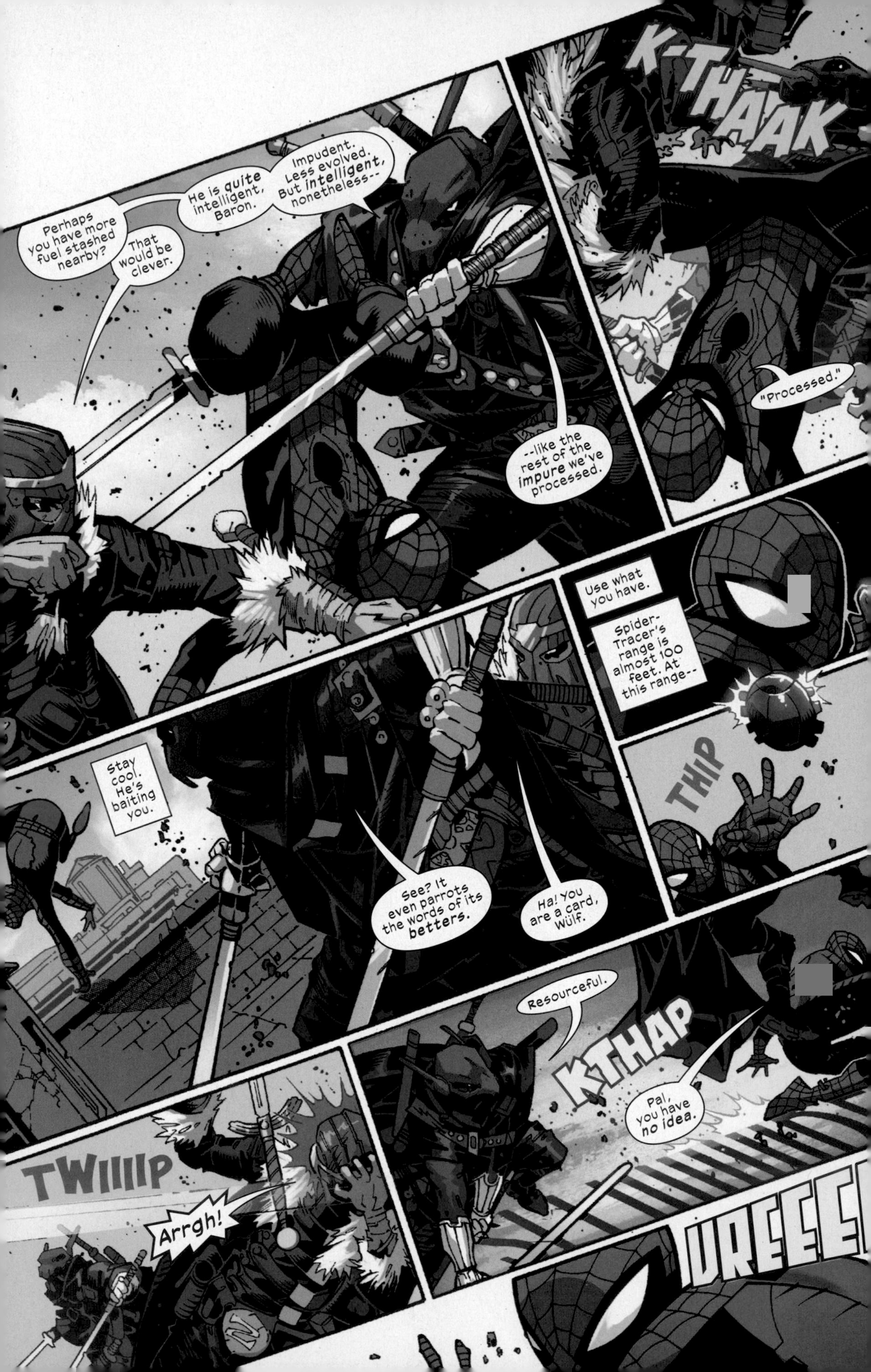

Perhaps you have more fuel stashed nearby?
That would be clever.
He is quite intelligent, Baron.
Impudent. Less evolved. But intelligent, nonetheless--
--like the rest of the impure we've processed.
K-THAAK
"Processed."
Use what you have.
Spider-Tracer's range is almost 100 feet. At this range--
THIP
Stay cool. He's baiting you.
See? It even parrots the words of its betters.
Ha! You are a card, Wülf.
Resourceful.
KTHAP
Pal, you have no idea.
TWIIIIP
Arrgh!
VREEE

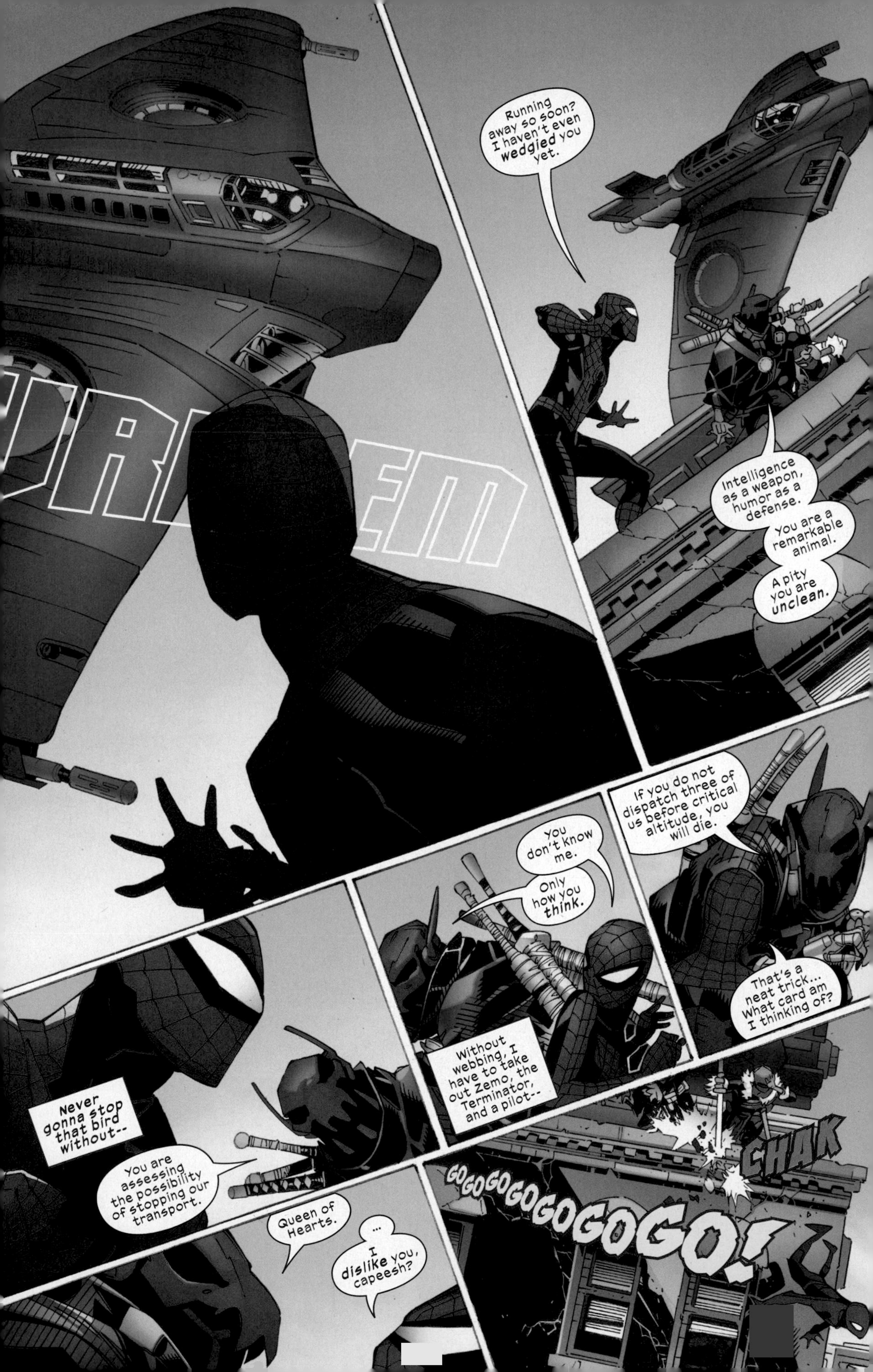
Running away so soon? I haven't even wedgied you yet.
Intelligence as a weapon, humor as a defense.
You are a remarkable animal.
A pity you are unclean.
If you do not dispatch three of us before critical altitude, you will die.
You don't know me.
Only how you think.
That's a neat trick... What card am I thinking of?
Without webbing, I have to take out Zemo, the Terminator, and a pilot--
Never gonna stop that bird without--
You are assessing the possibility of stopping our transport.
Queen of Hearts.
...
I dislike you, capeesh?
CHAK
GOGOGOGOGOGOGOGO!

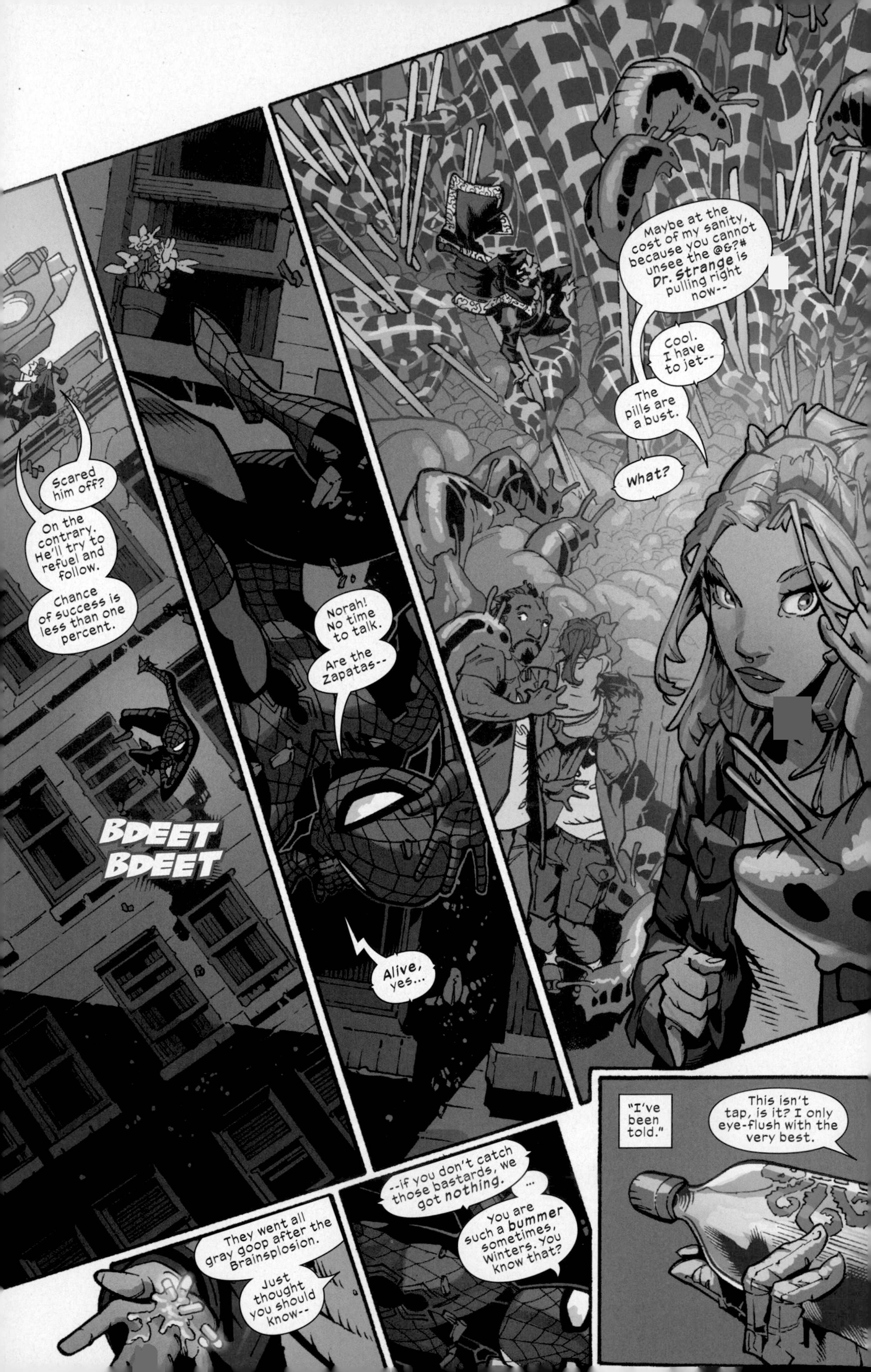

Scared him off?
On the contrary. He'll try to refuel and follow.
Chance of success is less than one percent.
BDEET BDEET
Norah! No time to talk.
Are the Zapatas--
Alive, yes...
Maybe at the cost of my sanity, because you cannot unsee the @&?# Dr. Strange is pulling right now--
Cool. I have to jet--
The pills are a bust.
What?
They went all gray goop after the Brainsplosion.
Just thought you should know--
--if you don't catch those bastards, we got nothing.
...
You are such a bummer sometimes, Winters. You know that?
"I've been told."
This isn't tap, is it? I only eye-flush with the very best.

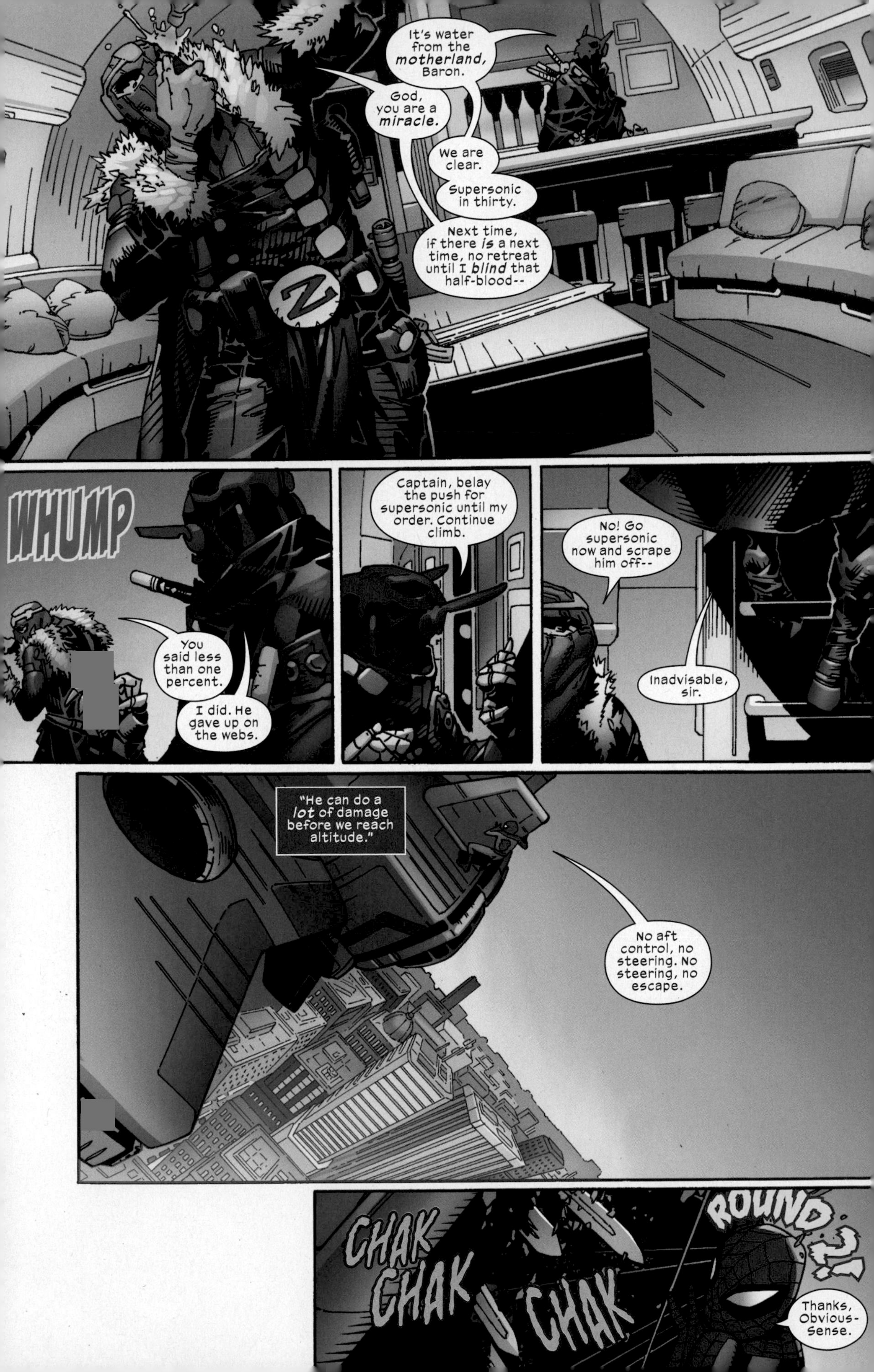

It's water from the *motherland,* Baron.
God, you are a *miracle.*
We are clear.
Supersonic in thirty.
Next time, if there *is* a next time, no retreat until I *blind* that half-blood--
WHUMP
You said less than one percent.
I did. He gave up on the webs.
Captain, belay the push for supersonic until my order. Continue climb.
No! Go supersonic now and scrape him off--
Inadvisable, sir.
"He can do a *lot* of damage before we reach altitude."
No aft control, no steering. No steering, no escape.
CHAK
CHAK
CHAK
ROUND
Thanks, Obvious-Sense.

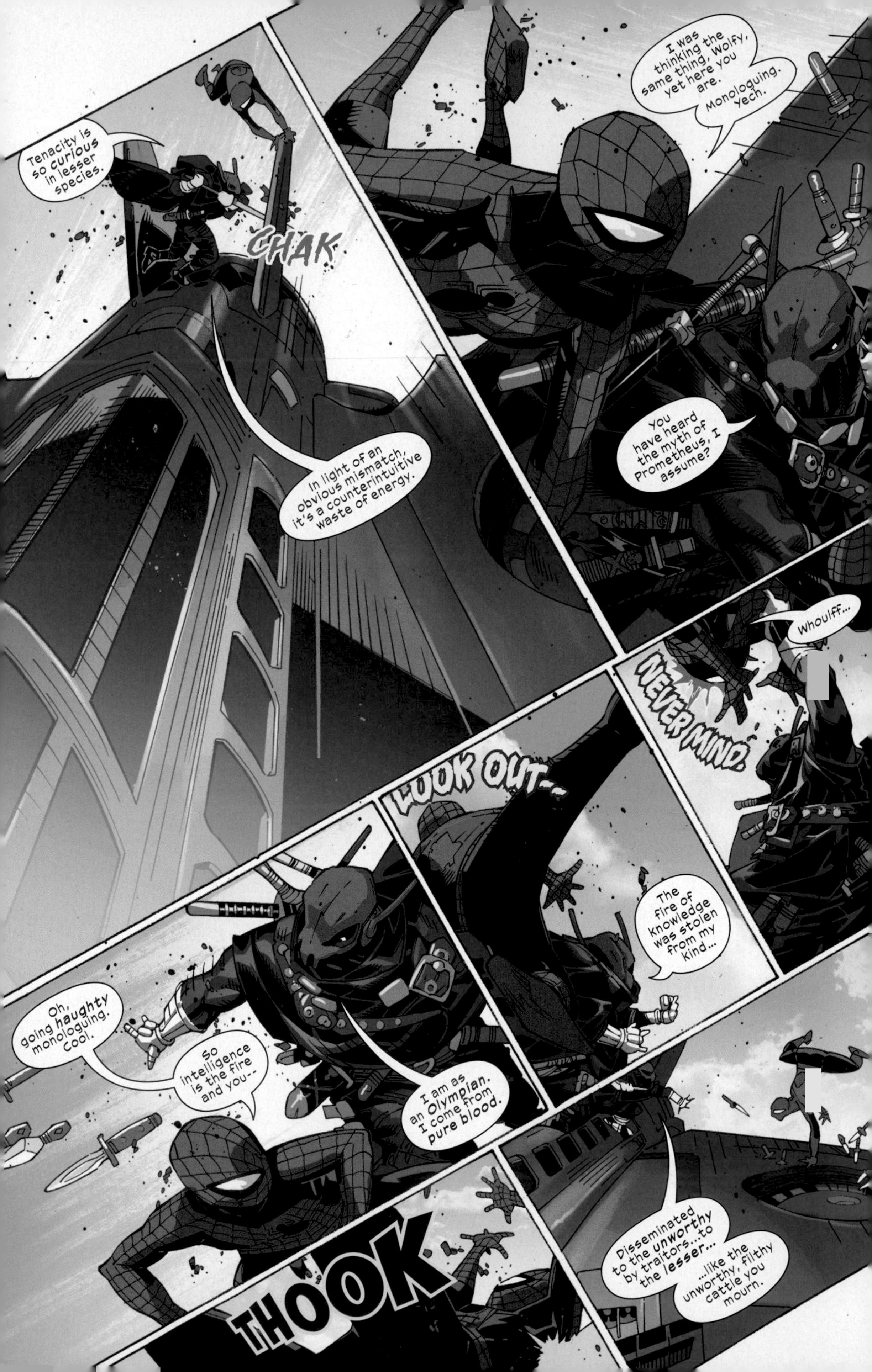
Tenacity is so curious in lesser species.
CHAK
In light of an obvious mismatch, it's a counterintuitive waste of energy.
I was thinking the same thing, Wolfy, yet here you are.
Monologuing. Yech.
You have heard the myth of Prometheus, I assume?
Whoulff...
NEVER MIND.
LOOK OUT--
The fire of knowledge was stolen from my kind...
Oh, going haughty monologuing. Cool.
So intelligence is the fire and you--
I am as an Olympian. I come from pure blood.
THOOK
Disseminated to the unworthy by traitors...to the lesser...
...like the unworthy, filthy cattle you mourn.

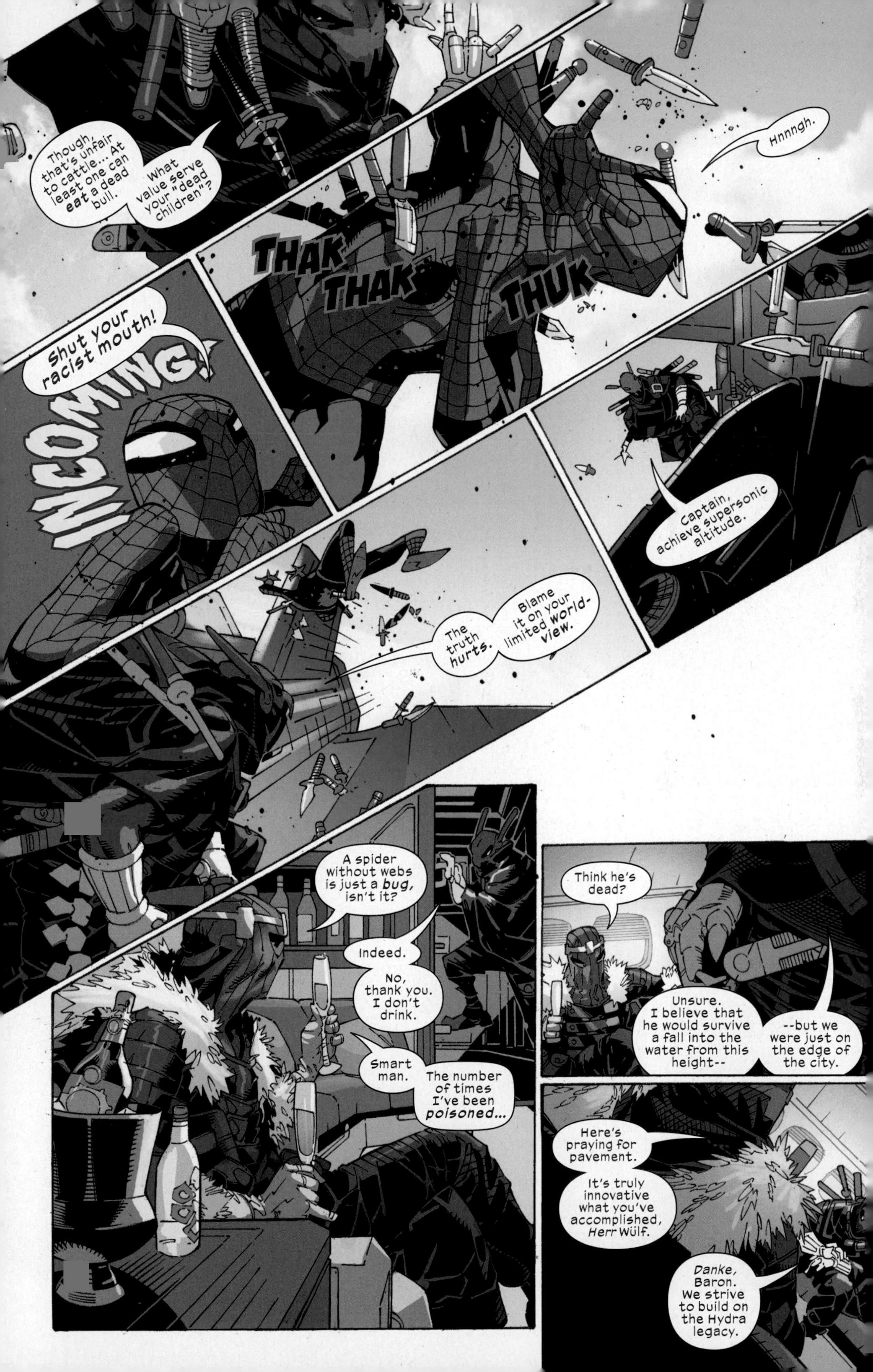

Though, that's unfair to cattle... At least one can eat a dead bull.
What value serve your "dead children"?
Hnnngh.
THAK
THAK
THUK
Shut your racist mouth!
INCOMING!
Captain, achieve supersonic altitude.
The truth hurts.
Blame it on your limited world-view.
A spider without webs is just a bug, isn't it?
Indeed.
No, thank you. I don't drink.
Smart man.
The number of times I've been poisoned...
Think he's dead?
Unsure. I believe that he would survive a fall into the water from this height--
--but we were just on the edge of the city.
Here's praying for pavement.
It's truly innovative what you've accomplished, Herr Wülf.
Danke, Baron. We strive to build on the Hydra legacy.

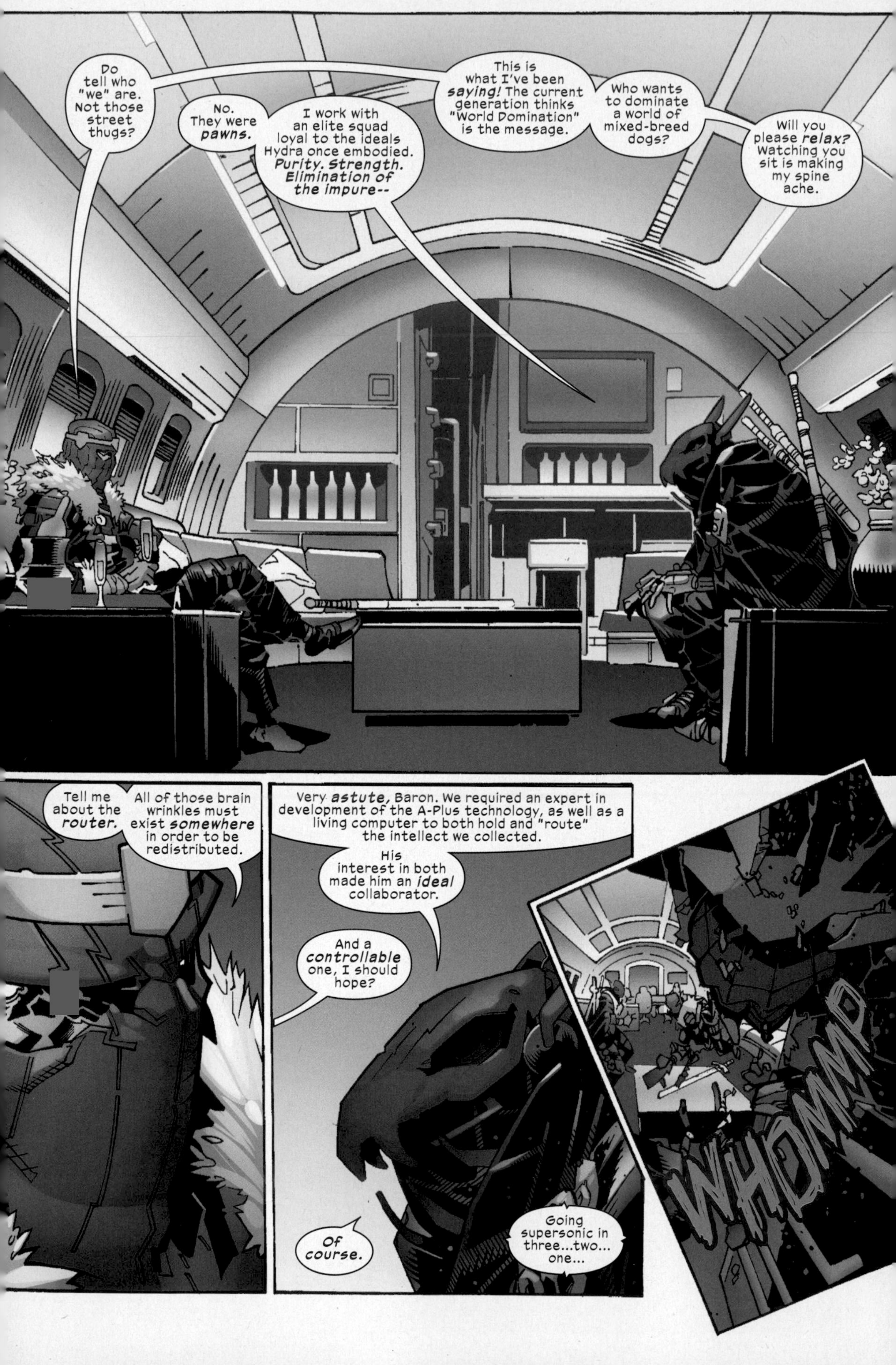
Do tell who "we" are. Not those street thugs?
No. They were *pawns.*
I work with an elite squad loyal to the ideals Hydra once embodied. *Purity. Strength. Elimination of the impure--*
This is what I've been *saying!* The current generation thinks "World Domination" is the message.
Who wants to dominate a world of mixed-breed dogs?
Will you please *relax?* Watching you sit is making my spine ache.
Tell me about the *router.*
All of those brain wrinkles must exist *somewhere* in order to be redistributed.
Very *astute,* Baron. We required an expert in development of the A-Plus technology, as well as a living computer to both hold and "route" the intellect we collected.
His interest in both made him an *ideal* collaborator.
And a *controllable* one, I should hope?
Of course.
Going supersonic in three...two... one...
WHOMP

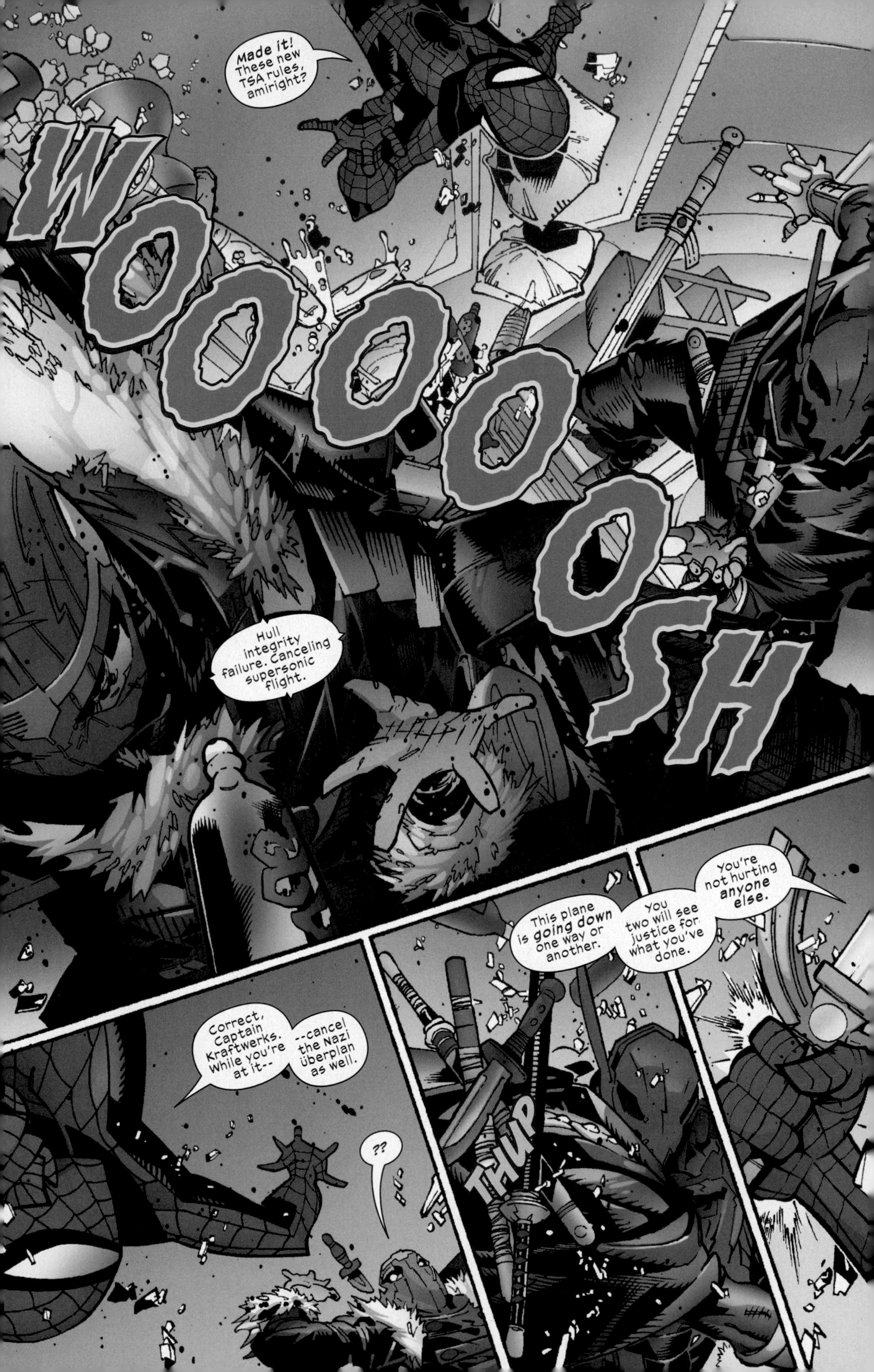
Made it! These new TSA rules, amiright?
WOOOOOOSH
Hull integrity failure. Canceling supersonic flight.
Correct, Captain Kraftwerks. While you're at it--
--cancel the Nazi überplan as well.
??
This plane is going down one way or another.
THUP
You two will see justice for what you've done.
You're not hurting anyone else.

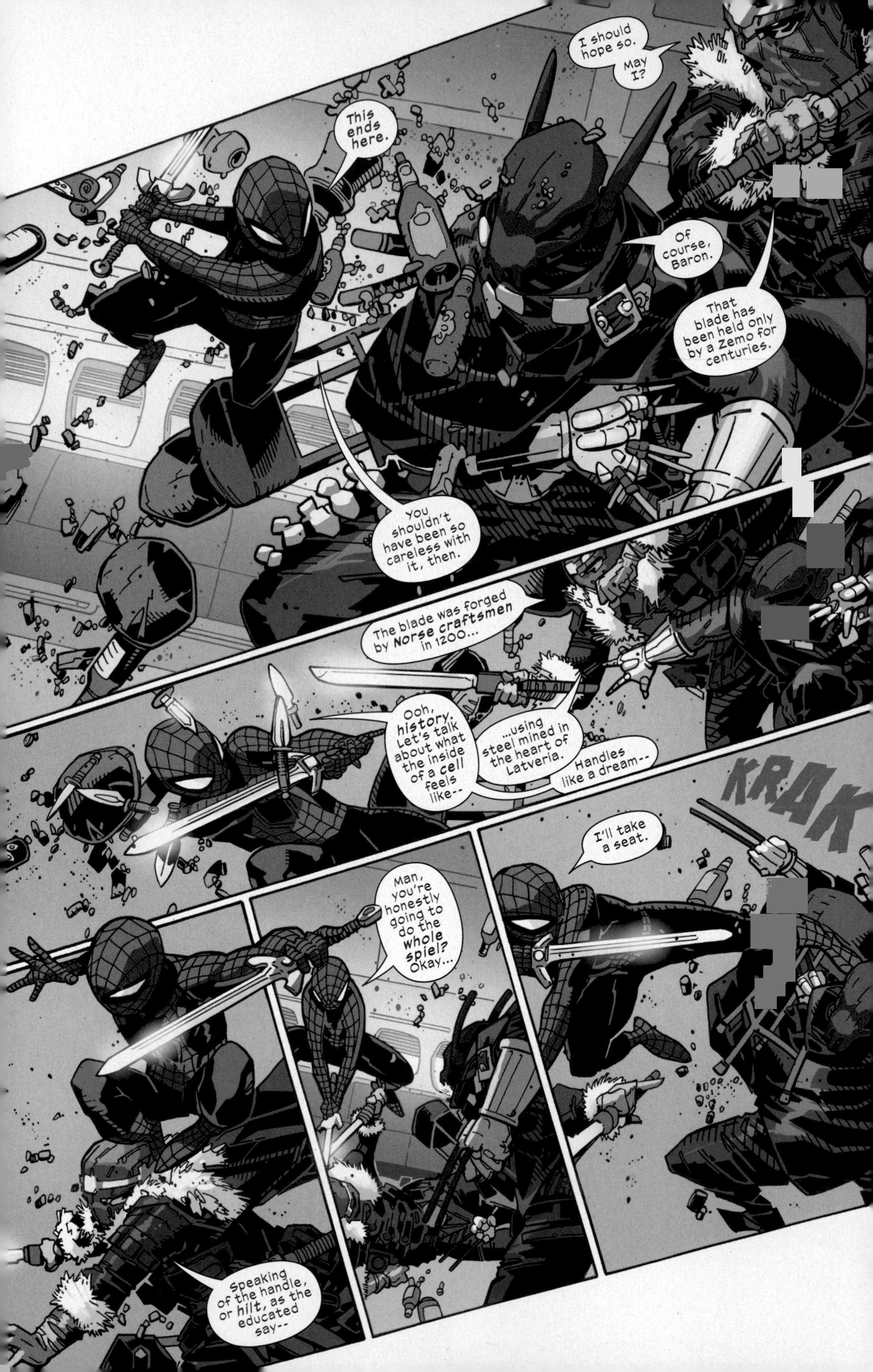
This ends here.
I should hope so.
May I?
Of course, Baron.
That blade has been held only by a Zemo for centuries.
You shouldn't have been so careless with it, then.
The blade was forged by Norse craftsmen in 1200...
Ooh, history. Let's talk about what the inside of a cell feels like--
...using steel mined in the heart of Latveria.
Handles like a dream--
Speaking of the handle, or hilt, as the educated say--
Man, you're honestly going to do the whole spiel? Okay...
KRAK
I'll take a seat.

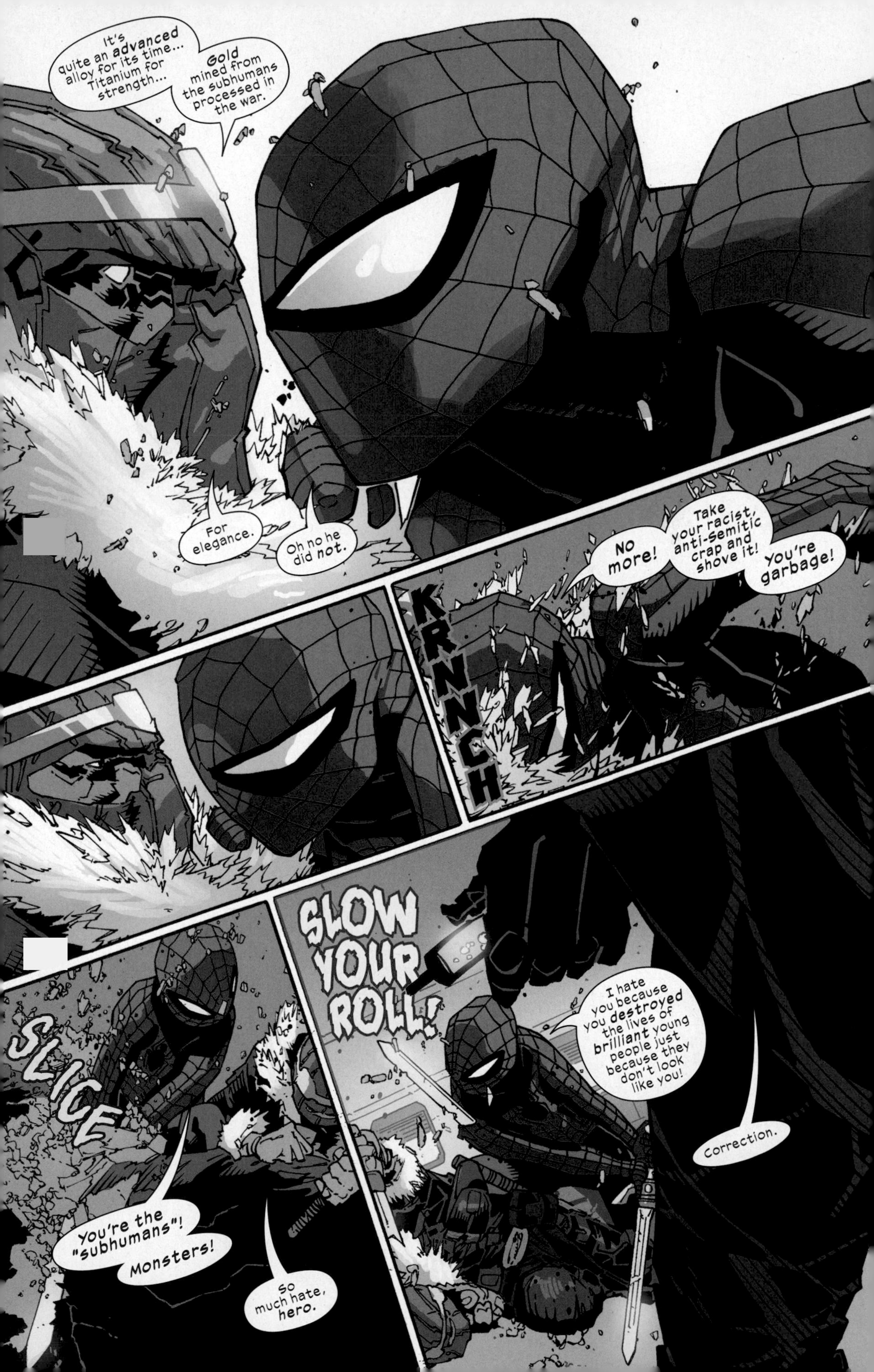

It's quite an advanced alloy for its time... Titanium for strength...
Gold mined from the subhumans processed in the war.
For elegance.
Oh no he did not.
No more!
Take your racist, anti-Semitic crap and shove it!
You're garbage!
KRNNCH
SLICE
You're the "subhumans"! Monsters!
So much hate, hero.
SLOW YOUR ROLL!
I hate you because you destroyed the lives of brilliant young people just because they don't look like you!
Correction.

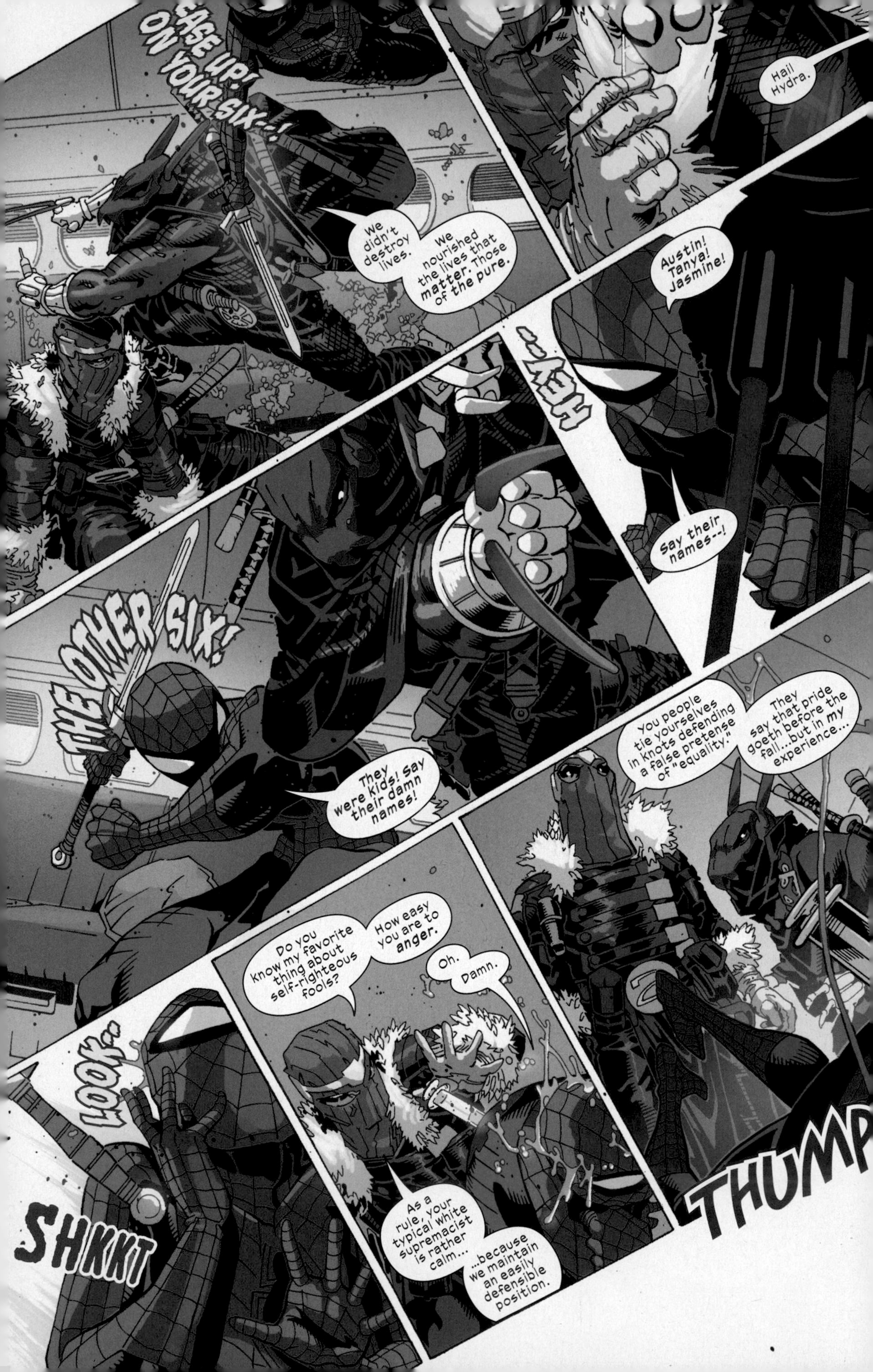
EASE UP! ON YOUR SIX--!
We didn't destroy lives.
We nourished the lives that matter. Those of the pure.
Hail Hydra.
Austin! Tanya! Jasmine!
HEY--
Say their names--!
THE OTHER SIX!
They were kids! Say their damn names!
You people tie yourselves in knots defending a false pretense of "equality."
They say that pride goeth before the fall...but in my experience...
Do you know my favorite thing about self-righteous fools?
How easy you are to anger.
Oh.
Damn.
LOOK--
SHKKT
As a rule, your typical white supremacist is rather calm...
...because we maintain an easily defensible position.
THUMP

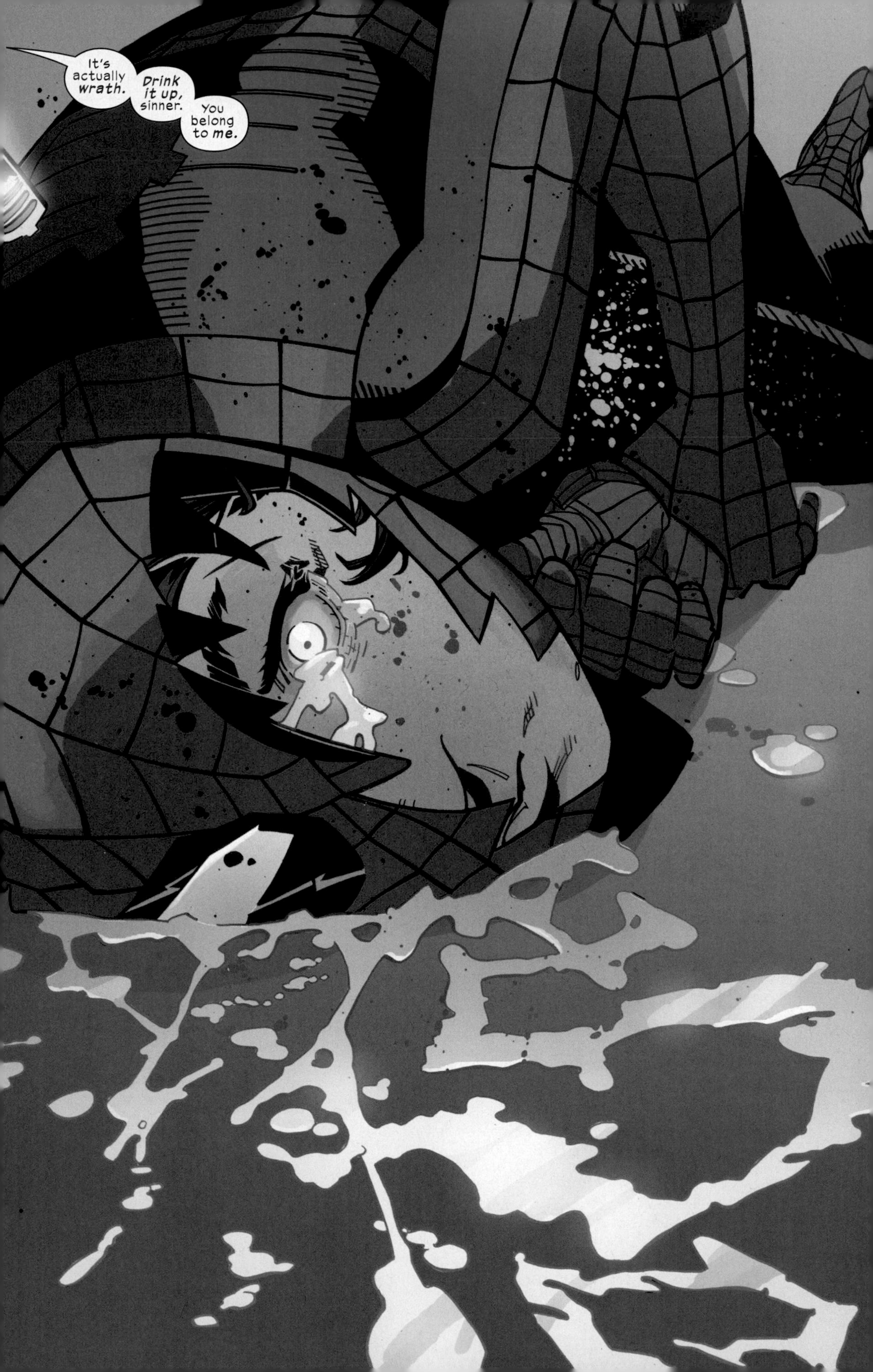
It's actually *wrath.*
Drink it up, sinner.
You belong to *me.*

5. THE SECRET LIVES OF SAVAGES CHAPTER TWO

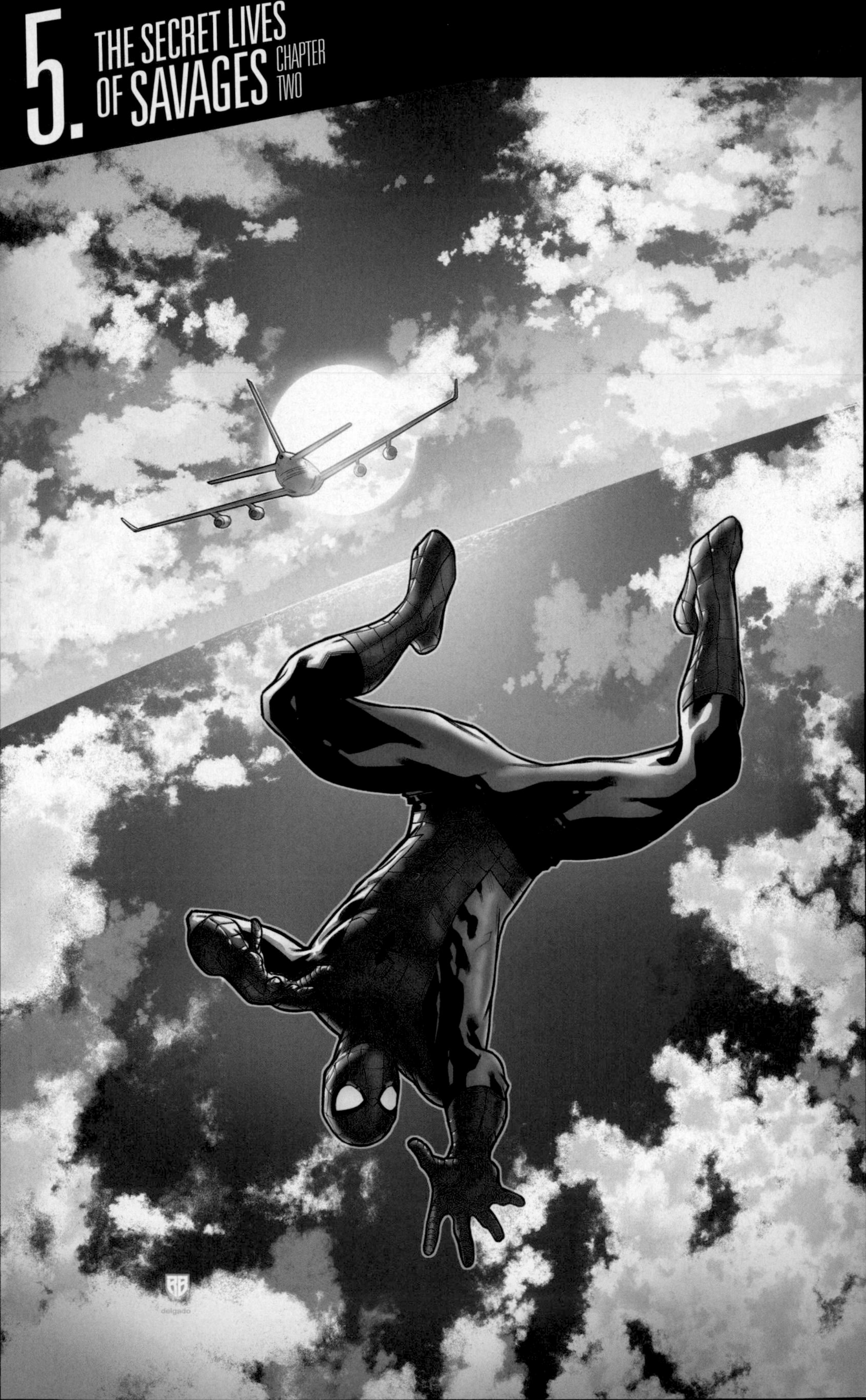

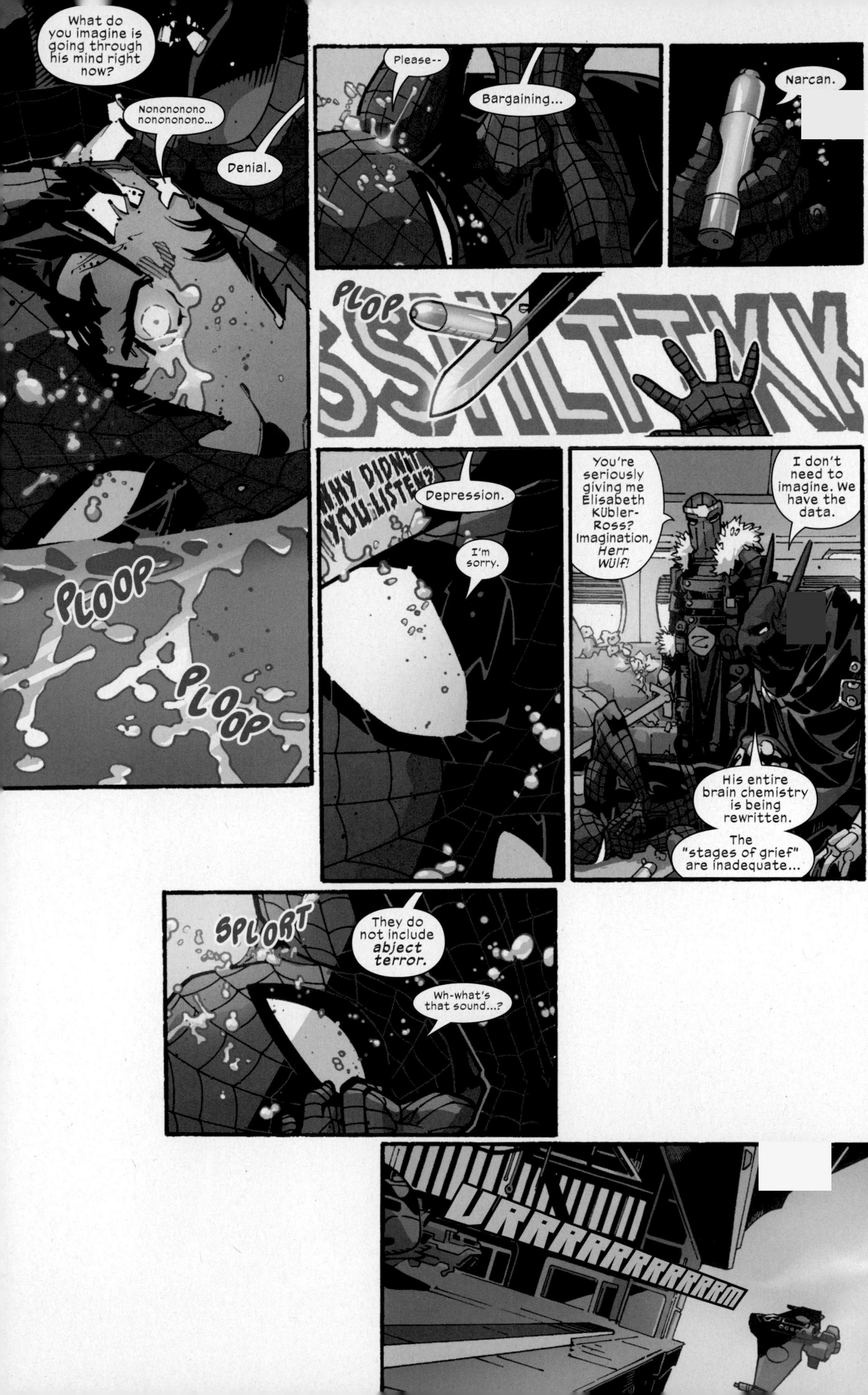

What do you imagine is going through his mind right now?
Nonononono nonononono...
Denial.
Please--
Bargaining...
Narcan.
PLOP
PLOOP
PLOOP
Depression.
I'm sorry.
You're seriously giving me Elisabeth Kübler-Ross? Imagination, *Herr* Wulf!
I don't need to imagine. We have the data.
His entire brain chemistry is being rewritten.
The "stages of grief" are inadequate...
SPLORT
They do not include *abject terror.*
Wh-what's that sound...?
URRRRRRRRRRRRRM

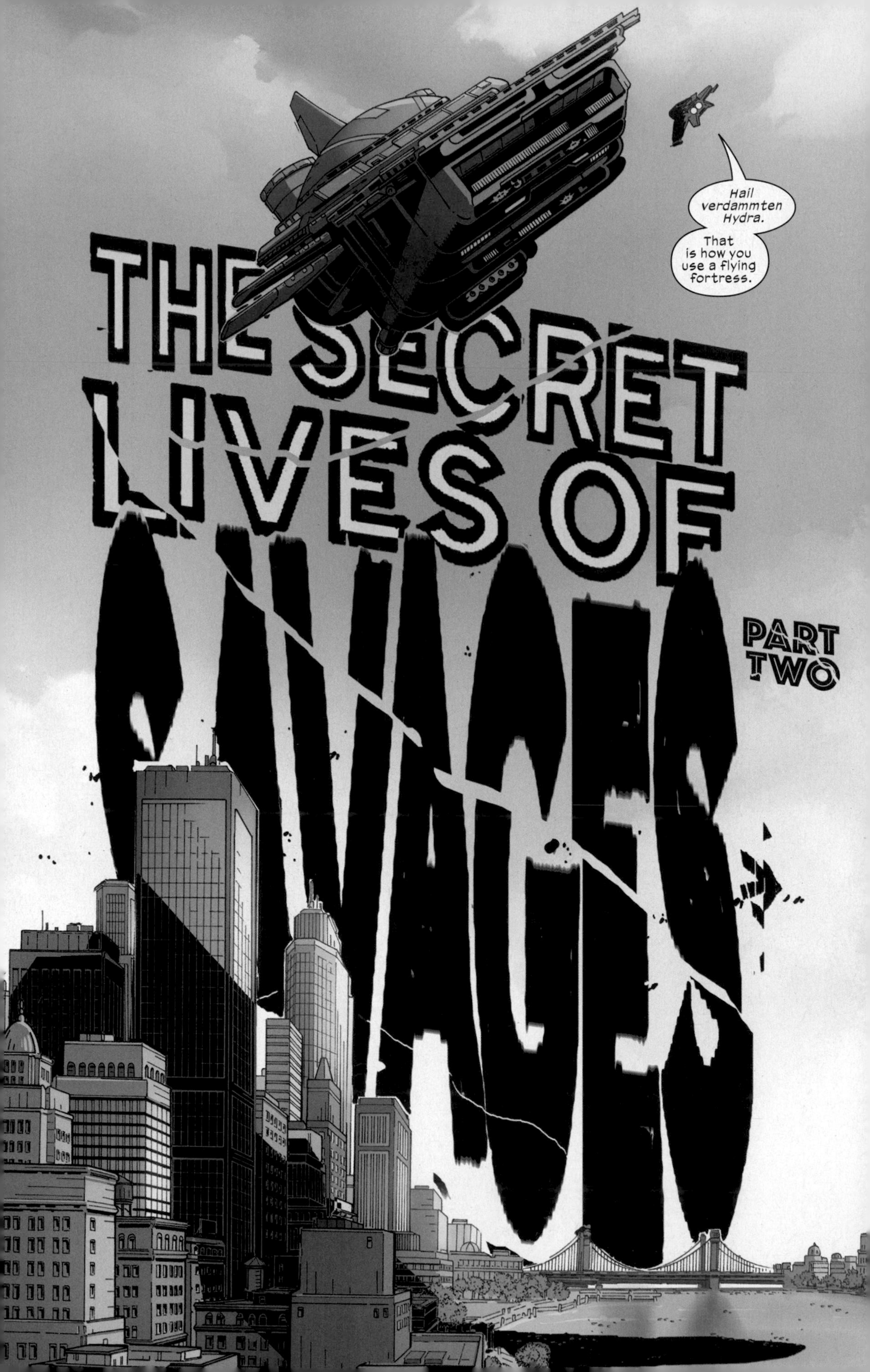
Hail verdammten Hydra.
That is how you use a flying fortress.
THE SECRET LIVES OF
PART TWO

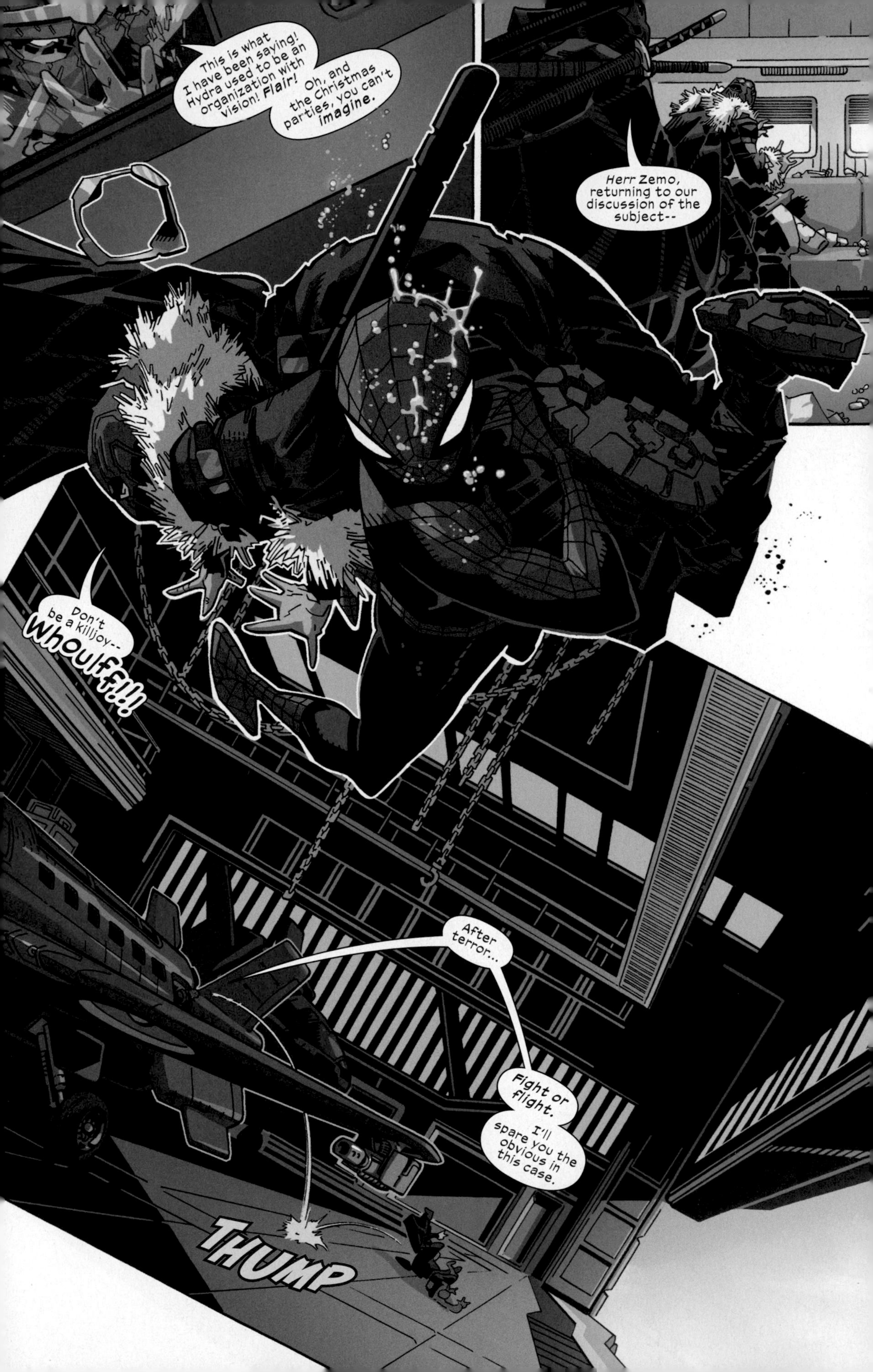
This is what I have been saying! Hydra used to be an organization with vision! Flair!
Oh, and the Christmas parties, you can't imagine.
Herr Zemo, returning to our discussion of the subject--
Don't be a killjoy--
Whoulff!!!
After terror...
Fight or flight.
I'll spare you the obvious in this case.
THUMP

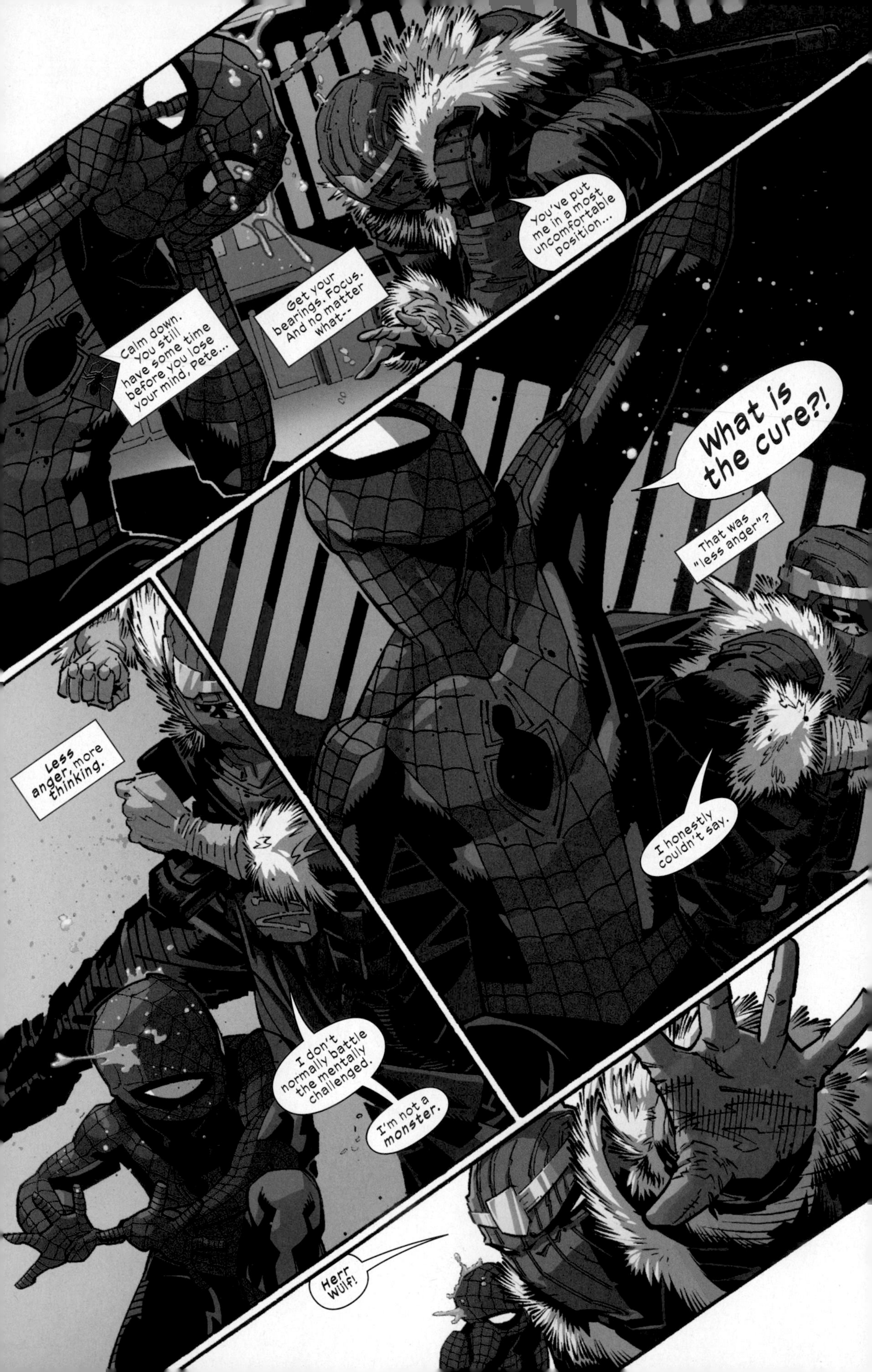
You've put me in a most uncomfortable position...
Calm down. You still have some time before you lose your mind, Pete...
Get your bearings. Focus. And no matter what--
What is the cure?!
That was "less anger"?
I honestly couldn't say.
Less anger, more thinking.
I don't normally battle the mentally challenged.
I'm not a monster.
Herr Wulf!

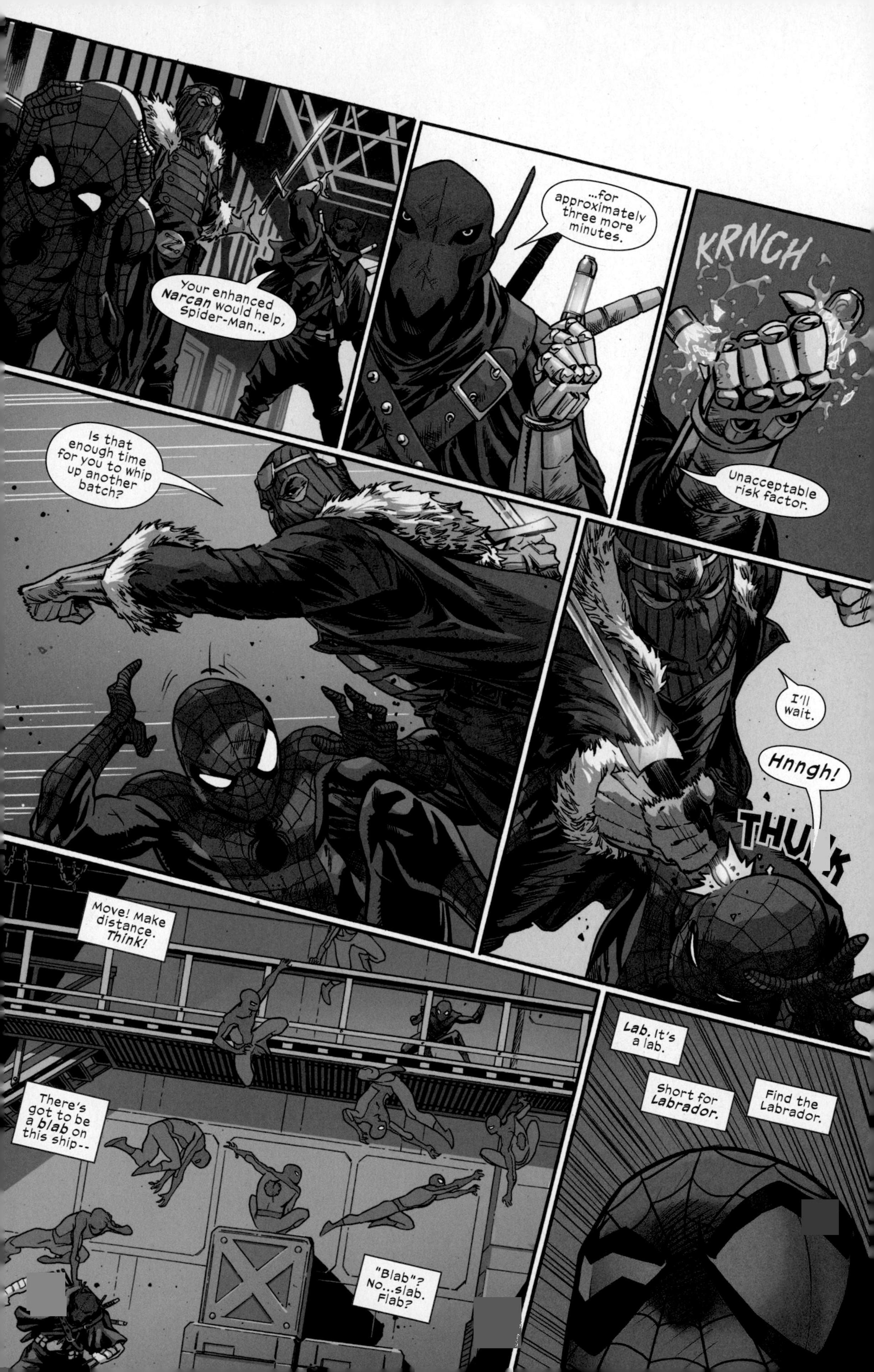
Your enhanced *Narcan* would help, Spider-Man...
...for approximately three more minutes.
KRNCH
Unacceptable risk factor.
Is that enough time for you to whip up another batch?
I'll wait.
Hnngh!
THU K
Move! Make distance. *Think!*
There's got to be a *blab* on this ship--
"Blab"? No...slab. Flab?
Lab. It's a lab.
Short for *Labrador.*
Find the Labrador.

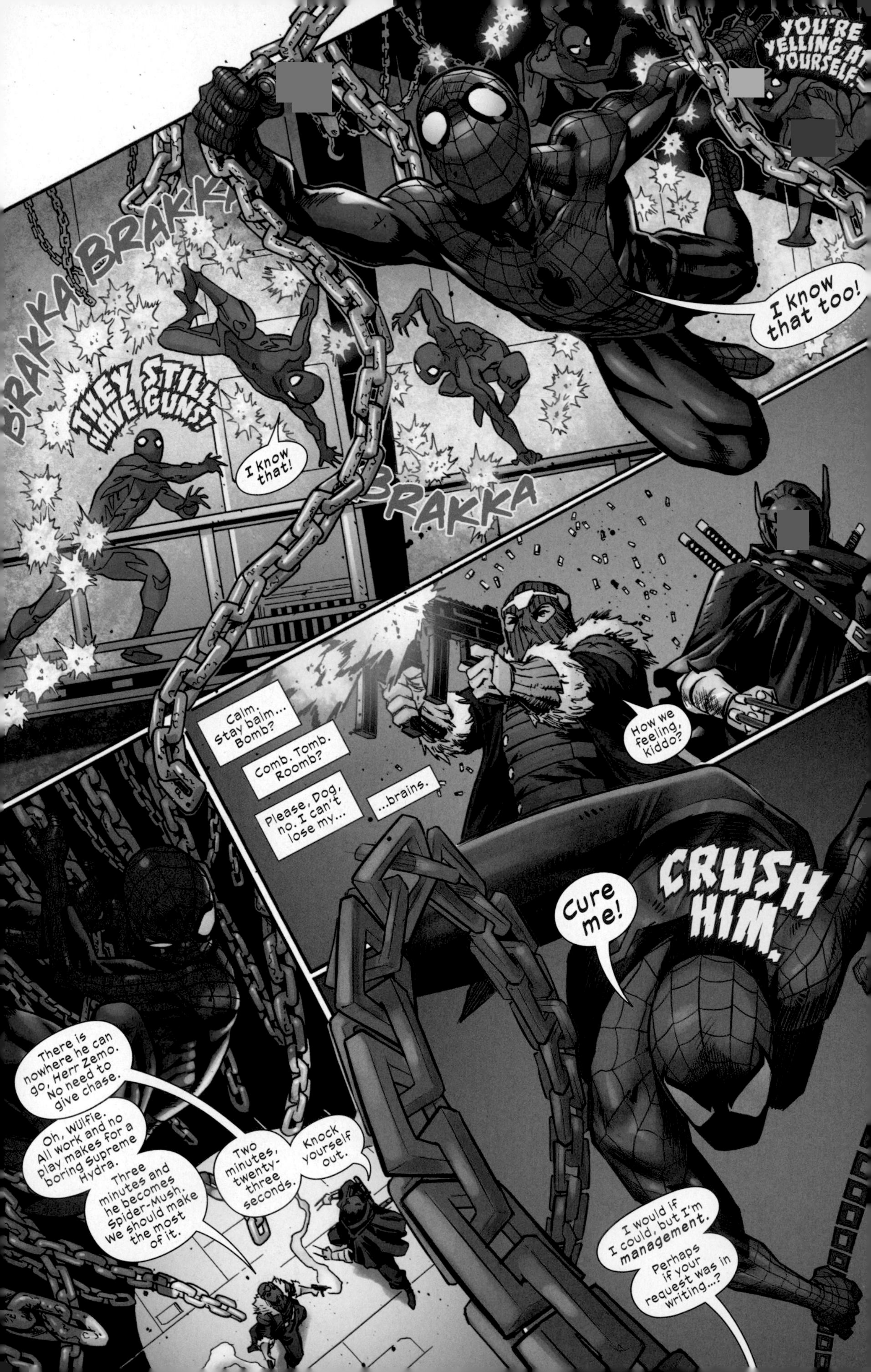
YOU'RE YELLING AT YOURSELF.
I know that too!
BRAKKA BRAKKA
THEY STILL HAVE GUNS!
I know that!
BRAKKA
Calm. Stay balm... Bomb?
Comb. Tomb. Roomb?
Please, Dog, no. I can't lose my...
...brains.
How we feeling, kiddo?
CRUSH HIM.
Cure me!
There is nowhere he can go, Herr Zemo. No need to give chase.
Oh, Wilfie. All work and no play makes for a boring Supreme Hydra.
Three minutes and he becomes Spider-Mush. We should make the most of it.
Two minutes, twenty-three seconds.
Knock yourself out.
I would if I could, but I'm management.
Perhaps if your request was in writing...?

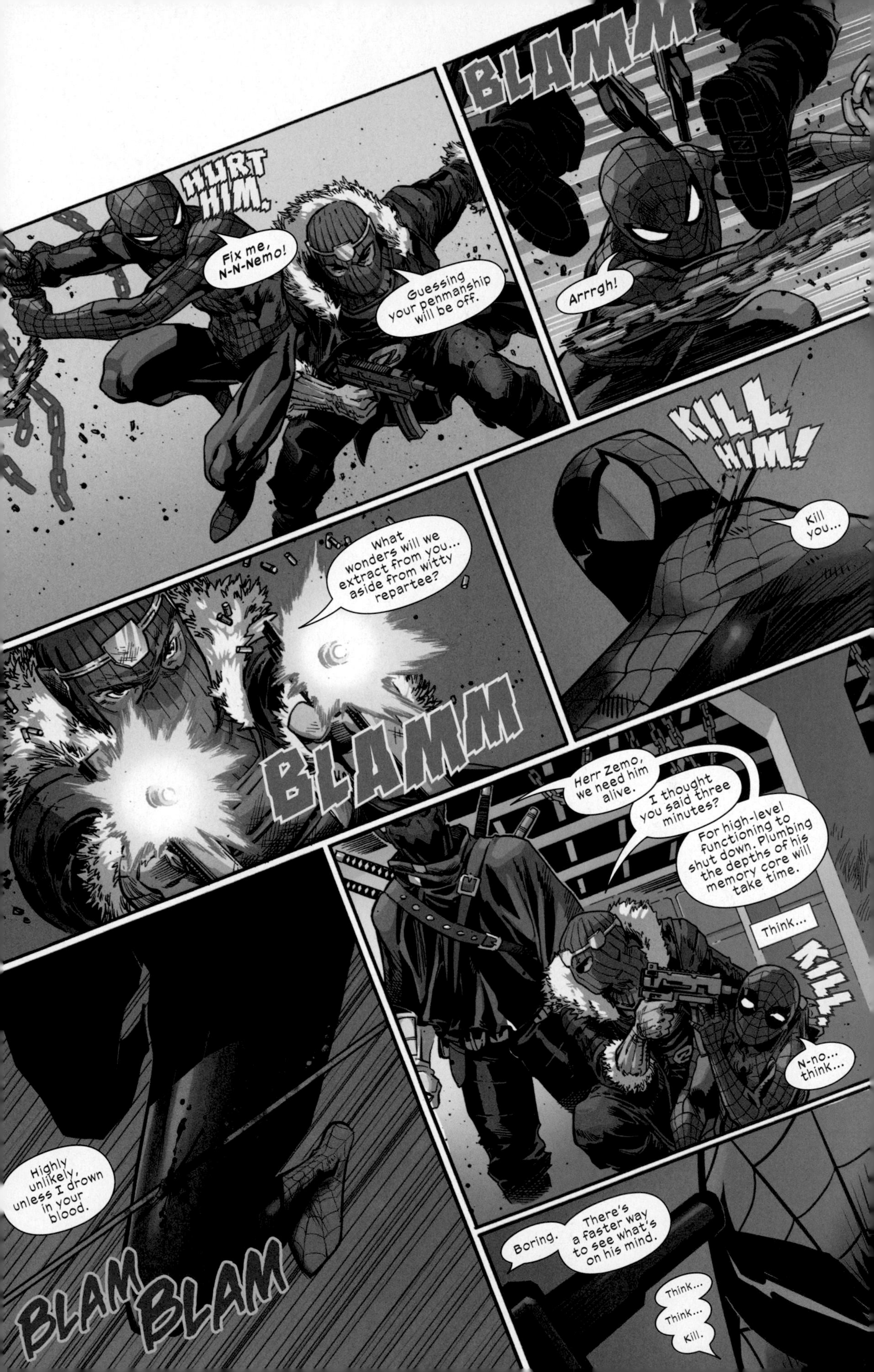
HURT HIM.
Fix me, N-N-Nemo!
Guessing your penmanship will be off.
BLAMM
Arrrgh!
KILL HIM!
Kill you...
What wonders will we extract from you... aside from witty repartee?
BLAMM
Herr Zemo, we need him alive.
I thought you said three minutes?
For high-level functioning to shut down. Plumbing the depths of his memory core will take time.
Think...
KILL.
N-no... think...
Highly unlikely, unless I drown in your blood.
BLAM BLAM
Boring.
There's a faster way to see what's on his mind.
Think...
Think...
Kill.

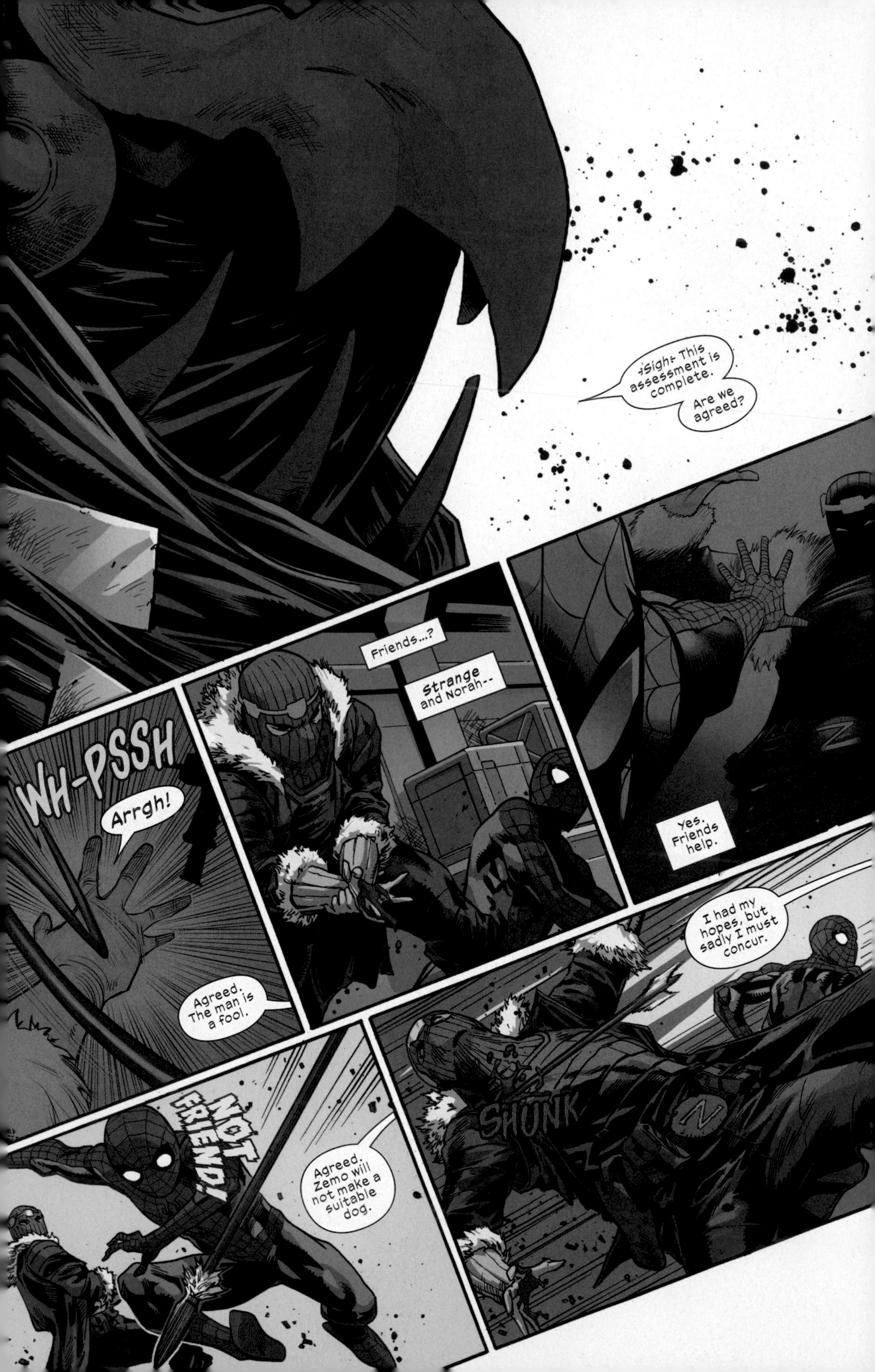
-Sigh- This assessment is complete.
Are we agreed?
Friends...?
Strange and Norah--
Yes. Friends help.
WH-PSSH
Arrgh!
Agreed. The man is a fool.
I had my hopes, but sadly I must concur.
SHUNK
NOT FRIEND!
Agreed. Zemo will not make a suitable dog.

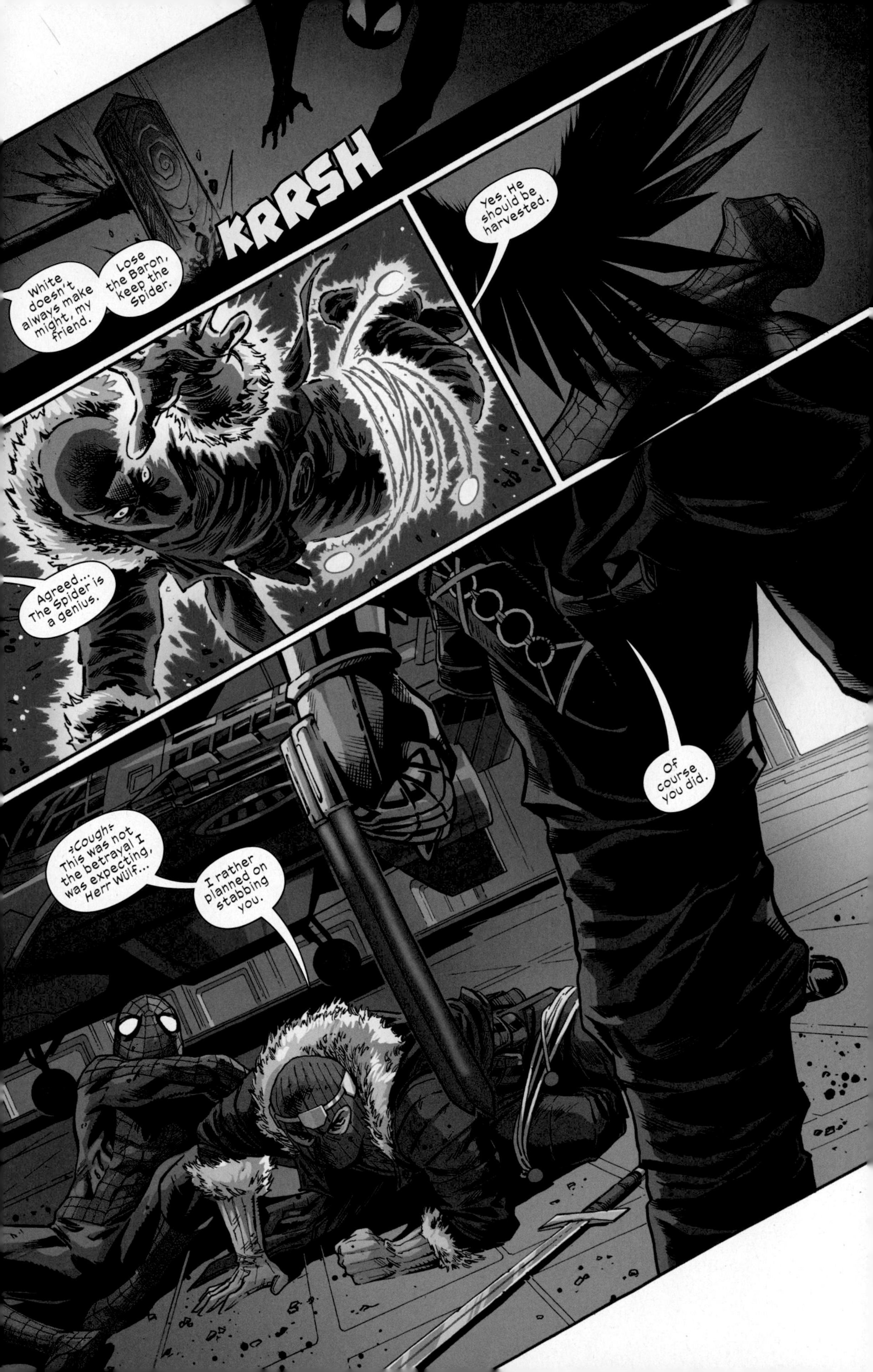
KRRSH
White doesn't always make might, my friend.
Lose the Baron, keep the Spider.
Yes. He should be harvested.
Agreed... The Spider is a genius.
Of course you did.
-Cough- This was not the betrayal I was expecting, Herr Wulf...
I rather planned on stabbing you.

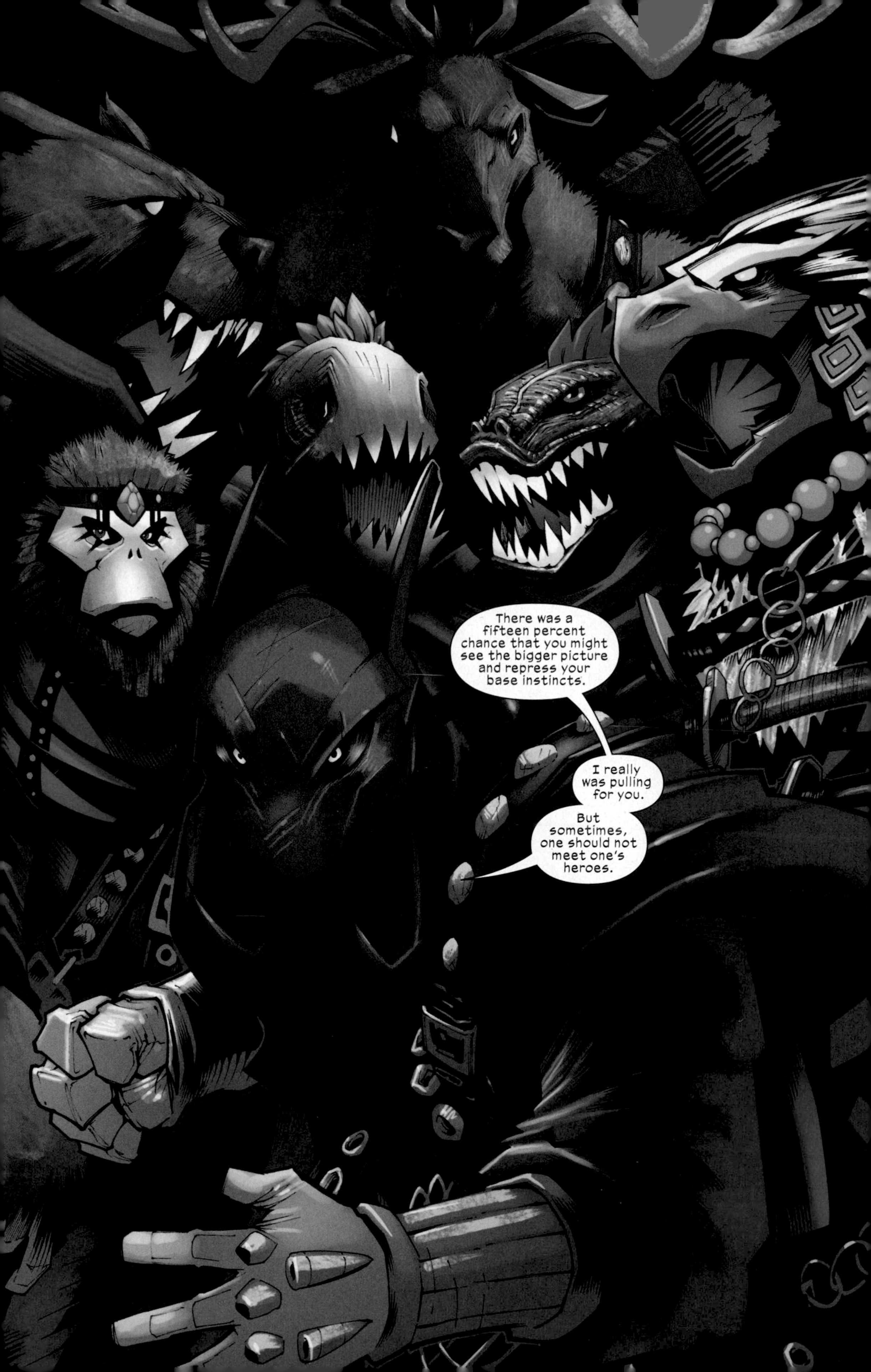
There was a fifteen percent chance that you might see the bigger picture and repress your base instincts.
I really was pulling for you.
But sometimes, one should not meet one's heroes.

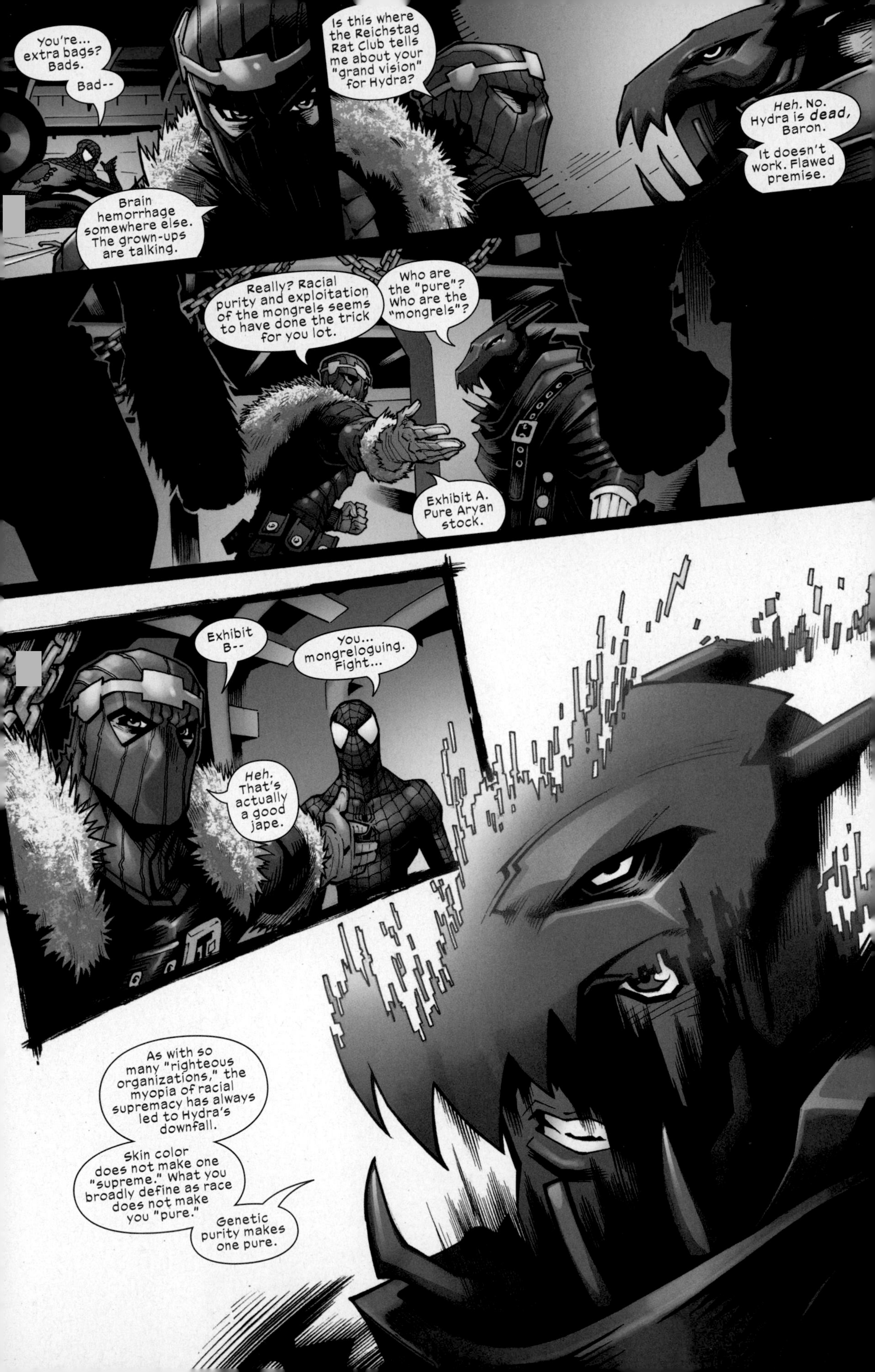
You're... extra bags? Bads.
Bad--
Brain hemorrhage somewhere else. The grown-ups are talking.
Is this where the Reichstag Rat Club tells me about your "grand vision" for Hydra?
Heh. No. Hydra is dead, Baron.
It doesn't work. Flawed premise.
Really? Racial purity and exploitation of the mongrels seems to have done the trick for you lot.
Who are the "pure"? Who are the "mongrels"?
Exhibit A. Pure Aryan stock.
Exhibit B--
You... mongreloguing. Fight...
Heh. That's actually a good jape.
As with so many "righteous organizations," the myopia of racial supremacy has always led to Hydra's downfall.
Skin color does not make one "supreme." What you broadly define as race does not make you "pure."
Genetic purity makes one pure.

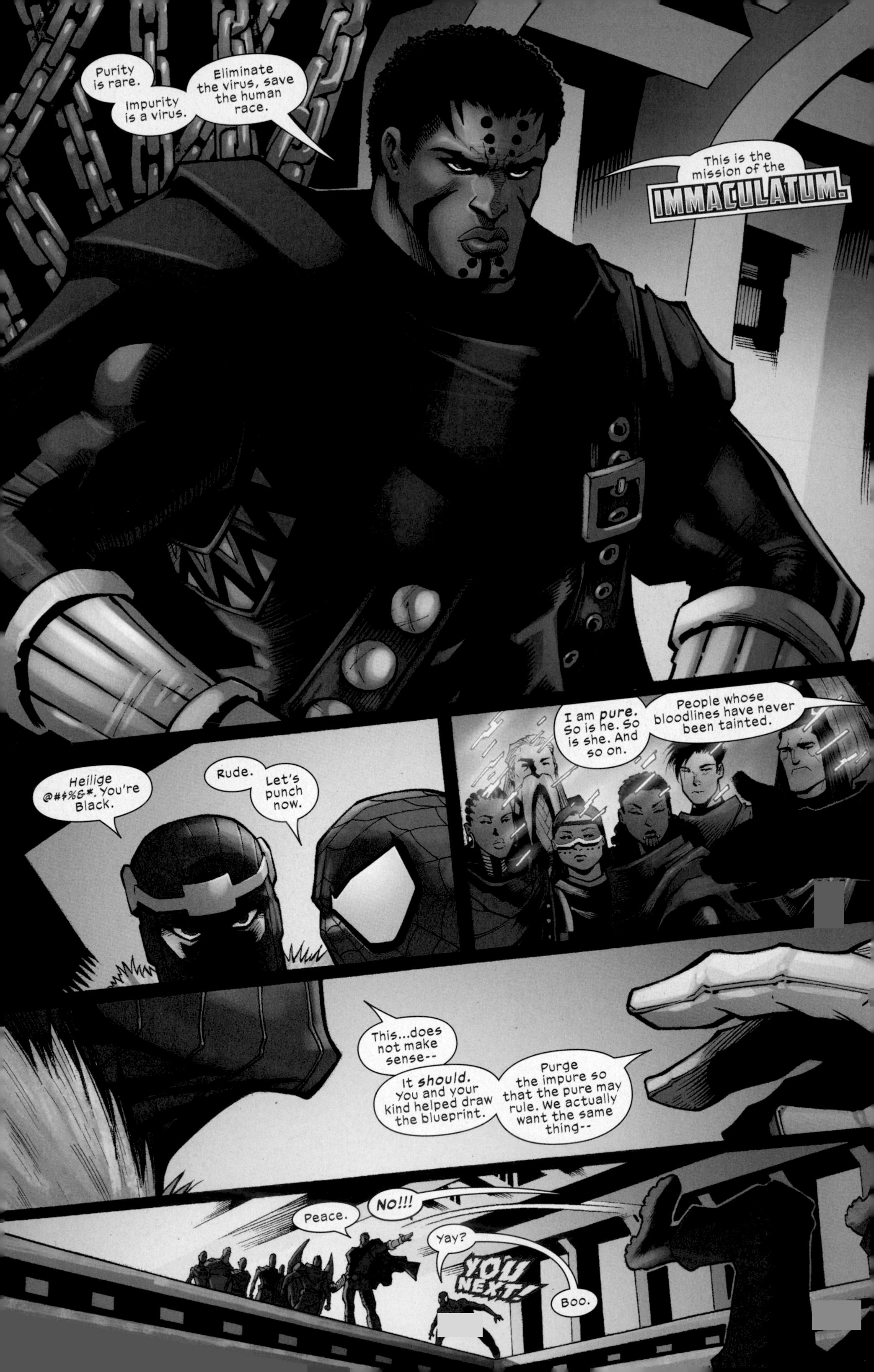
Purity is rare.
Impurity is a virus.
Eliminate the virus, save the human race.
This is the mission of the
IMMACULATUM.
Heilige @#$%&*. You're Black.
Rude.
Let's punch now.
I am pure. So is he. So is she. And so on.
People whose bloodlines have never been tainted.
This...does not make sense--
It should. You and your kind helped draw the blueprint.
Purge the impure so that the pure may rule. We actually want the same thing--
Peace.
NO!!!
Yay?
YOU NEXT!
Boo.

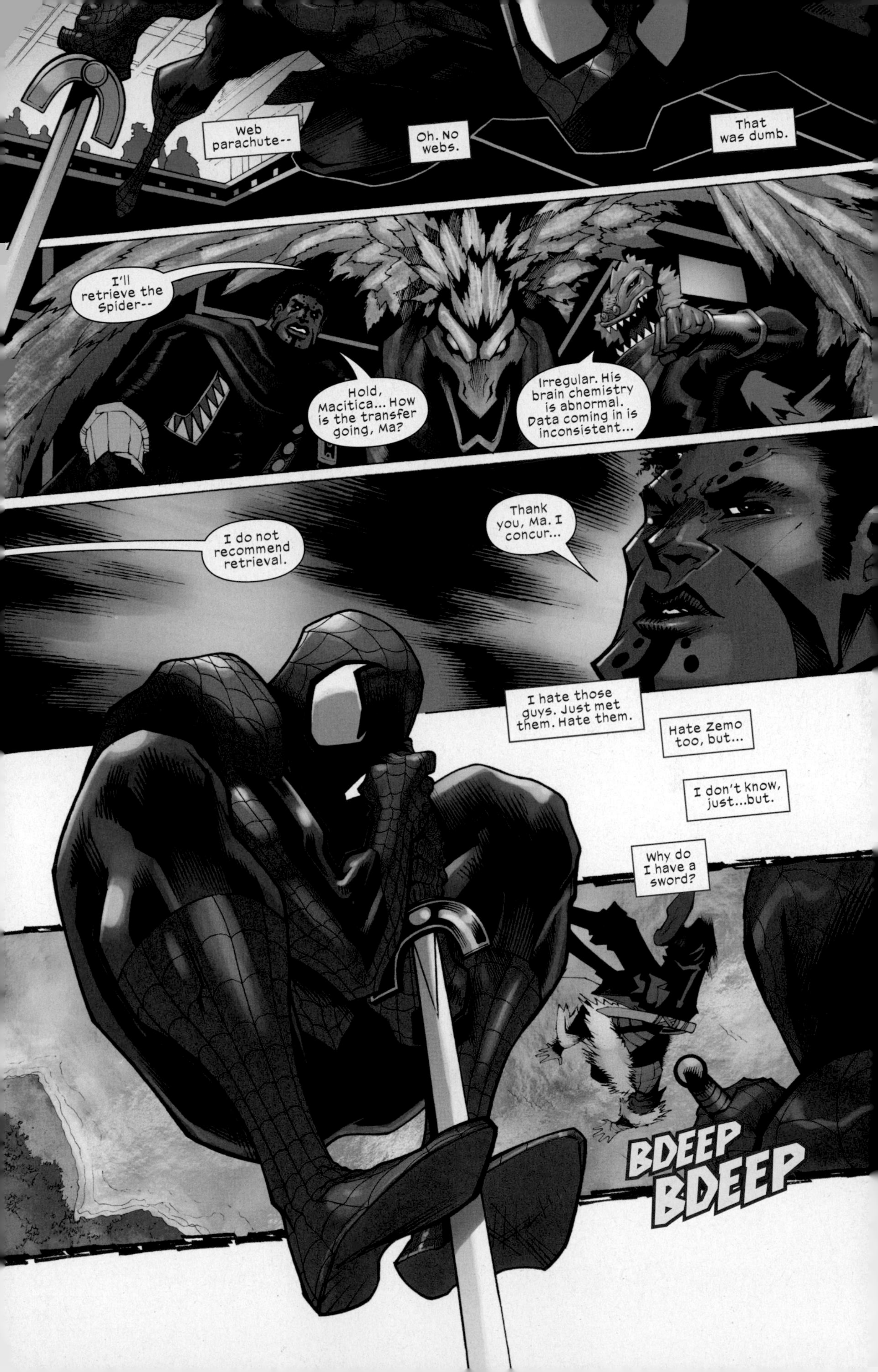
Web parachute--
Oh. No webs.
That was dumb.
I'll retrieve the Spider--
Hold, Macitica... How is the transfer going, Ma?
Irregular. His brain chemistry is abnormal. Data coming in is inconsistent...
I do not recommend retrieval.
Thank you, Ma. I concur...
I hate those guys. Just met them. Hate them.
Hate Zemo too, but...
I don't know, just...but.
Why do I have a sword?
BDEEP BDEEP

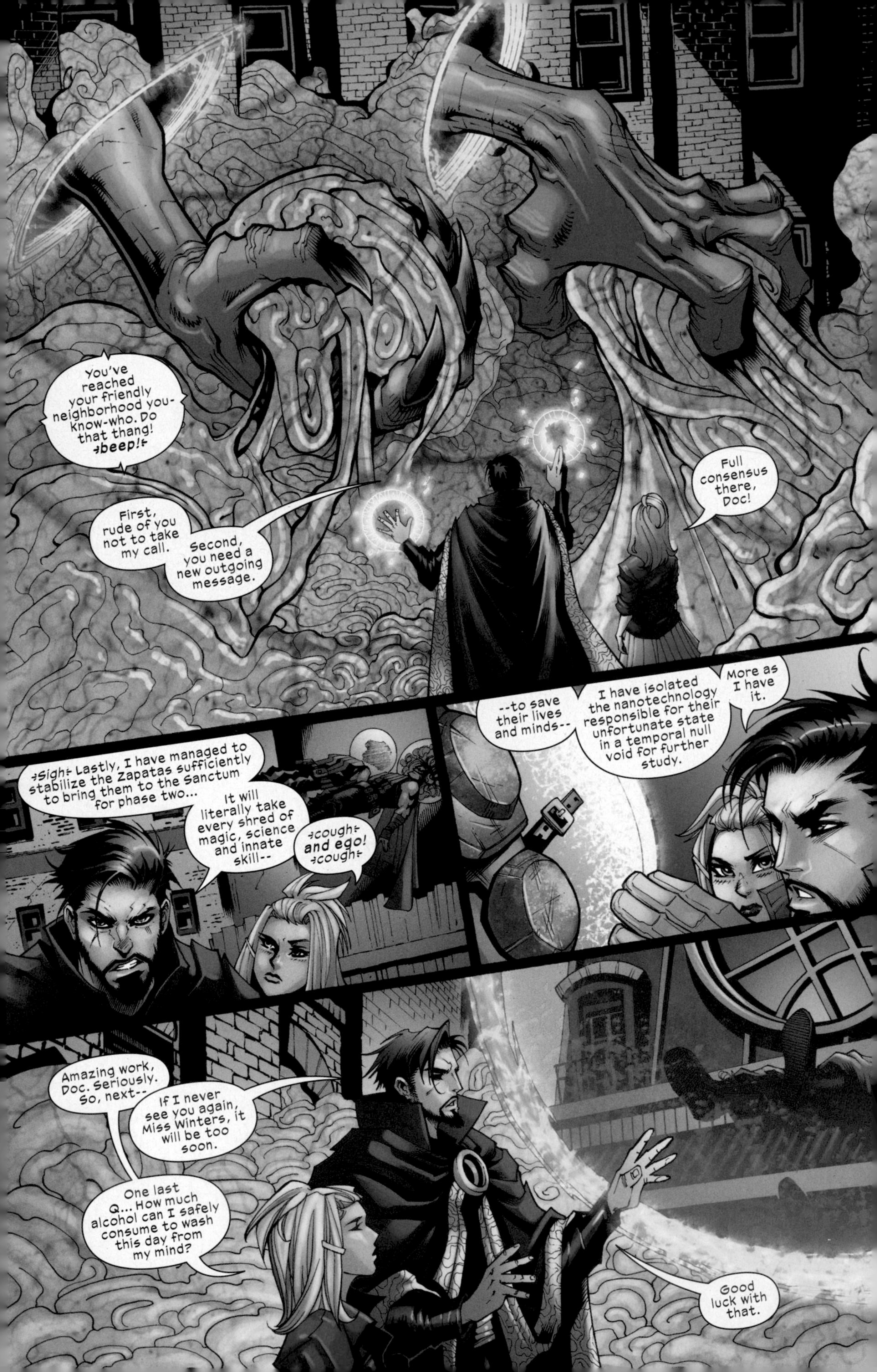

You've reached your friendly neighborhood you-know-who. Do that thang! ≠beep!≠
First, rude of you not to take my call.
Second, you need a new outgoing message.
Full consensus there, Doc!
≠Sigh≠ Lastly, I have managed to stabilize the Zapatas sufficiently to bring them to the Sanctum for phase two...
It will literally take every shred of magic, science and innate skill--
≠cough≠ and ego! ≠cough≠
--to save their lives and minds--
I have isolated the nanotechnology responsible for their unfortunate state in a temporal null void for further study.
More as I have it.
Amazing work, Doc. Seriously. So, next--
If I never see you again, Miss Winters, it will be too soon.
One last Q... How much alcohol can I safely consume to wash this day from my mind?
Good luck with that.

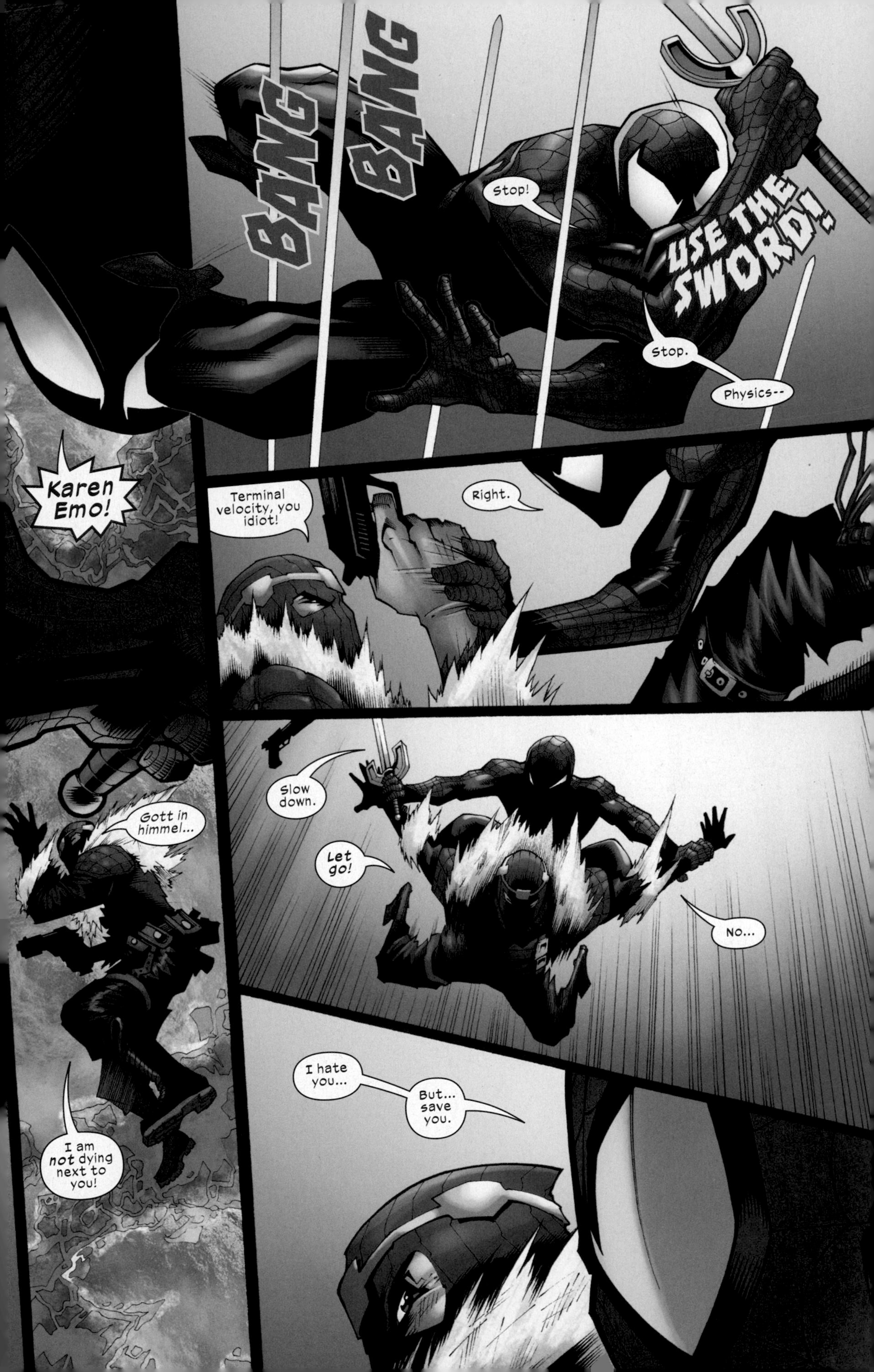
BANG
BANG
Stop!
USE THE SWORD!
Stop.
Physics--
Karen Emo!
Terminal velocity, you idiot!
Right.
Gott in himmel...
Slow down.
Let go!
No...
I am not dying next to you!
I hate you...
But... save you.

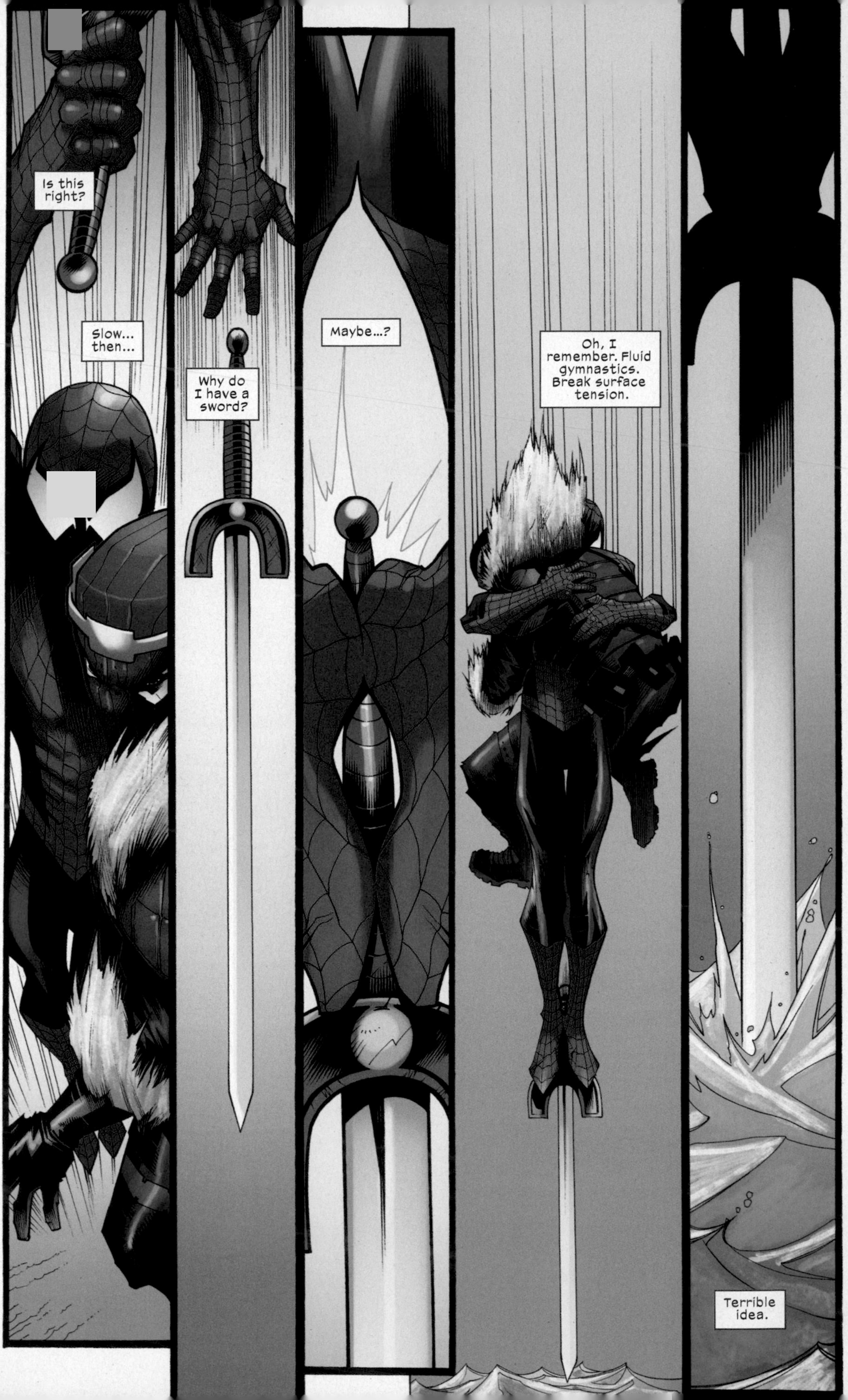
Is this right?
Slow... then...
Why do I have a sword?
Maybe...?
Oh, I remember. Fluid gymnastics. Break surface tension.
Terrible idea.

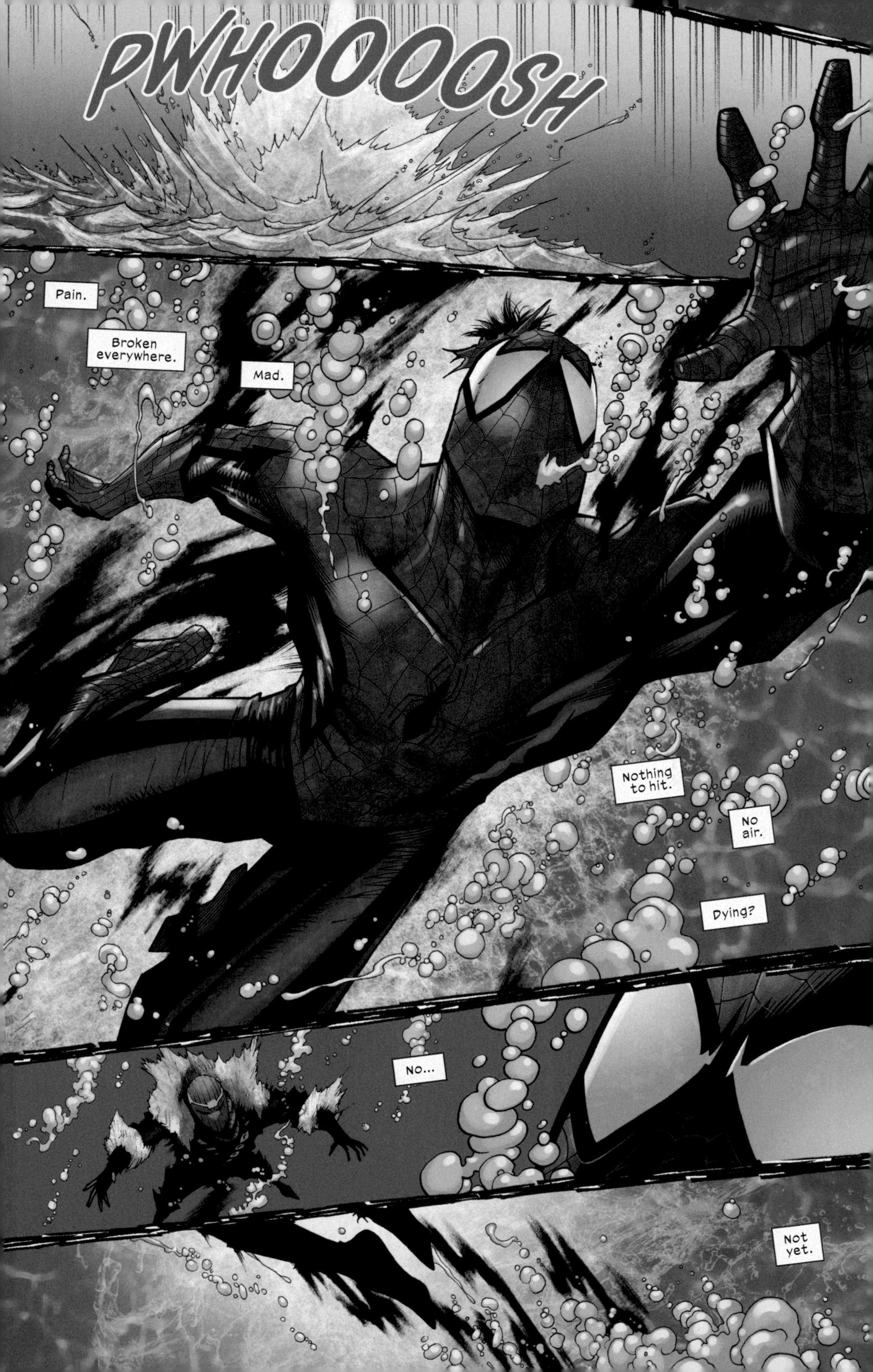
PWHOOOOSH
Pain.
Broken everywhere.
Mad.
Nothing to hit.
No air.
Dying?
No...
Not yet.

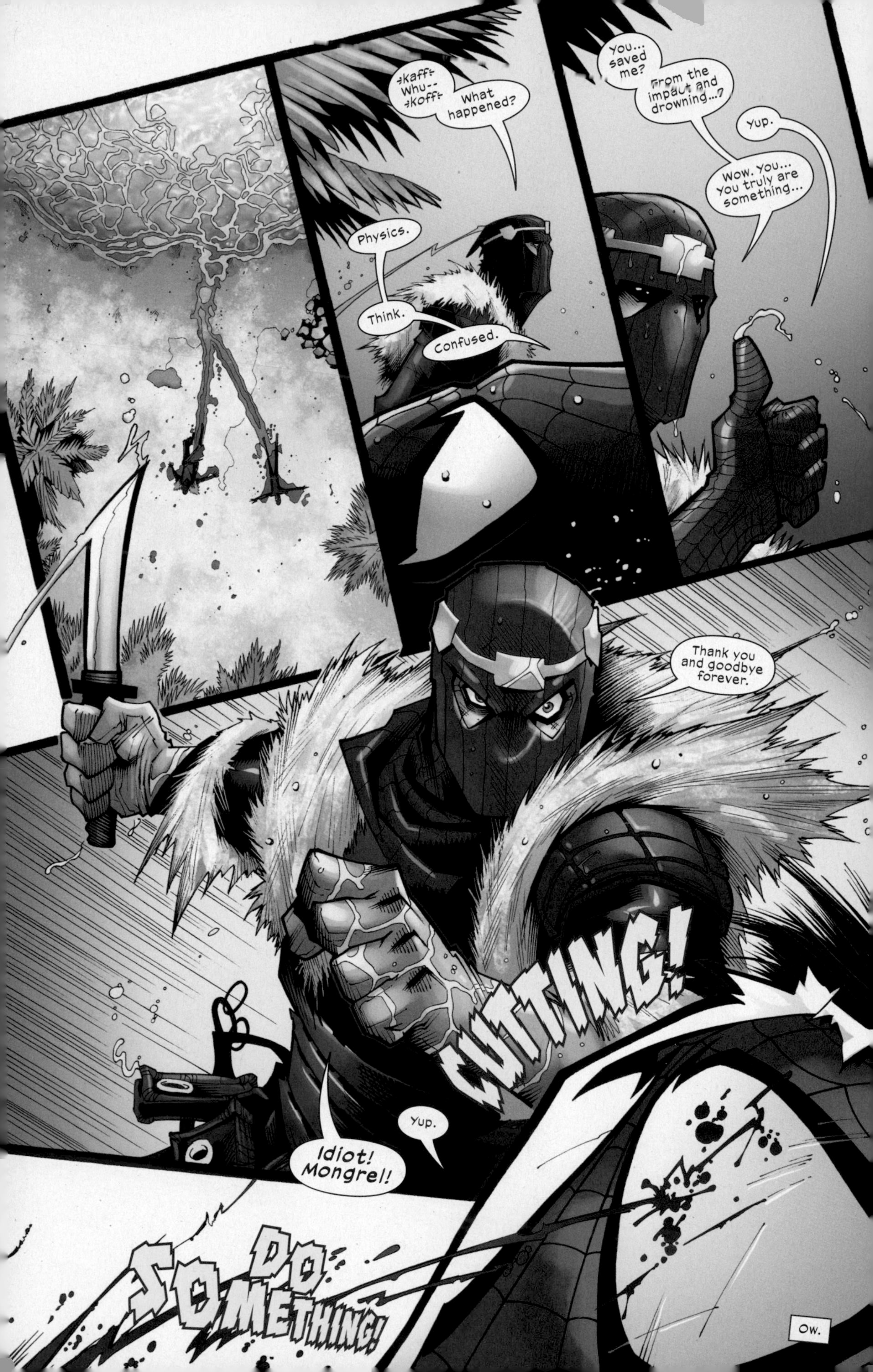

kaff Whu-- *koff*
What happened?
Physics.
Think.
Confused.
You... saved me?
From the impact and drowning...?
Yup.
Wow. You... you truly are something...
Thank you and goodbye forever.
CUTTING!
Yup.
Idiot! Mongrel!
DO SOMETHING!
Ow.

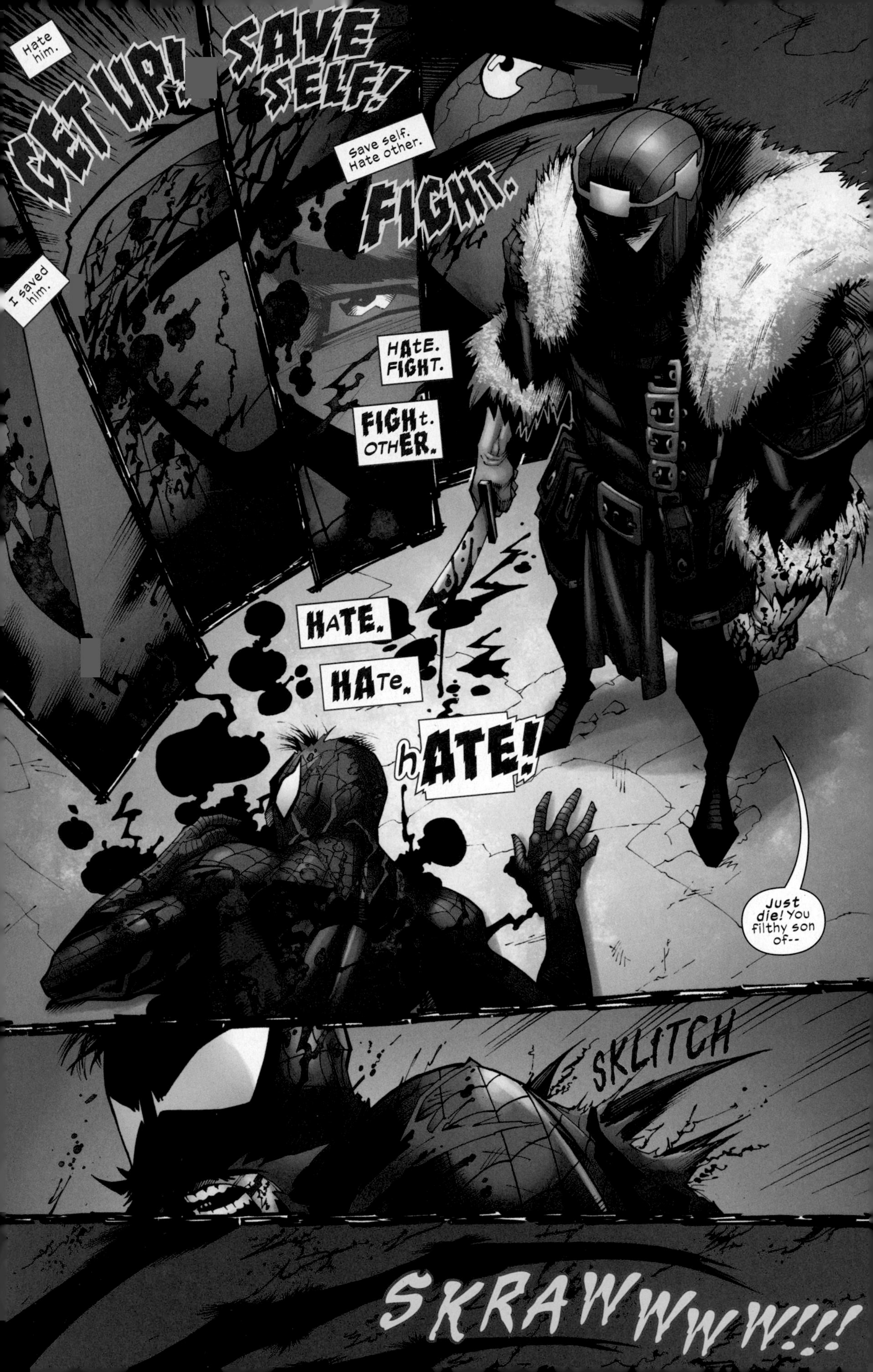
Hate him.
GET UP!
SAVE SELF!
Save self. Hate other.
FIGHT.
I saved him.
HAte. FIGHT.
FIGHt. OTHER.
HATE.
HATe.
hATE!
Just die! You filthy son of--
SKLITCH
SKRAWWWW!!!

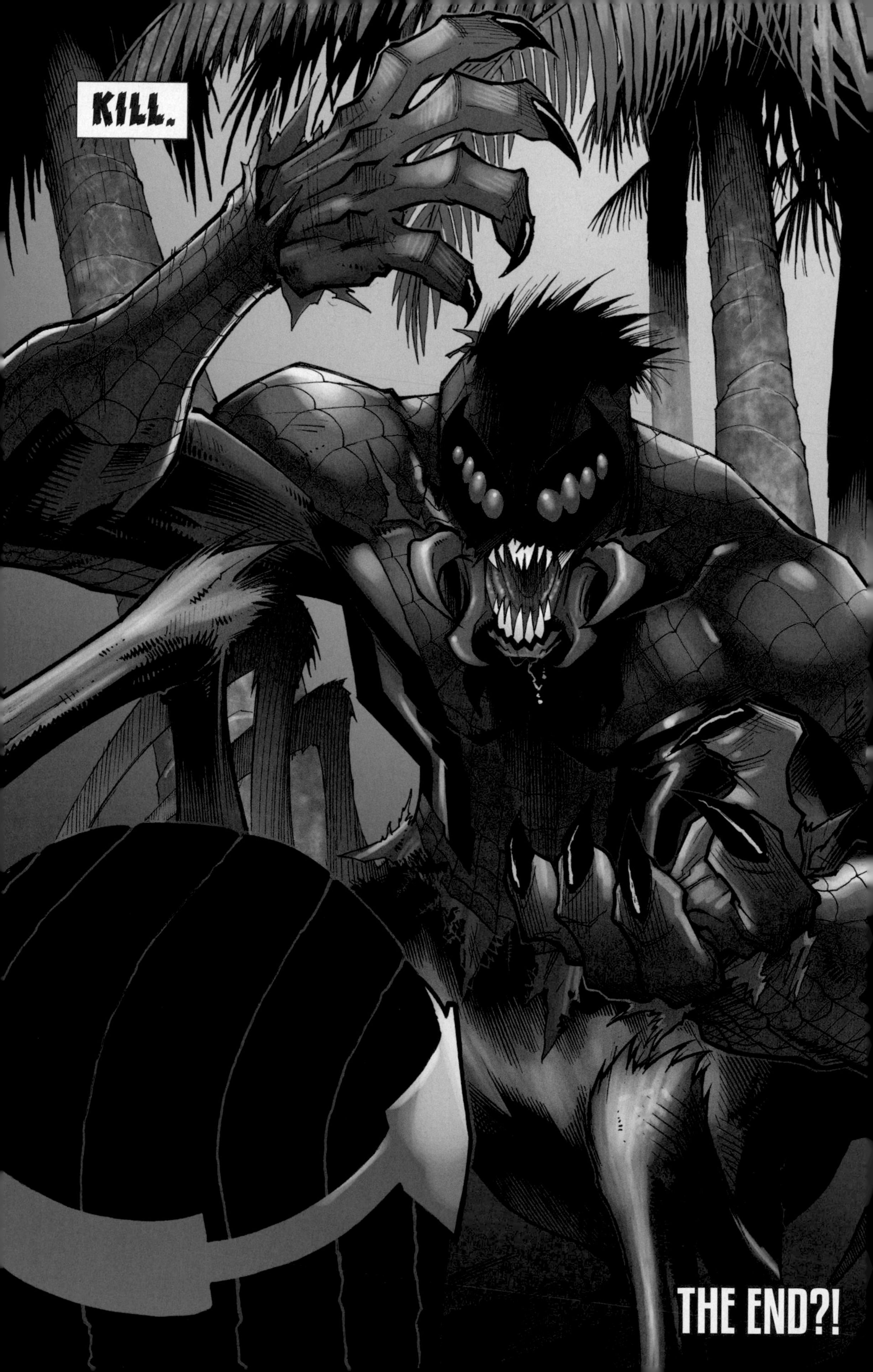
KILL.
THE END?!

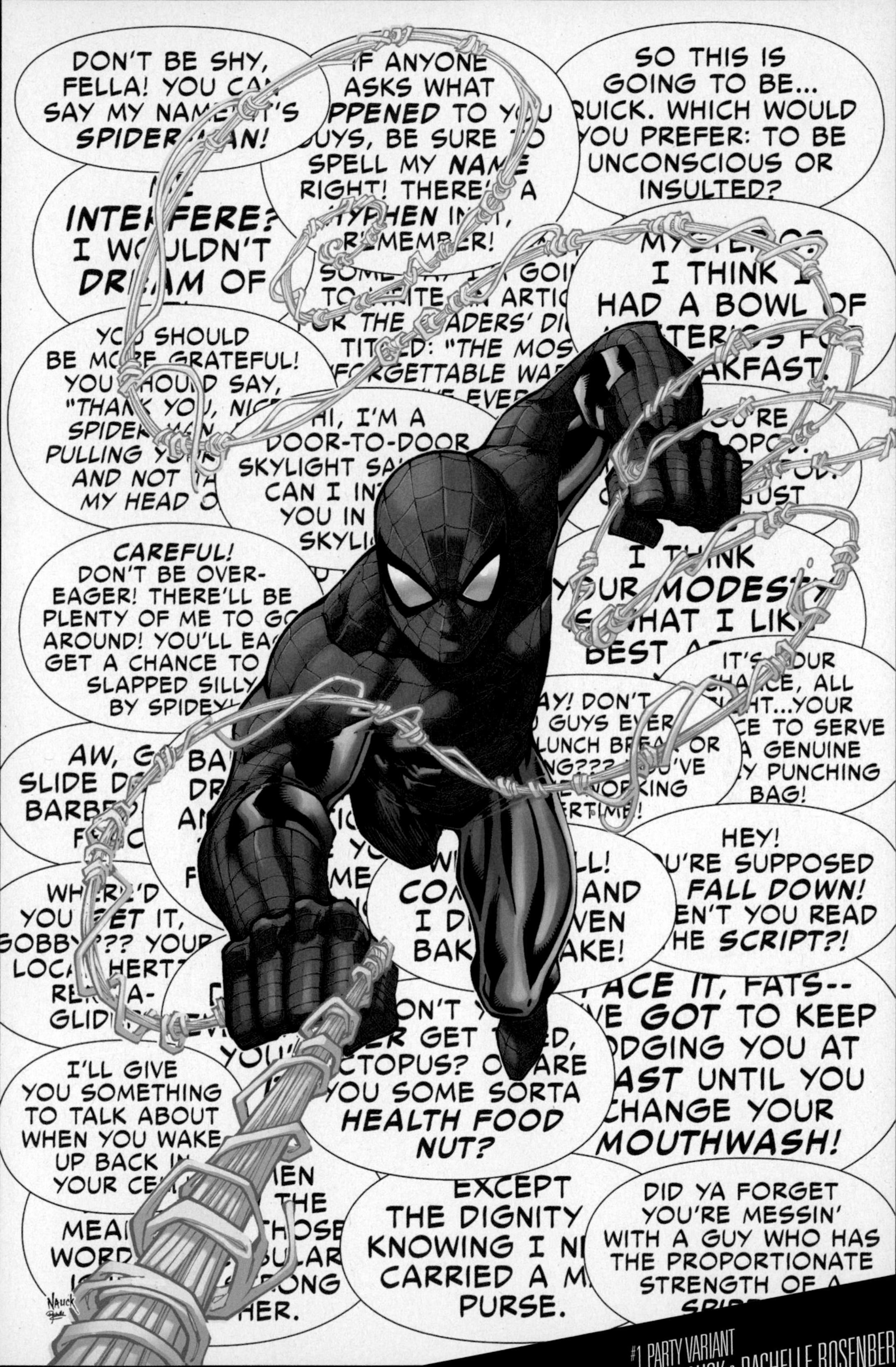
DON'T BE SHY, FELLA! YOU CAN SAY MY NAME! IT'S SPIDER-MAN!
IF ANYONE ASKS WHAT HAPPENED TO YOU GUYS, BE SURE TO SPELL MY NAME RIGHT! THERE'S A HYPHEN IN IT, REMEMBER!
SO THIS IS GOING TO BE... QUICK. WHICH WOULD YOU PREFER: TO BE UNCONSCIOUS OR INSULTED?
INTERFERE? I WOULDN'T DREAM OF
I THINK I HAD A BOWL OF
YOU SHOULD BE MORE GRATEFUL! YOU SHOULD SAY, "THANK YOU, NICE SPIDER-MAN, PULLING YOUR AND NOT MY HEAD
HI, I'M A DOOR-TO-DOOR SKYLIGHT SA CAN I IN YOU IN SKYLI
CAREFUL! DON'T BE OVER-EAGER! THERE'LL BE PLENTY OF ME TO GO AROUND! YOU'LL EA GET A CHANCE TO SLAPPED SILLY BY SPIDEY!
I THINK YOUR MODESTY WHAT I LIK BEST
IT'S YOUR CHANCE, ALL RIGHT...YOUR CE TO SERVE A GENUINE PUNCHING BAG!
DON'T GUYS EVER LUNCH BREAK OR VE WORKING RTIME!
AW, SLIDE BARB
HEY! YOU'RE SUPPOSED FALL DOWN! EN'T YOU READ HE SCRIPT?!
WHERE'D YOU GET IT, GOBBY??? YOUR LOCAL HERTZ RENT-A-GLIDER
AND I EVEN BAKE AKE!
FACE IT, FATS-- WE GOT TO KEEP DODGING YOU AT LEAST UNTIL YOU CHANGE YOUR MOUTHWASH!
I'LL GIVE YOU SOMETHING TO TALK ABOUT WHEN YOU WAKE UP BACK IN YOUR CE
DON'T YOU EVER GET TIRED, OCTOPUS? OR ARE YOU SOME SORTA HEALTH FOOD NUT?
EXCEPT THE DIGNITY KNOWING I N CARRIED A M PURSE.
DID YA FORGET YOU'RE MESSIN' WITH A GUY WHO HAS THE PROPORTIONATE STRENGTH OF A
HER.
NAUCK

#1 PARTY VARIANT
TODD NAUCK & RACHELLE ROSENBER

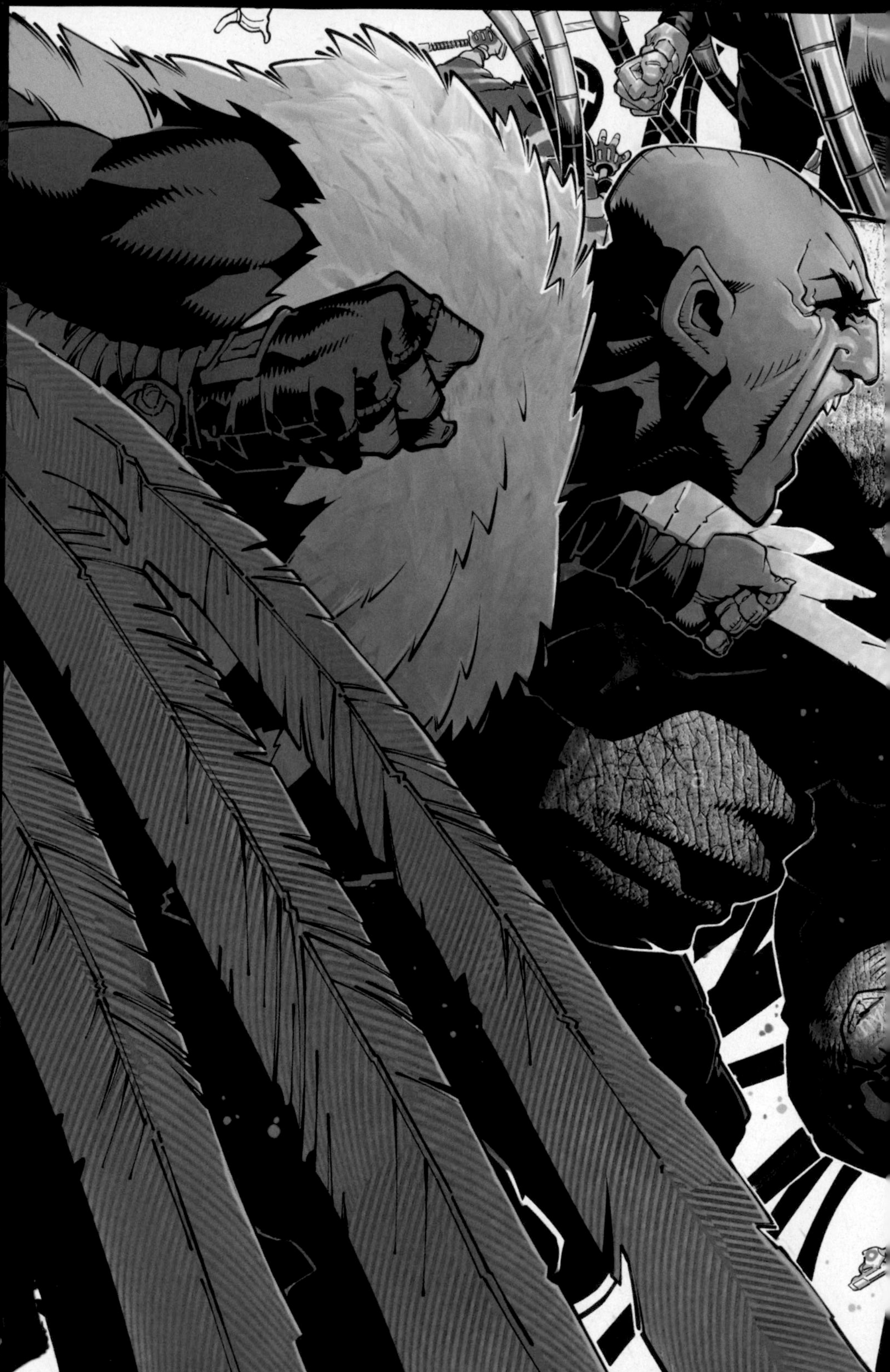

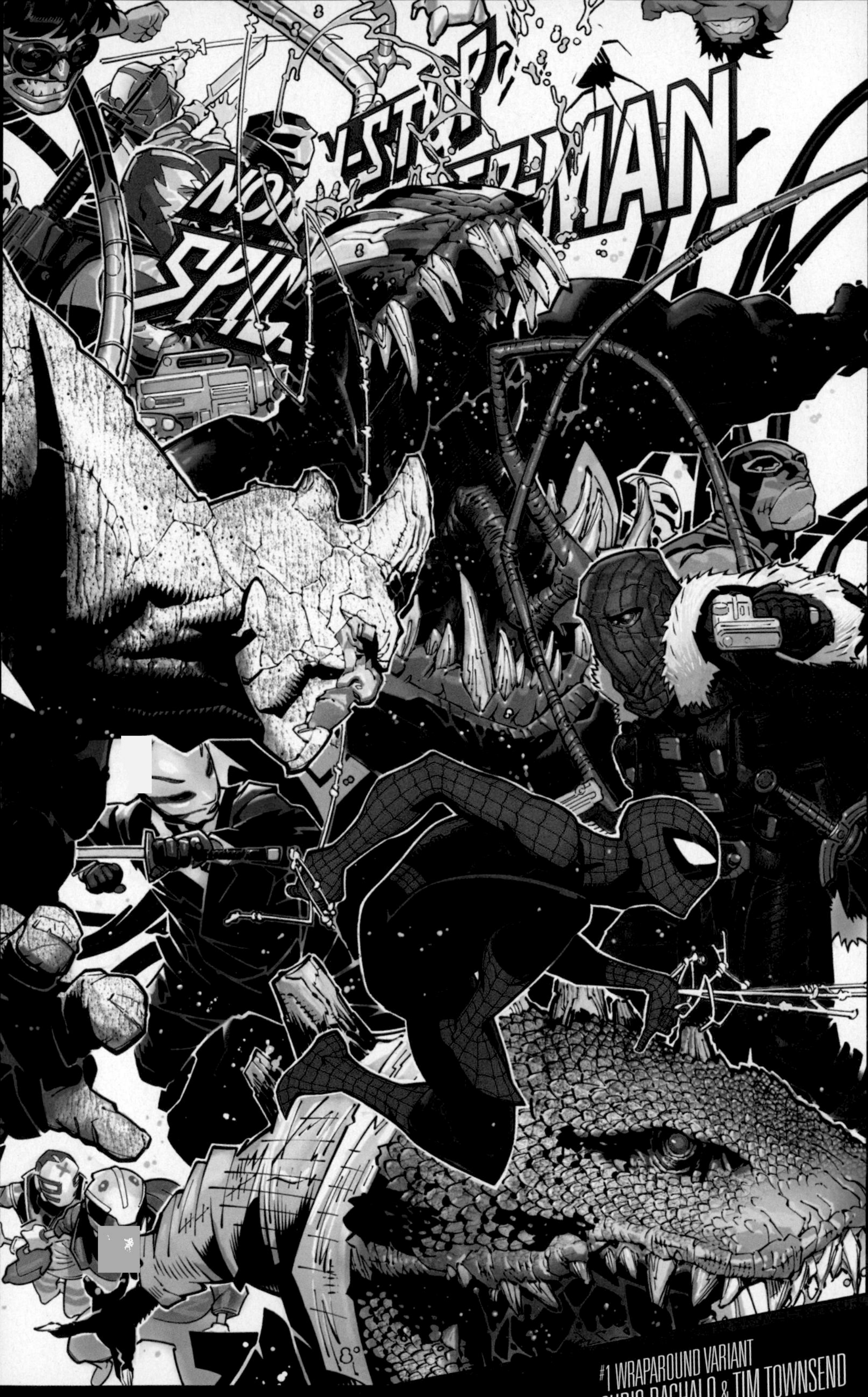

#1 WRAPAROUND VARIANT
CHRIS BACHALO & TIM TOWNSEND

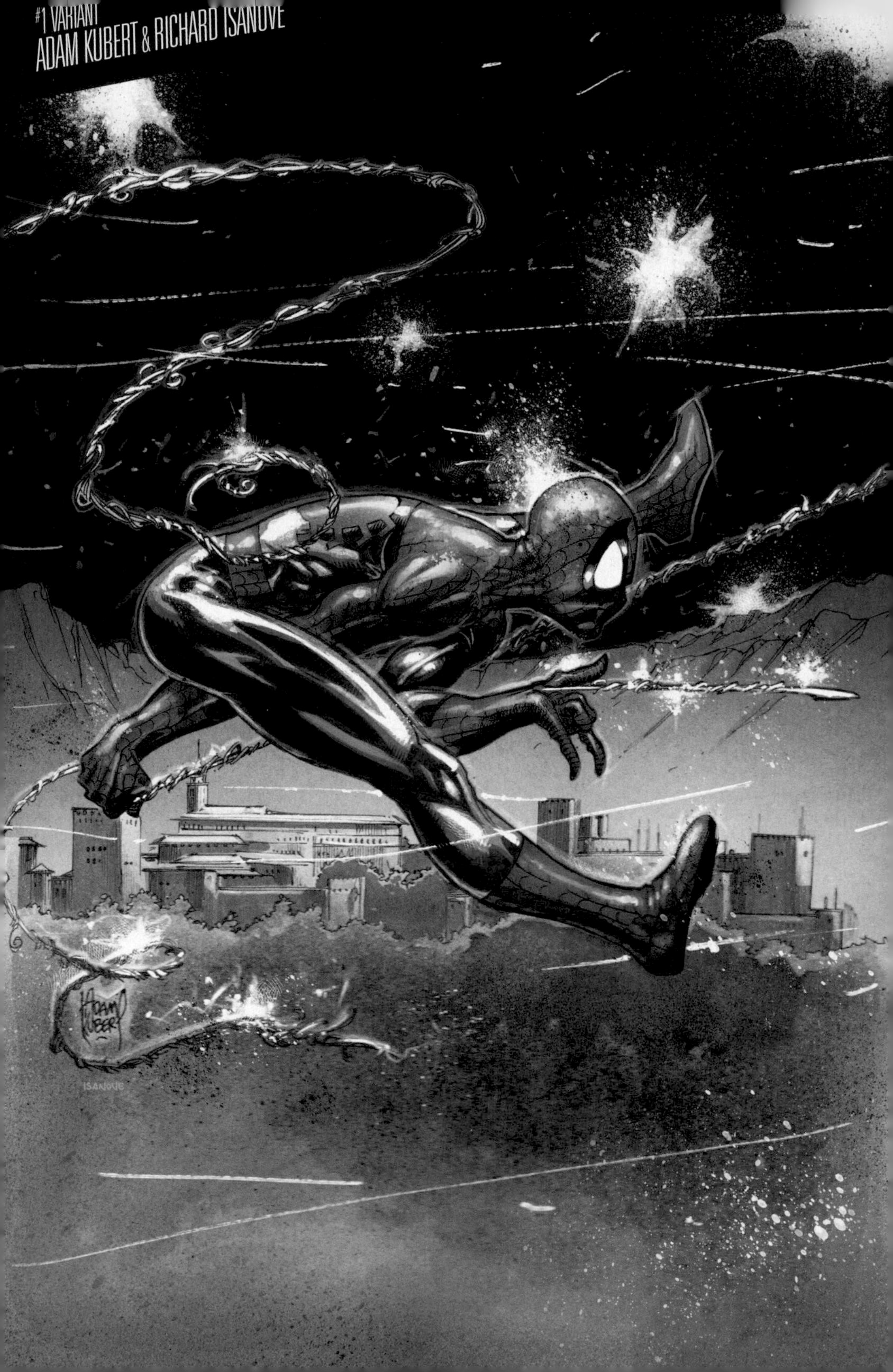

#1 VARIANT
ADAM KUBERT & RICHARD ISANOVE

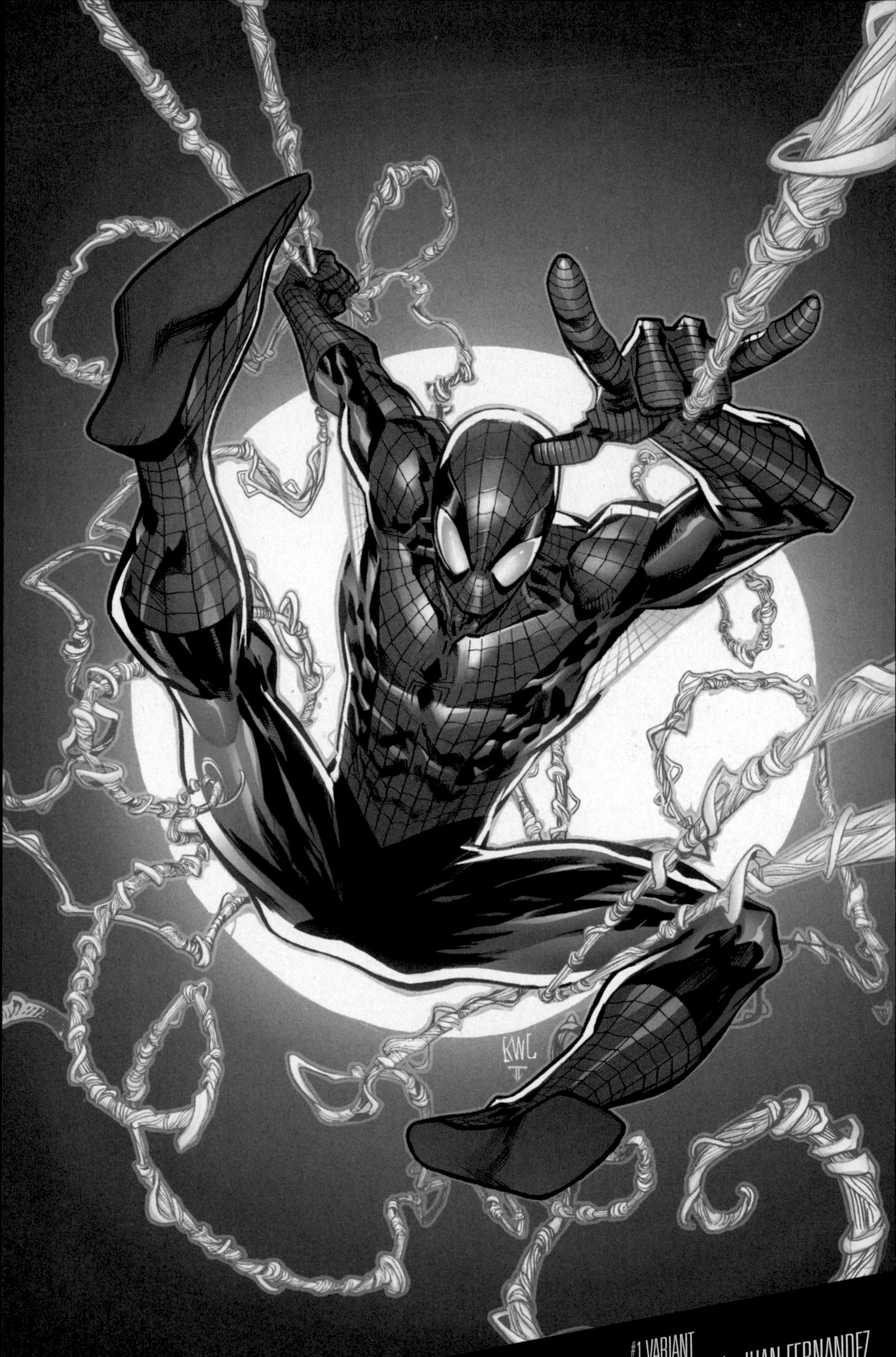

#1 VARIANT
KEN LASHLEY & JUAN FERNANDEZ

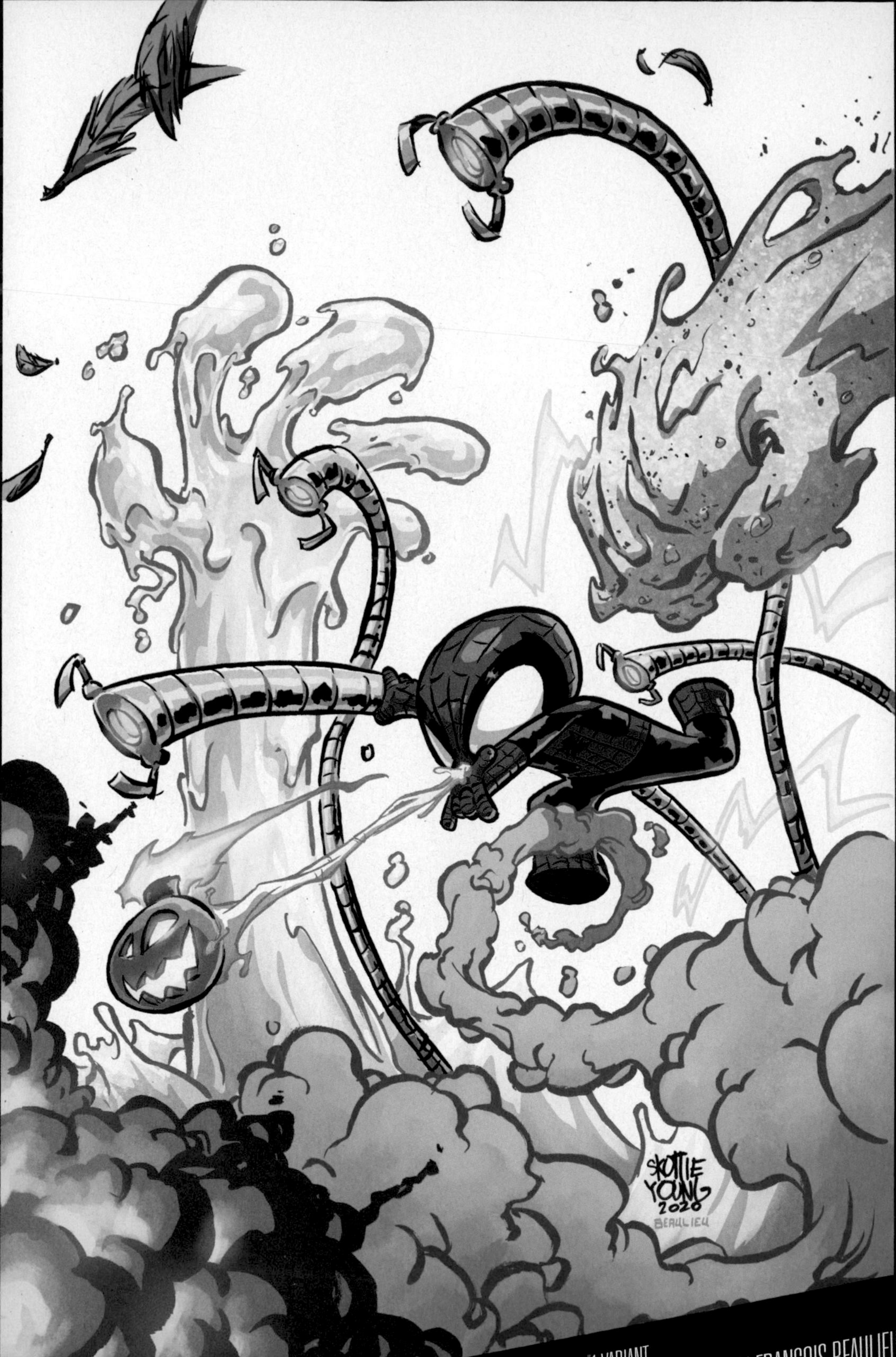
SKOTTIE YOUNG 2020
BEAULIEU

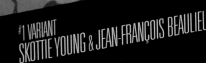

#1 VARIANT
SKOTTIE YOUNG & JEAN-FRANÇOIS BEAULIEU

#1 VARIANT
GREG LaROCQUE & CHRIS SOTOMAYOR

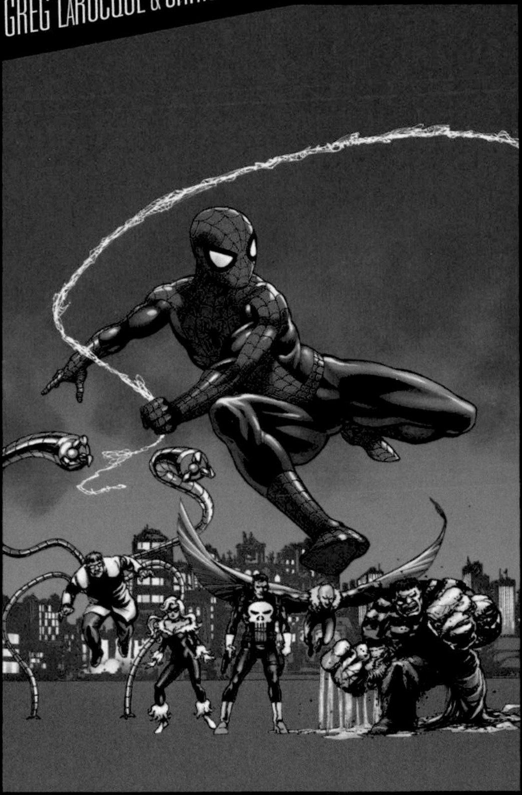

#1 HIDDEN GEM VARIANT
LARRY LIEBER, FRANK GIACOIA & CHRIS SOTOMAYOR

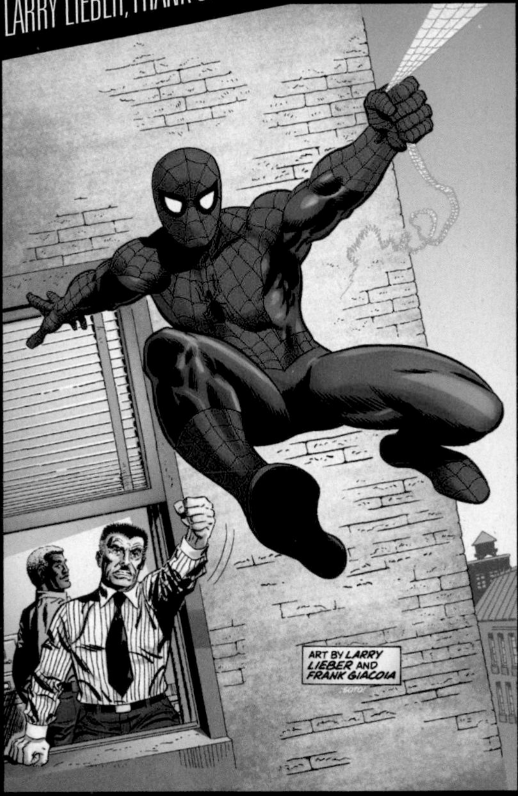
ART BY LARRY LIEBER AND FRANK GIACOIA

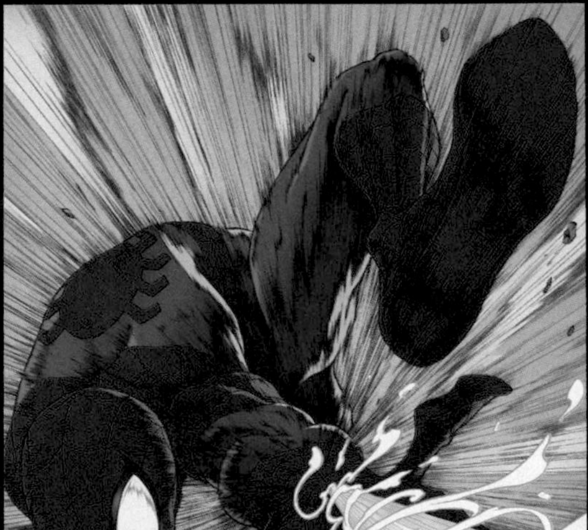

#2 VARIANT
TAKASHI OKAZAKI & RICO RENZI

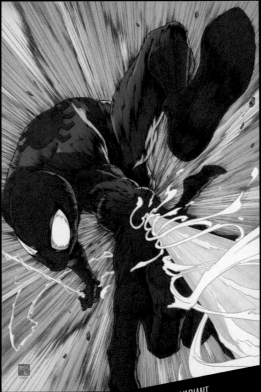

#3 VARIANT
CHRIS BACHALO & TIM TOWNSEND

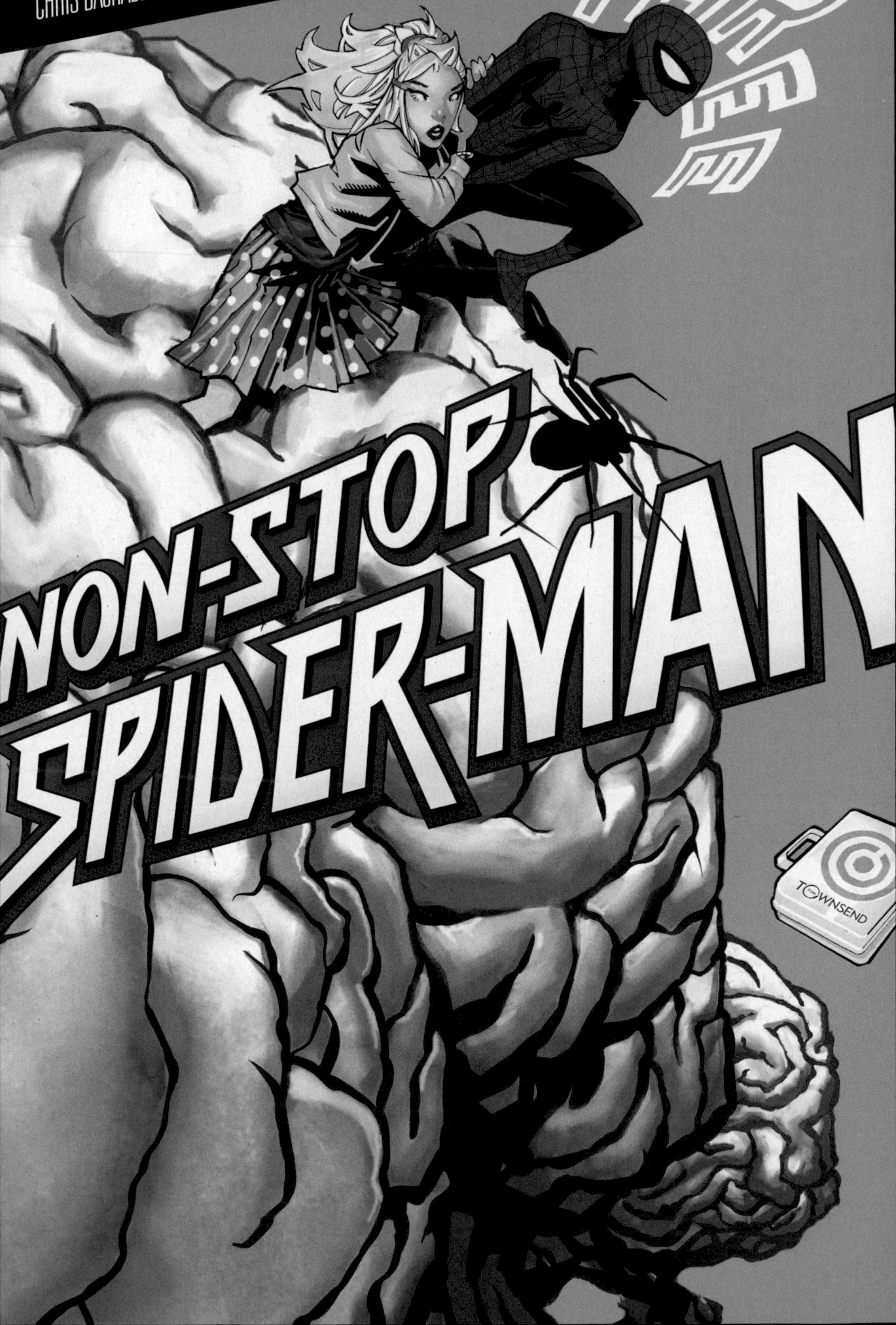
THREE
NON-STOP SPIDER-MAN
TOWNSEND

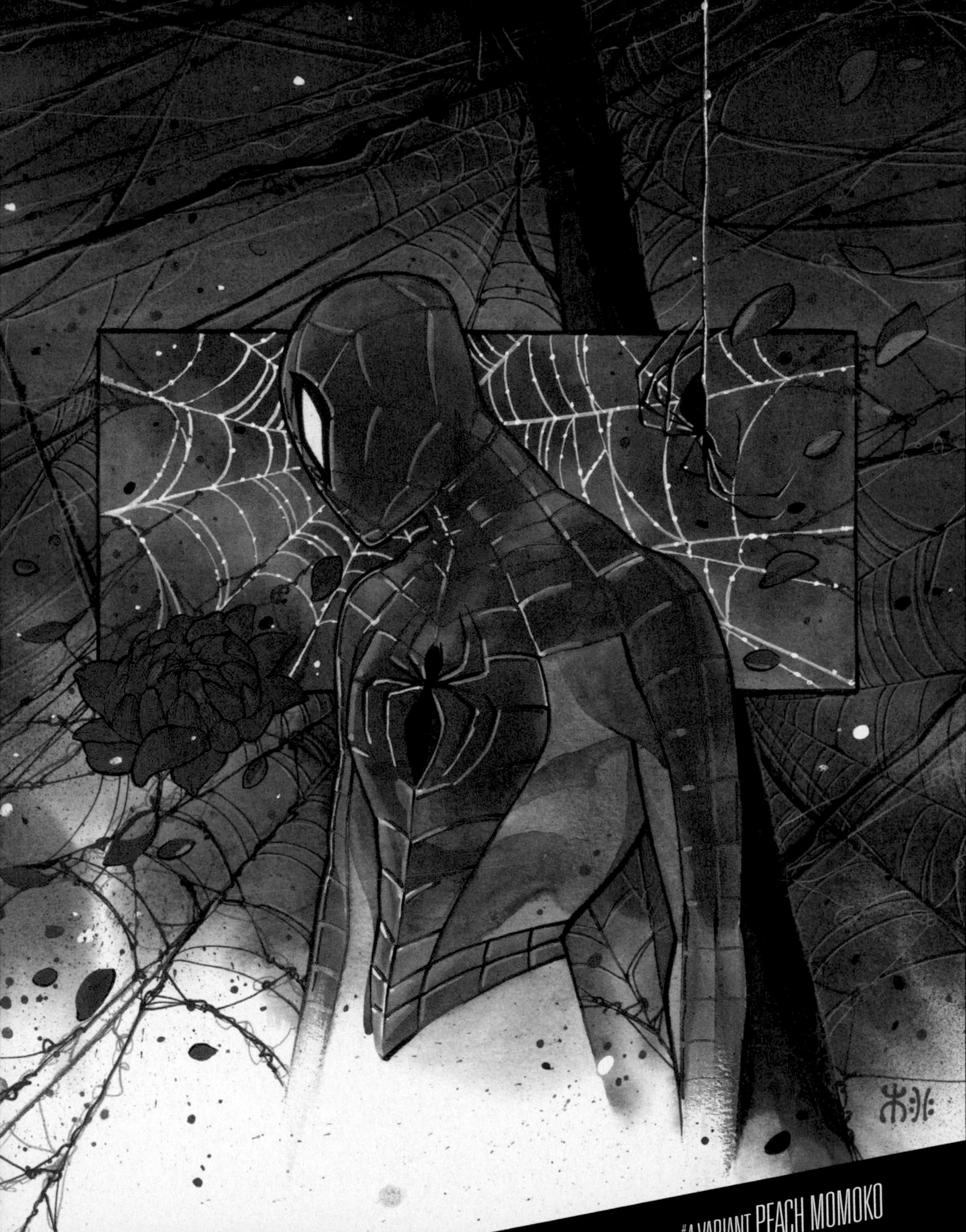

#4 VARIANT PEACH MOMOKO

#5 VARIANT KAEL NGU

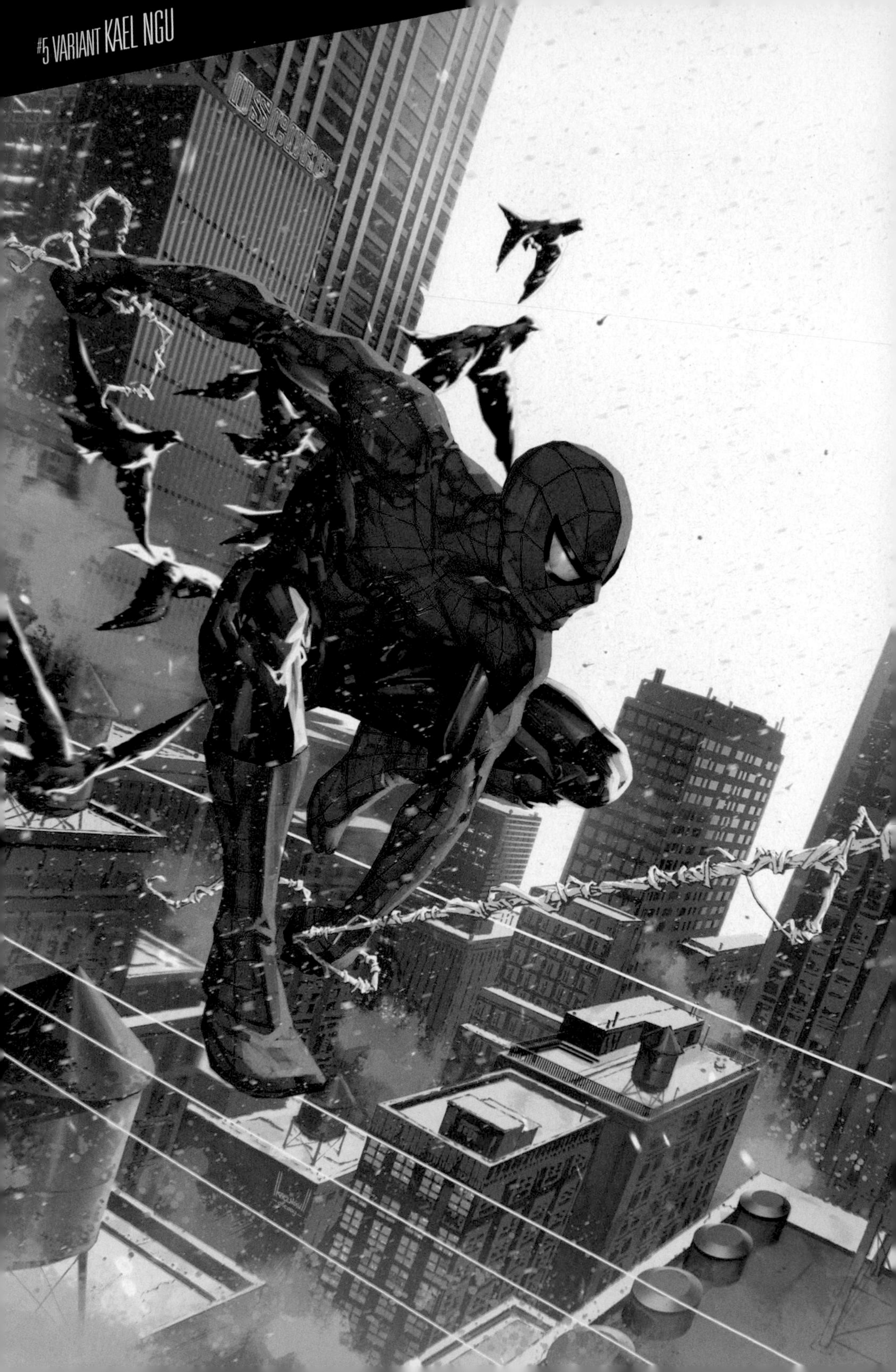